1979

Heritage of the
Graphic Arts

Heritage of the Graphic Arts

Arts A selection
of lectures delivered at
Gallery 303, New York City
under the direction of
Dr. Robert L. Leslie

Edited by Chandler B. Grannis

R. R. Bowker Company
New York & London, 1972

Published by R. R. Bowker Co. (A Xerox Education Company)
1180 Avenue of the Americas, New York, N.Y. 10036
Copyright © 1972 by Xerox Corporation
Library of Congress Catalog Card Number: 69–19210
International Standard Book Number: 0–8352–0213–5
Printed and bound in the United States of America.

Contents

v

To the Memory of

Frederic G. Melcher, 1879-1963

Editor of the Publishers Weekly,
bibliophile and Typophile,
one-time bookseller, who
throughout his life inspired others
with his own endless delight
in reading and in the look and
the feel of good books.

Dr Robert L. Leslie, presiding at a Gallery 303 lecture.

Foreword

THE MASTERS of the graphic arts who form the subjects of these lectures have long delighted me with their individuality, their realism, and their strong principles. How did they begin? What experiences did they have which changed the focus of their visual imagination? Why is one man elegant in style, another lyrical, another full of fantasy, but each grounded in one reality—the certainty of the direction in which he wanted to go?

Much of my career has been spent in working directly with people, both as an educator and in the world of printing. My experiences with the details of people's lives have taught me that the great example—that of an estimable personality—is of value to us all in helping us to come to terms with ourselves. Here in these lives are the struggles, the intolerance, the frustrations, the betrayals, to which we are all heirs: but these lives have not been destroyed, but enriched and conjoined with creative power. How did they make order out of their own distorted environments? How can we use their experiences?

One snowy day in January 1965, I visited Alice and Rollo Silver in their home in Boston. As we looked at the books in Rollo's study we spoke of these things, and lamented that few young people working in the graphic arts know of the giants to whom they are indebted. I said that I wished a lecture series about these artists and their work could somehow be arranged. The Silvers responded immediately by suggesting that Dorothy Abbe might be gracious enough to lecture on Dwiggins. Within a few minutes Dorothy was on the phone, had consented, and the lecture series was begun. With the enthusiastic cooperation of many friends I scheduled the rest of the series. The first series was so successful that I was encouraged to arrange another . . . and another . . . and another. . . . As this volume goes to press, thirteen series have been completed.

The successive series were given the name "Heritage of the Graphic Arts." This may seem a strange title to bestow at the height of what Stanley Morison has termed an age of effort by graphic artists of all kinds to emancipate their metier from dogma. Nevertheless, I am proud that the word *heritage* figures in the title, because it points to the value which should be given to tradition in this and every age. As Morison defines it, tradition is another word for unanimity about fundamentals which has been brought about by the trials, errors, and corrections made over many centuries. I am proud to have been able to organize these series of talks because they gave me exceptional opportunities to see, analyze, and discuss the trials, errors, and corrections made by some great masters who have been active in the graphic arts during the past hundred years.

My special thanks to Paul A. Bennett, whose counsel and criticism were constructive and helpful, and in whose memory the sixth Heritage series was named; to Paul Standard, who gave me guidance; to a host of friends who acted as a committee; to Leo Joachim, editor of *Printing News*, for his close cooperation and advice; and to The Composing Room, Inc., until its recent merger the sponsor of the Heritage of the Graphic Arts series.

Robert L. Leslie
Director, Gallery 303

Preface

By the time this volume went to press, several years after its conception, that irrepressible impressario of typographic lore and graphic arts education, Dr. Robert L. Leslie, had organized more than a dozen successive series of lectures under the title "Heritage of the Graphic Arts."

The chapters of this book are edited versions of twenty-two out of the many lectures that Dr. Leslie has arranged. Taken mainly from the earlier series, they were chosen partly because of their availability in written form at the time of original editing; partly because they stood up without primary dependence on illustration, even though they were virtually all presented as slide lectures; but mainly because of their high interest and representative nature in the broad area covered.

The lectures are presented here roughly in chronological order in terms of the subject matter. But the lectures were not given in topical sequence, and the chapters in this book do not have to be read in sequence either.

In whatever order they are read, two impressions will doubtless stand out. One is that the typographic renaissance which flowered into the past decade was brought about by an extraordinary group of talented personalities, English, Continental, and American, many of whom knew one another and freely acknowledged one another's influence, even when they sharply disagreed.

The other major impression or idea, especially evident in the first chapter and the final three, seems to be that the patterns of excellence set during the typographic renaissance are challenged by the new technology of film, tape, and computer; but that they remain decisive because their excellence rests upon function—upon the overriding aim of clarity in communication.

Grateful acknowledgment for the use of numerous illustrations is owed to many sources, and these are cited in the captions and in several footnotes.

The editor wishes to express his appreciation, for much help and great patience, to the lecturers, particularly Paul Standard and Max M. Stein; to his colleagues at *Publishers' Weekly;* to the Bowker book editorial department; to the designer of this volume, Peter Oldenburg; to Jack Schulman, Horace Hart, Burton Carnes, Jack Rau, Alexander S. Lawson, the Strathmore Paper Company, and others who helped with numerous details; and above all to Dr. Leslie himself. The editor, however, is the responsible party if editing and picture selection are found to be debatable or derelict.

Heritage of the
Graphic Arts

Hermann Zapf.

THE EXPRESSION OF OUR TIME IN TYPOGRAPHY

by Hermann Zapf

I WOULD LIKE to talk about the expression of our time in typography. What I have in mind is to give a short and general summary of the typographic art of the last 500 years and, in addition, some of the late developments that in my opinion are leading more and more toward a programmed phototypography.

Furthermore I shall try to answer whether or not today's printing types, and typography as such, represent a true image of our technical progress and the taste and spirit of our time.

Moreover, I should like to analyze whether, and how far, the typographical form and content of a book, a newspaper or any other printing product conforms to our ideas concerning contemporary industrial design. For illustration I have chosen from the long list of great printers and famous personalities: Gutenberg, Ratdolt, Bodoni and William Morris. Each represents his age as a creator and shows the taste and the spirit of his time.

About 1440, according to many technical studies, Gutenberg invented the art of printing at Mainz, beginning with the first contemporary report in the *Cologne Chronicle* of 1499.

But Gutenberg did not invent printing. From the year 868, fifty years after the death of Charlemagne in Europe, there had been printed books

Hermann Zapf, calligrapher, typographer and teacher, is the designer of many typefaces, including Palatino, Melior, and Optima. He is the author-designer of *About Alphabets, Manuale Typographicum* and other basic works. Lecture given May 2, 1966.

in China. These, however, were in the form of rolls, and produced without the use of movable types.

Cicero, who lived from 106 to 43 B.C., had a vision of printing by means of single letters. Let me quote a passage from his book *De Natura Deorum:* "He who believes this (that a world full of order and beauty could be formed by the fortuitous concourse of solid and individual bodies) may as well believe that a great quantity of the one-and-twenty letters, composed either of gold or any other matter, thrown upon the ground, would fall into such order as to form the Annals of Ennius." Remember this was written 900 years before the appearance of Chinese printing and 1,500 years before Gutenberg. When Gutenberg made his first prints in 1445, the Chinese were already beginning to print their great edition of the *Tao Canon*, which they finished in 1607 (after 162 years, and in 5,485 volumes). It is said that in Korea books were printed with single characters as early as 1392—a century before Columbus arrived in America, fifty years before Gutenberg.

What Gutenberg did was to invent typecasting and mass production—many years before Henry Ford. For the first time in history a true technical system of mass production was applied: from a punch (the patrix) cut in steel, a mold (the matrix) was produced. A variable instrument, the original core of Gutenberg's invention, made it possible to produce letters in whatever quantity with the utmost precision. The entire complex of Gutenberg's invention also included the metal used for casting, the system of justifying, the press and the special ink for the printing of his books.

From Gutenberg's time to the year 1500—that is, a period of almost fifty years—there were more than 1,000 printers in some 200 places in Europe. Over 35,000 works, some quite voluminous, were printed during the Incunabula period, with an overall total of ten to twelve million copies. This figure is astonishing indeed when we bear in mind that cultural life was restricted in those days to monasteries and the courts of rulers, and that only a very small percentage of the population of Europe could read.

We may state that modern times began with the distribution of books, and that here began a revolution of the human mind. The printing of books prepared the ground for education on a broad basis, spreading progressively to all social classes. The diffusion of technical and social knowledge was possible only through the invention of the art of printing, as was the propagation of the Christian faith by means of the Bible printed in various languages. The Bible very soon became the household book of the masses. The invention of printing conveyed great discoveries and deepened knowledge of foreign countries. It led to spiritual revolutions, the Reformation, the French Revolution, and in this century to the theories of Einstein.

In the year 1455, Gutenberg completed the printing of the 42-line Bible in Mainz. The great models towards which he strove were the handwritten books of the monks in the Middle Ages. One such manuscript, dating from the middle of the fifteenth century, is now owned by the Library of Congress in Washington. His invention enabled Gutenberg to produce Bibles faster and cheaper. It initiated a true revolution in bookmaking.

The first printed books, like Gutenberg's Bible, were very strongly influenced by their handwritten originals. It was the great achievement of Erhard Ratdolt that he turned away from imitating manuscripts to create the pure typographic book, in accordance with the technical possibilities of printing—that is, the laws and rules of design inherent in typographic material. In 1476, Ratdolt moved from Augsburg to Venice, which was the center of economic and spiritual life in Europe at that time. In 1482, Ratdolt printed the first scientific book, an edition of Euclid, which introduced geometric diagrams in combination with the text. Ratdolt was the first to use gold in his prints, and printed with color plates, in order to avoid the illumination of the wood blocks by hand.

There is another book on mathematics printed by Ratdolt. The Chinese, however, are said to have printed a mathematical book in 1083—exactly 400 years earlier.

Four years before Ratdolt arrived in Venice, Nicolas Jenson had printed his edition of Pliny's *Natural History* in his famous roman type. In 1494, Aldus Manutius founded his printing firm in Venice. He was the first printer to use an italic, which appeared in 1501 in his handy pocket-size editions.

The books of the three great Venetian printers, Jenson, Ratdolt, and Aldus, show a wonderful harmony of style, form and content. Only a few decades after Gutenberg, a pure typographical form had crystalized. The *Hypnerotomachia Poliphili*, printed by Aldus in 1499, is a typical book of the Renaissance period, showing a unity of content (text) and form (type, typography and illustration) which truly reflects the vitality of spirit and intellect of that time.

The year 1492 is a very important year in history: Columbus landed in America. The Moors lost Granada, their last stronghold in Spain, and were forced to leave Europe. Leonardo da Vinci made drawings for a flying machine that anticipated the inventions of centuries ahead. And Anton Koberger printed Hartmann Schedel's *Weltchronik*, generally known in the English-speaking world as the *Nuremberg Chronicle*, with 645 woodcuts. His typography and illustrations, characteristic of that period, show perfect harmony. The layout pages for this book are still in the possession of the City Library in Nuremberg.

The sixteenth century presents us with a number of important publications in which the great ideas of the Renaissance are contained. In 1516, Thomas More's *Utopia* was first published in Latin. A German translation followed in 1524, an Italian version in 1548, a French one in 1550, and an English edition in 1551. In 1522, the Bible translated by Martin Luther was printed by Melchior Lotter at Wittenberg. At Basle, in 1543, Operinus printed *De Humani Corporis Fabrica*, by Andreas Versalius. Also in 1543, Nicolaus Copernicus published at Nuremberg his theory of the planetary orbits. In the same year Garamond finished his famous Greek typeface in Paris.

Let us now pass on to the seventeenth century, the age of science, the age in which among other things the first computers were conceived. In 1632 and 1638—a few years before his death—Galileo Galilei published the first textbook on physics, his own dialogues about the new science. In 1652, Pascal invented the first calculating machine for addition and subtraction. In 1694, Leibniz, one of the great personalities of the seventeenth century (he had exchanged letters with more than 1,000 contemporaries) also produced a calculating machine. It was Leibniz, too, who discovered electrical sparks on a sulphur ball (1672). In 1678, he planned the program of a universal scientific sign language with logical calculating rules. Ornaments in architecture, book illustrations, tools, nearly everything reflected the style of the period. We may observe the same forms of ornaments on the maps published by Blaeu (Amsterdam 1650) or in title pages used in Antwerp by Moretus, the son-in-law of Plantin.

A wonderful example of typography in the early eighteenth century is the edition of *Ordonnance du Roy*, printed by the Imprimerie Royale in Paris (1733). In 1727, J. H. Schulze discovered the light sensitivity of silver salts, which proved a century later to be the basic prerequisite of photography. In 1752, Franklin demonstrated that lightning is a form

Page from the *Hypnerotomachia Poliphili*, printed by Aldus, Venice, 1499.

Et quiui le ualue doro referate, in feme introrono. Ma io me affermai sopra il fancto & riuerendo limine. Et cum uigilanti ochii, nel amantiffimo obiecto imobilemente in fixi refpectante, uidi la monitrice iubente, che la mia polia uero myropolia fe geniculaffe sopra il fumptuofo pauimento, & cum fincera deuotione coricarfe.

Il quale pauimento era mirabile tuto di gemme lapidofo, orbitaméte compofito, cú fubtile factióe, cum multiplice & elegante innodatióe po litamente diftincto, opera officulatámete taffelata, difpofita in uirente fo glie, & fiori, & auicule, & altri animali, fecúdo che opportuno era il grato colore delle ptiofe petre fplendido illucente, cú perfecto coæquamento, dalle quale geminato rimonftraua quelli che erano intrati.

Sopra quefto dunque la mia audacula Polia, denudati religiofamente gli lactei genui, cum fumma eleganþia genuflexe. Piu belli che unque ue deffe la Mifericordia ad fe dedicati. Per laquale cofa ifteti fo fpefamente at tento cú gli filenti labri. Et per non uolere gli fancti litamenti interrópere & le ppitiatione contaminare, & interrumpere le foléne fæe, & il mysterio fo minifterio, & le arale cerimonie perturbare, gli i probi fofpiri da ualido amore in fiammati debitamente incarcerai.

Hora dinanti di una fanctificata Ara, nella mediana dil facrulo operofamente fituata, di diuina fiamma lucente, geniculata humilmente fe ftaua.   La

BELOW LEFT   Page from Hartmann Schedel's *Weltchronik* (the *Nuremberg Chronicle*) printed by Anton Koberger, Nuremberg, 1492.

BELOW RIGHT   The original layout sheets are extant, and can be seen in the City Library of Nuremberg.

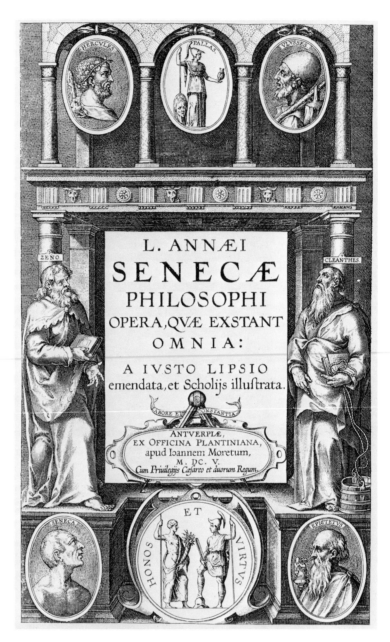

A title page from the Plantin Office, printed by Johann Moretus, Antwerp, 1605, showing typical ornamentation.

of electricity. In the middle of the eighteenth century, electrical and mechanical machines were used as fashionable toys. An "automatic" designing machine, now in the Musée d'Histoire in Neuchatel, was constructed by Leschot and Jaquet-Droz (Paris, 1722–1774). The mechanism was "programmed" for different drawings; note that this was done about 200 years ago.

In 1767, Giambattista Bodoni took over the printing office of the court of Parma. During the first years he copied Fournier. I will illustrate this by comparing the title pages of Fournier's *Manuel Typographique*, published in 1766, and Bodoni's type specimen *Fregi e Majuscole* of 1771. No doubt we would never have heard of him and he never would have gained his great reputation in the history of printing had he continued copying Fournier. However, after 1789, the year of the French Revolution, he began developing his own style. The editions of the following years are full of greatness, full of simplicity: this is pure typography without ornaments. Later works show the true genius of Bodoni: the classic form which he created out of the spirit of that time; a unity of style and form in letters and arrangement; no clinging to the styles of the past but a true expression of his era. It is not difficult to detect in Bodoni's new style the intellectual change in Europe following the French Revolution.

The nineteenth century marks the beginning of industrialization: the technical perfecting of the steam engine by Bodoni's contemporary, James Watt (1736–1819) and the first weaving machine of Cartwright (1784) demonstrate the advance from manual work to industry, and in 1801, Jacquard invented the mechanical loom. This loom was controlled by punched cards representing the code of the design to be woven.

The field of graphic arts, also, was enriched during the nineteenth century by new devices. Among these were Bramach's paper-producing machine, invented in 1805. In 1814, the first cylinder printing press constructed by Koenig was used for printing the *Times* with an output of 1,100 copies per hour. The first issue of the *Times* was dated November 29, 1814. The Columbian Press was invented by Clymer in 1817. The invention of different systems of typesetting machines—the first one by William Church 1822—and the discovery of photography are milestones in the evolution of our trade. The great exhibition in London, 1851, demonstrated the leading position of England as an industrial power.

There are other important inventions of the nineteenth century which were the foundation for far-reaching developments. For example, the year 1837 brought the invention of the electric telegraph by Samuel F. B. Morse, followed by the Morse code in 1840, the jubilee year of Gutenberg's invention. It was only a small step from the Morse code and the Braille alphabet for the blind, 1829, to the punched cards of Hollerith in 1886 and the punched tape. In these coding systems, the single characters of the alphabet form a certain code combination which bears no similarity at all to the traditional forms of the alphabet.

A good example of the problems in the field of arts in the nineteenth century is provided by the life and work of William Morris (1834–1896). His background was influenced by the first industrial revolution in England with all its fundamental economic and social changes. The typical contradictions of that era are to be found within his personality.

During the years 1821–1823, A. C. Pugin published in London the *Specimens of Gothic Architecture* and thereby stimulated the great neo-Gothic movement of the nineteenth century, not only in architecture but also in all other fields of art. The study of medieval architecture and art influenced Morris's thought, as did the philosophy of Karl Marx.

William Morris tried to swim against the stream of industrial development, just as Ruskin did in his opposition to the railways. Morris demonstratively used the handpress and handmade paper. One might expect a man so deeply involved in socialistic ideas to do something for the people, perhaps to invent the pocket-sized book for printing good literature at low cost. Instead, he produced books for the rich upper classes, people who collected his editions, but hardly ever read them.

It was William Pickering, with his Chiswick Press, who inspired Morris to establish his own printing press in the 1890s. In 1840, Pickering had selected the Caslon Roman of the early eighteenth century as his printing type. Thus historicism, already evident in architecture, entered the field of typography.

And now in the twentieth century, about 500 years after Gutenberg's invention, the era of photocomposition, or cold type, starts. The last twenty years have brought about greater and deeper changes than did the 500 years following Gutenberg. Photocomposition has proved a revolutionary new development. Two Japanese, Mokichi Ishii and Nubuo Morisawa, filed patents for the first usable photocomposing machine in 1924. In 1929, the Hungarian Edmund Uher began work on his Uhertype and showed this form of photocomposition for the first time in 1936.

It was only after World War II, however, that photocomposition reached a state of economic importance. The Photon-Lumitype was invented in 1948. Today, we are in a position to produce more than a million characters per hour by using new photocomposing machines in conjunction with a computer. They use cathode ray tubes for reproduction, and their only mechanically moving parts are those affecting film transport.

Mass production has increased the output of printed matter many times since Gutenberg's day. On August 22, 1962, less than five years after the first artificial satellite, news from the *New York Times* was transmitted via Telstar to Paris at a speed of 1,000 words per minute, sixteen times faster than the usual communication speed by transatlantic cable. Since April 9, 1965, "Early Bird" has helped to build a communication bridge between the hemispheres.

On February 14, 1962, the *Arizona Journal* made the first attempt at computer composition. The *Los Angeles Times* and a growing number of other newspapers are printed today by automated composition methods.

Possibly synthetic paper will have to be produced in order to meet the growing needs of the paper industry. The development of plastics during the past twenty years has been enormous and has replaced in certain applications such classic materials as iron, copper, and wool.

Printing has never been the sole medium for distributing knowledge and information, and now it shares this function with electronic media of communication.

Let us again refer to the time when Gutenberg lived and worked. A monk might need his whole life to produce a book. He could not have foreseen machines capable of producing thousands of books within some hours. The scribe of the Middle Ages was followed by the manual compositor. Some 450 years later, the machine operator conquered the printing room.

Today, photocomposition has taken over part of his job. Techniques of photocomposition, combined with computers, have opened new perspectives of printing. The steady rise of production costs, caused in part by rising wages with shorter working hours, is quickening the pace and will very soon lead to composing techniques even more mechanized and automated. The growing world population necessitates a growing production of books, especially in the field of technical literature. Around 1640, at the time of Galileo, world population was about 600 million; in 1850, at the time of William Morris, 1,200 million; today about three billion people are estimated to populate the globe. By the year 2000, world population is expected to reach more than six billion.

The increasing production of books is also influenced by the rapid progress of science and technology. Roughly 50 percent of all books today are textbooks. Future decades will show an even greater increase in this field.

We have to face the new facts in book production and newspaper composition and find a way to live with them. Is it really unrealistic or heretical to say and to believe that the standard production of books, and especially that of pocket-sized books, can be solved by computer programs? Individual book sizes, measures of type area, point sizes and leading can certainly be kept variable in spite of the standardization of book sizes. Nobody need be restricted in his creative ideas. Page and volume calculation can be done by the computer in extremely short periods of time.

This, of course, calls for certain assumptions which we will have to accept in the future. It excludes fancy ideas and typographical playing about. A well-prepared manuscript is an absolute must; the classic working method of some authors, who only get their best ideas after they receive the galley proofs, has no place here. The time is not far off when the manuscript—handwritten or typewritten—will be put into a reading machine which, via a computer, will produce the information necessary for book production on paper or magnetic tape. The computer will also be programmed to correct automatically typographical and grammatical errors, check the logic of thoughts, prepare an index of names and conceptions, compare dates, and even translate the complete work into any foreign language.

It is only a matter of time until the large and expensive computer installations which we have to use today to do this work will be replaced by small, special-purpose computers of moderate size and price, suitable for everyday use. We should face this new trend realistically; computers have not done away with any habits as yet, they have only changed them, replacing manual functions with electronic operations. "Creative thinking, however, will never be replaced by an electronic computer," we are assured by an authority, IBM.

Eventually, computer typography is bound to be more exact than the orthodox work of a compositor. The automated machine can execute all and any functions of a compositor. Without fail it complies with the programmed information and instructions fed to it. Putting in running heads, chapter headings and folios, captions and subtitles, picking out references and footnotes, it can at the same time eliminate widows, hyphenations breaking over a page, and other typographical taboos. It even thinks continually; no longer will one need to search for a good compositor to replace the man not working with necessary care. There will be no questions such as whether or not, in a large volume, all lines with caps are spaced equally, or, in complicated composition, all specifications and details have been observed. There will be no anxiety any more about the compositor remembering all your instructions and passing them on to his colleague in the next shift. A computer can be programmed for any requirements of composition, including hyphenation; theoretically it can produce steady and perfect composition even when digesting complicated technical or scientific literature.

The responsibility of the book designer will be larger in the future. He will no longer be an unnecessary cost factor, but will direct the whole orchestra to avoid the mistaken decisions that mean additional costs and loss of time. If his concept is correct, the same paper or magnetic tape can be used for the "fine" edition as for the cheap pocket book. Already today, text alterations can be easily inserted for new editions by merging the information of an original tape with information from a correction tape.

When considering the advance of technical evolution we should not forget that in our line of business the typeface and typography are of basic importance. Do people think about this? Perhaps the layman does not, but the professional should. The Bauhaus style introduced a new idea into design in the twenties: "function and simplicity." This concept should again inspire our ideas for today and the future as we develop the techniques of computer- and phototypography. Our objective should be a typography aimed at legibility and clarity, self-evident in disposition, free of unnecessary "extras" or ornaments. The disappearance of superfluous ornaments and fancies in favor of a clear concept of typography need not necessarily end in a sterile typographic outlook. That dogmatic "one-size typography" which you see in some places is dangerous; it requires the reader himself to distinguish between important and unimportant news.

We do not want to strive for uniformity of printed things—from the catalog of a steel company, or the jacket of a pocket Shakespeare or Goethe, to the ads for cosmetics. Yet we certainly will not be able to make progress by hanging on to the historic elements in typefaces or in ornaments for their own sake. Years ago, W. A. Dwiggins tried to shake typography out of its conservative tendencies, saying:

"We all love the old printers. They did such fine things before we came along that we can't help harking back to them and trying to get some of their quality into the things we do. Each of us has his own pet moment in printing and no one of us can quite escape the temptation to work out his designs in the style of his favorite time.

"But if we are to design our books—our trade editions of today—on a basis of function—if the text is presented to us to be read now, in this year, we have to put those old loves aside. Our design is contemporary. It can't help being so. You can't copy and repeat successfully even the most beautiful typography of another time—because you did not live in that time."

The Art Nouveau Exhibition of 1952 at Zurich and in the Museum of Modern Art in 1960 suddenly reawakened a love for the letter forms used at the turn of the century. Today it is sometimes difficult to find out at once whether you have in front of you printed matter dating from the year 1906 or 1966.

Does typography keep in step with technical advances? Unfortunately, we cannot answer this question affirmatively without an element of doubt. If you just look around you will find excellent examples in architecture, in industrial design, demonstrating our modern way of thought. Certainly you will also find quite a number of bad examples: television sets in imitation Renaissance or Chippendale; printed matter showing forms and the spirit of the nineteenth century.

The stream of printed matter with which the individual is confronted day by day in the form of newspapers, magazines, and periodicals will soon overwhelm him. When Gutenberg lived, a day had only twenty-four hours, and this fact will not be changed in 1984 or 2066. Yet, in each scientific field and discipline, hundreds of news items are being published day by day in magazines, newspapers and scientific publications. Add to this the news reports broadcast via radio and TV and you will agree that the total amount of information facing the individual human being by far exceeds his capacity to take it in.

To return to the problems of design, compare an August 1914 copy

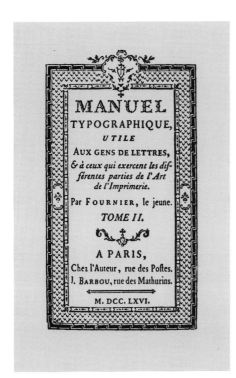 

ABOVE LEFT   Title of Fournier's *Manuel Typographique*, Paris, 1766.

ABOVE RIGHT   Title of an early type specimen of Bodoni, Parma, 1771, in imitation of Fournier, before Bodoni developed his own style.

of the *Times* printed in London, with the *Times* of October 3, 1932, redesigned by Stanley Morison. Between these dates the paper changed from Cheltenham to Times Roman. Or compare a copy of the *New York Times* printed in 1927, shortly after the time when Lindbergh crossed the ocean, with newspapers printed thirty years later, when the first Sputnik was launched.

Are the enormous changes in this world and the changes in our way of thinking reflected in any way in many newspapers of today? To my mind there are newspapers whose typography lags decades behind the modern and advanced information and news which they contain.

Since we use the most up-to-date facilities in computerized composition it is only logical, in consequence, to redesign the typography of newspapers. Not only for the sake of a modern look, but more so for greater legibility, this will be the next step to be taken. Sometimes only minor modifications improve things, without changing the complete image of the paper.

The time has come for us to consider ways and means of creating a new form of newspaper, allowing the individual reader to find the most important news—as far as he is concerned—by using typographical means for better survey. These newspapers should be styled in such a way that the required details can be found at a glance. Many of today's newspapers do not provide information-at-a-glance for the reader. The news published does not show any sequence in accordance with its importance, but is printed without orderly thought, the confusion of the reader being even increased by advertisements which interrupt articles and subjects. I plead, contrary to today's concept, for a clear distinction between essential news text and purely explanatory information. Each newspaper, each technical magazine, should be equipped with a detailed index on the front or back page. As time advances, an index will grow more important if only for the purpose of saving time. We must remember that millions of people are influenced by newspapers every day; it is, in my opinion, their responsibility not only to tell the truth, but also to educate the public's taste a little.

If we are to work out new rules and new systems for computerized photocomposition, we must not forget that it is important to free ourselves from the chains of a conservative typographic past. We should show our respect for the typography of the past by not using it as a cheap source of ideas as the Renaissance builders used antique buildings of Rome for quarries. When things are changing, when architecture and industrial design are showing themselves in new suits, typography should not stand aside. Yet, bound by tradition, we do not seem to be able to see new developments around us.

I think, therefore, that new printing types based on our knowledge of historic letter-forms and designed for the needs of the special printing conditions of today should also be an expression of the time in which we live. I purposely avoid the word "modern," I simply mean that a new type must reflect the spirit of today as well as it is reflected in architecture, in art and industrial design. I am not thinking of a standard typeface, or of uniformity. There is need for a large variety of types for all the different purposes of advertising, book printing, commercial printing, newspaper and magazine printing, and so on.

The world is changing more rapidly now than ever before in the past—too fast, it often seems, to permit logical industrial planning. It is common today to consider scientific progress only in the light of the possibilities of its practical application. The challenge of tomorrow, however, will be met not by people operating the most modern equipment, but by those who employ the engineers most capable of running these machines to perfection.

The printing industry is able—as are the other communications media like radio and television—to represent an enormous power factor. It is in a position to influence millions of people. This places upon us an even heavier burden of responsibility than other industries must carry.

William Morris.

WILLIAM MORRIS

by E. Willis Jones

USUALLY THOUGHT OF as an Englishman, William Morris had in him on both sides of his family—and evident throughout his hectic life—the wild blood of the Welsh.

Often referred to as the founder of the private press movement, William Morris (1834–1896) was by no means its originator. That honor goes to one back in the later years of the fifteenth century when Englishmen could not spell "well" without adding an "e." I refer, of course, to that other printing William—William Caxton.

And too, there had been several other notable private presses in the eighteenth and nineteenth centuries, well before the advent of Morris and his Kelmscott Press. There was the press at Passy, France, the proprietor of which was Benjamin Franklin. Another press of the era, producing truly fine books, was that at Strawberry Hill, operated by the great and worldly Horace Walpole. Then there was the Lee Priory Press, principally recording the writings of its owner, Sir Edgerton Brydges, from 1813 to 1823. And there was the Auchinlech Press, of about the same period, an avocation of Sir Alexander Boswell, the son of Johnson's Boswell. The excellent Hafod Press in Wales had Thomas Jones as it proprietor. All of these were important in their way, though they were but toys of wealthy men. Each did his cultural bit affecting a narrow circle, but none (possibly barring Caxton) made a major contribution in either a literary or a graphic sense.

The only other one of note was that charmer, The Daniel Press, a

E. Willis Jones, designer, winner of the Harvard-Bok award in typography, was founder and first president of the Art Directors' Club of Chicago. Lecture given November 4, 1965.

truly amateur operation worked throughout the last quarter of the nineteenth century by the Provost of Worcester College, Oxford, the Reverend C. H. O. Daniel. Typographically, his main contribution was in his inspired use of the resurrected Fell types, particularly its italic.

But, none of the works of these men and their presses were *felt*. They were so personal that they excited neither emulation nor much interest, and the main stream of printing went sluggishly on its downhill course right into the nineties.

And then came William Morris, who in a very positive way redirected and clarified that stream, affecting the forward course of printing and typographic design on two continents. Imitations of his work were weak and futile, but he had lifted a veil and elevated the sights of thinking craftsmen. And that influence continued. Bruce Rogers told of his inspiration, as did many others—even D. B. Updike.

It even filtered down to such as I; though I'll admit that my first Kelmscott book was acquired quite by accident. At a private library auction sale, a bundle of six miscellaneous press books knocked down to me for seven dollars contained a jewel hidden within an unobtrusive cardboard box: the sixth Kelmscott book, *A Dream of John Ball* by Morris. Soon after, I bought a Doves Press book, one of the thin ones, and my love affair with private press books had begun. It remained at white heat for over twenty years, resulting in a collection of over a thousand volumes—most bought at sacrifice of necessities.

One does not fall in love only with the beauty of such books. An admiration for their diversity of concept also results, and a curiosity about the men who created them. I never missed an opportunity to hear, meet and talk with some of those greats: Bruce Rogers, Fred Goudy, Carl Rollins, Stanley Morison, and others.

In listening, and in reading about the private press movement, I found that all seemed to lead back to the work of one man, William Morris. But this raised questions. How was it that even the first books from his hand showed none of the bumblings common to initial efforts of many later private press operators? Where did he acquire his affinity for ornamentation? Why did he wait until his mid-fifties to begin the bookmaking adventure that was to influence all printing?

A quick survey of his other achievements gives clues, but not answers. Besides being widely regarded as a cultured intellectual, he was well known as a writer and poet, a political leader in the beginnings of the Socialist movement, a leading artisan and designer responsible for a

revival of hand crafts, and a businessman, head of a firm making the
finest of furniture, wallpapers, chintzes, tapestries, ceramics, and glass-
ware—even stained glass windows for churches.

He has been called "one of the most elusive problems ever put before
the student of human nature." The life story of this intense being is
fascinating. We can only touch on the high spots, but it may inspire
some of you to want to learn more.

Some of our younger people might logically ask, "Why?" None of us
today would think of patterning our typographic concepts on Morris's
Kelmscotts. We can't consider for commercial use such a luxury as handmade paper, and few printers know how to handle it. Handpresses and
wood engravings are for dilettantes. And, except for limited use, hand
composition is no more. So why look back at Morris and his works? I
will try to answer.

Can it be conceded that the study of anything that will help us to
develop or hold on to an attitude of craftsmanship in our work is on the
good side? This man Morris not only inaugurated a new era of craftsmanship, he created and forged it. Should we not let his feelings for the
right impression of good type on fine paper, the harmonious relationship
of two facing pages, serve us as constant inspiration?

Since the first years of the sixteenth century, there had been, he felt,
no period of bookmaking worth emulating. So he went back for inspiration to the world of the manuscript, where every dot was made with
loving care. Though not speaking of books at the time, he expressed his
feelings this way: "Once, every man that made anything made it a work
of art besides a useful piece of goods, whereas now only a very few
things have even the most distant claims to be considered works of
art."

Holbrook Jackson said: "Morris would have us learn that . . . it was
the same spirit that guided alike the hand and brain of the potter as that
which moved the masons to build edifices which are still the glory and
pleasure of mankind." It seems evident as we look at his life story that
the motive power of all his labors was a discontent with all forms of
mediocrity. To find out how he got this way we must start at the
beginning.

As I have said, Morris was of Welsh ancestry. He was born on March
24, 1834, in an Essex countryside village, now a part of East London.
His father was doing well as a London discount broker. As the family
fortunes grew, there were moves to larger homes with larger grounds,

but still in the pleasant countryside of the Lea Valley and Epping Forest. Young William roamed the woods and fields, developing a deep and lasting love for all of nature—trees and flowers, birds, streams, and sky. He had a playsuit patterned after medieval armor and rode his pony, sure that he was a knight errant.

When William was eight, his father took him on a tour of ancient Kentish churches. The impression of their beauty, that of Canterbury Cathedral in particular, was so strong that he never forgot them. In fact, throughout his life, his retentive memory held images in the minutest detail.

At fifteen, a year after his father's death, he entered a preparatory school, Marlborough College. During several years there, he used the libraries on architecture and archaeology and roamed the countryside dotted with ancient ruins, but gave little energy to school work. His biographer, J. W. Mackail, says that he "gained more knowledge about silkworm's eggs and old churches than in exact scholarship."

He was a confirmed loner—usually wandering with just himself for company. The one thing that brought him a form of popularity with his schoolmates was his telling of tales. His highly developed imagination created romances, armored knights in high adventure or woodsmen who knew the mysteries of the deepest forest.

He was a handsome, sturdy lad with exceptional strength and, belying the dreamer that he was, a shouting voice and gusty temper. A schoolmaster stated that in the game of singlestick, young Morris's bill for broken sticks exceeded the total of all the other players.

It was this bundle of concentrated energy that went up to Oxford at nineteen with the intention of taking holy orders—typical of many young men entering Oxford at this time. But, unlike most, Morris's ecclesiastical feelings, though deep-rooted, stemmed from love for the medieval church ritual and the physical, architectural church itself. Along with these was a burning desire to remove evil from the earth and to help improve living conditions for all men. At one point he was set on a plan to devote his fortune to the founding of a religious order.

But somehow this ardor cooled, partly because of new friends who had given up the thought of taking holy orders. Among these were two sensitive, creative, artistic, young men, Charles Faulkner and Edward Burne-Jones, destined to be lifelong friends. And it may also have been due to his becoming immersed in writing—wholeheartedly, as he did all things. Even at twenty-one, both his poetry and prose were skillful and stately. He wrote of his first love, nature, with passionate feeling—words flowing from his pen freely. As writing took precedence over religion, he made an important step: the founding of a magazine, *The Oxford and Cambridge Gazette*. Though groups from both universities were to have collaborated, most work was by Oxford men during its one year of monthly publication. It was Morris's baby, even to its full financing, and he was an ardent contributor: a total of five poems, eight prose tales and three articles.

An important facet of this adventure was that he was made aware of degrees in the character and quality of printing, the work having been fortunately placed with one of the few good printers, The Chiswick Press. Charles Whittingham, the proprietor, had in the previous decade revived the use of Caslon type, and it was put to use here. Cover, title page and makeup showed a desire to rise above standards of the period. Morris, though he did not create the dress for his baby, was aware of its superiority.

The year of the magazine was his senior year. The two previous years' vacations had been spent in jaunts through northern Europe; the first time alone, traveling the byways of Belgium and northern France. The next trip was made with Burne-Jones and another friend. A major interest of both trips was ancient cathedrals, which Morris described as "the grandest, the most beautiful, the kindest and most loving of all the buildings that the earth has ever borne." At this time Morris was influenced also by Ruskin's philosophy in his *Stones of Venice*, particularly the chapter "On the Nature of Gothic."

So it is not surprising that in his senior year he decided on architecture as a career, and applied for and got an apprenticeship to an Oxford Diocese architect, G. E. Street, who, like Morris, was a strong advocate of thirteenth century forms. Street soon moved to London and Morris went along. His friend Burne-Jones had preceded him and was studying with the popular painter and poet, Dante Gabriel Rossetti. The two friends took rooms together and Morris, inspired by Jones and Rossetti, began experimenting with several forms of crafts. The art of illumination in manuscripts of the Middle Ages had always fascinated him, and now he practiced it while studying examples in the Bodleian Library. He moved on to clay modelling, then to carving in both wood and stone.

Continuing architecture and carrying on his new interests proved impractical, so he reluctantly gave notice to his employer. But his year there had been well spent. In a lecture of later years he declared, "Architecture would lead us to all the arts . . . If we take no note of how we are housed, the other arts will [suffer]. A true architectural work is a building duly provided with all the necessary furniture, and decorated . . . according to the use, quality and dignity of the building." (Sounds a bit like another man of Welsh blood, our own Frank Lloyd Wright!)

Now another phase began. Jones had progressed so well that Rossetti said of him, "He is doing designs that quite put one to shame . . . Aurora Leighs of art. He will take the lead in no time." Association with Rossetti and Jones brought on a burning desire to attempt painting, and this Morris did for the next two years with his usual intensity, though still keeping on with the other crafts as well as doing some writing.

While at Street's he had made a friend of Philip Webb, also employed there. When Webb visited the Morris-Jones quarters he suggested during a bull session that he could help them fix it up. Since there was nothing to be bought suitable to their tastes, Morris and Webb designed and made furniture, drapes and other accoutrements—and here we have the first efforts of the future, famous firm of decorators. Yes, Morris was very happy, doing just fine. And then he got married!

Well, it wasn't that abrupt; he fell in love first. It came about in this way: Morris became discouraged in his efforts to master painting, realizing that it was not in him to reach the perfection of Rossetti. An inferiority complex? Perhaps, but his tendency to shift from one art form to another when the first could not be quickly mastered may have been the means of keeping his creative impulses constantly fresh.

But, just as Morris was on the point of quitting, a group of young painters, all former Oxonians, persuaded the roommates to join a project of creating a huge mural in the Debating Room of the newly built Oxford Union Society. It was to have been a brief affair, but stretched into months of work.

During one night of relaxation, he met his Dream Girl during an intermission at the Oxford Theatre. He was twenty-three, she was eighteen. Morris stayed on in Oxford to court her—and to return to a blaze of poetry and prose inspired by this English version of a Greek goddess. Her name was Jane Burden. Rossetti painted a portrait of her soon after and described her as possessing "a face for a sculptor, a face

for a painter, a face solitary in England . . . at once tragic, mystic, passionate, calm, beautiful and gracious," which sounded like, and later proved to be, the voice of love. We shall assume that the figure was in keeping with such a face.

During his first year of marriage, Morris's first book was published—*The Defence of Guenevere and Other Poems,* full of drama, melody and sheer beauty, according to published praise by none other than Robert Browning. But the book was a flop; the public ignored it (though later it was much read and acclaimed as close to Morris's best). His reaction to its initial failure was to renounce poetry for eight years.

With his marriage came the building of a home—the Red House, as it came to be called, at Upton in Kent. The romantic, fifteenth century Flemish-style design was created by his friend Webb—red brick with steep tiled roofs, Gothic gables and porches and four-sided towers, the whole topped with many chimneys. Morris and Webb planned the interior and its furnishings and were soon joined by a band of artists and craftsmen, a sort of brotherhood that had gradually surrounded Morris. A factory could not be found to build what they designed, so the work was executed by the brotherhood. Morris's discontent with mediocrity in all crafts and a disgust for the shoddy had been building up over the years and now that it struck him personally, he solved it characteristically.

He founded a business firm, "Morris, Marshall, Faulkner & Co., Fine Art Workmen in Painting, Carving, Furniture and Metals." Actually there were seven partners, the others being Rossetti, Jones, Webb, and Madox Brown. These were the men who were soon to revolutionize the handcrafts not only of Britain, but of continents. In 1861, their workshop-showrooms were set up in Red Lion Square, but business meetings and creative sessions were held at the Red House. Every room there exhibited the results of their individual and collective talents, and the sessions of execution were mingled with boisterous horseplay as the wine flowed freely.

Though business increased, it was not enough. The rich man's toy had now to more than pay its way, for Morris's income from the family copper mines was decreasing steadily. Then an attack of rheumatic fever settled the matter. Red House was sold at a good profit, and they moved to town into a huge house on Queen's Square, Bloomsbury, that soon included workshops and showrooms. Unintentionally, Morris was now emulating the medieval craftsmen he so much admired—living and working under the same roof with his workmen. He found that it suited him, too, for he loved work as intensely as he abhorred idleness.

During the five years at the Red House, the handsome Mrs. Morris had continued to serve as a model for Rossetti's illustrations and paintings, and his portraits of her were many. But she had also found time to produce two little girls, so in the new home there were other sounds besides the thump of looms and the whirr of bobbins.

Some of us remember when most American homes boasted a round dining table (a Morris creation) and when the lounge chair of the head of the household was called a Morris Chair. Every night after dinner, my great-uncle settled into one of those leather marvels, with its adjustably reclining back, to listen to the Gramophone. His chair, I believe, was a genuine Morris, but most, like the dining tables, were American-made copies.

The success of these and other soundly built but more beautiful pieces, plus a craze that developed for Morris chintzes and wallpapers, brought such prosperity to the firm that more factory space was acquired.

Somehow, during all this, Morris made time to return to his earliest love—the writing of poetry. His new work depicted a sixteenth century dream world—tales of men driven from Europe by the Black Death and going forth to seek a better land, an Earthly Paradise—and that became the title. But one episode, about Jason and his search for the Golden Fleece, became so long that it was published as a separate book. *The Life and Death of Jason* was an immediate success and encouraged the now acclaimed author to complete *The Earthly Paradise*. Its several volumes were published during the following three years.

Now Morris began to take some interest in the physical appearance of his books. He and Burne-Jones planned an illustrated edition of *The Earthly Paradise* involving 500 wood engravings. Morris designed many initial letters, and Jones drew more than one hundred illustrations. As these were in process of being cut into wood, the whole project, for some unknown reason, was abandoned.

Another of his activities was a return to the art of the illuminated manuscript, brought on by a new and close friendship with F. S. Ellis, an expert on the subject as well as a bibliophile. Ellis had also been the publisher of the third editions of Morris's recent books. While plunging into illumination and calligraphy with his usual abandon, Morris was also beginning an intensive study of the language and literature of Iceland, and was soon to make the first of two extensive tours there.

But before leaving for Iceland he found and acquired Kelmscott Manor, a large old Elizabethan stone house, thirty miles from Oxford. Its grounds included beautiful gardens and a boathouse on the river, complete with boats. Oddly enough, a joint tenancy agreement with Rossetti was arranged. Oddly, because most inquirers into the subject agree that Rossetti had, for all these years, been in love with the beautiful Jane. Whether it went farther is not known, but it is hinted that some force, such as submerged jealousy, drove Morris to fill his every waking hour with a multiplicity of interests and labors.

In view of these speculations, it is interesting to note that only a year after the Kelmscott Manor period began, there was published Morris's greatest long poem, *Love Is Enough*—a riotous ecstacy of love. In this year, 1892, the Morrises moved out of the Queen's Square workshops into a home on the west side of London. In 1874, the joint tenancy of Rossetti at the Manor came to an end, and was taken over by Morris's publisher-friend, F. S. Ellis.

During these several years, though continuing most of his other creative works, this amazing man was able to write several Icelandic romances and somehow to balance it all with an equally intense interest in an expanding business. It had grown so that employees numbered nearly 3,000. But to Morris it was not just manufacturing, it was art. For instance, because his woven materials were not right unless the colors were perfect, he took an interest in the craft of dyeing and went to the Staffordshire dye works for three months to master the technique.

Now came an unpleasant period. Three partners, including Rossetti, were demanding equal shares in the business which had recently taken the name of Morris & Company, even though Morris, by his capital investment and by most other criteria, was the principal owner. In 1875, the partnership was dissolved along with severance of friendships with Marshall, Brown and Rossetti.

And now too, at the age of forty-three, he found circumstances forcing him toward a civic consciousness. Because of his love for ancient buildings, he resented their being restored and renovated beyond recognition. They were "sacred monuments of the nation's growth and hope" and he became the leading spirit in founding "The Society for the Protection of Ancient Buildings." And, making himself known as a fighter for civic causes, he was brought into others. He entered into a fight against the replanting of some of England's famous and ancient forests which he had always loved so well. Next, in 1876, he was drawn into politics, becoming an active member of the "Eastern Question Association" whose purpose was to force the Government to be on the side of humanity rather than conventional diplomacy in its relations with the affairs of Turkey and the surrounding lands. All these new interests he pursued with his usual gusto.

Then, in the year following, when England seemed on the point of war with Russia, he published a plea to "the working men of England"—speaking against his own class, the rich, who would have nothing to lose by war, and who would "if they had the power . . . thwart your just inspiration, would silence you, would deliver you bound hand and foot forever to irresponsible capital."

That did it! He became known as the declared champion of the laboring man and of the downtrodden democracy of England. He didn't realize that during the next eleven years most of his energy would be directed toward making the Socialist movement a force to be reckoned with.

But in reality, it had begun seventeen years before at Red House when that small band of craftsmen initiated a revolution against conditions of labor under which things were made. Hear one of Morris's socialistic statements: "It is right and necessary that all men should have work to do which shall be worth their doing, and be of itself pleasant to do; and which should be done under conditions as would make it neither over-wearisome nor over-anxious. If Society could or would admit that simple claim, the face of the world would be changed." That was in 1877.

After a year in politics and a short vacation in Italy where his family had been wintering, he arranged for their move into a town house—a large Georgian one in Upper Mall, Hammersmith, which he named Kelmscott House. For the next eight years he was absorbed only in business and in the vicissitudes of the Socialist cause, traveling and lecturing endlessly. A siege of ill health resulted, and with it a realization that his dream of a better world for the working man could not come about without years of strife.

In seeking respite, it was natural for him to return to writing—first in a translation of the *Odyssey*, and then, by beginning the writing of what biographer Mackail called "the flower of his prose romances," *A*

Dream of John Ball, a medieval tale—but with a Socialist slant—dealing with men of the past who had the courage to fight for their liberty. All of Morris's prose writings to follow were to have the same qualities of pagan wildness.

An increased interest in the typographic treatment of his books was now brought about by association with a neighbor, Emery Walker, owner of a wood engraving business and very well versed in the technique of printing. They had become close friends through mutual interest in Socialism, and now that a new book, *The House of the Wolfings,* was ready for typesetting, Morris sought Walker's advice. As a result, at the Chiswick Press, a type modeled on an old Basle font was used, with Caslon for chapter initials. The title page treatment of full-width lines of capitals placed at the top of the page would be used in all of Morris's books to come.

And then came the spark that was to light the fire that became a conflagration—The Kelmscott Press. Emery Walker was asked to deliver a lantern-slide lecture at the New Gallery of The Arts & Crafts Society on the technique of letterpress printing. Though he invited Morris to attend, his quiet, shy nature kept him from discussing the talk in advance. So, on that mid-November evening in 1888, Morris heard ideas expounded that greatly excited his craftsman's soul. As they walked home together, his questions brought answers that further stirred him.

In the following year, the friends saw the next book through the press, modifying a lowercase "e" and using shoulder notes instead of headings. This, *The Roots of the Mountains,* Morris proudly called the best looking book since the seventeenth century. The bug had truly bitten.

Another neighbor, T. J. Cobden-Sanderson, later the proprietor of the Doves Press, liked to claim that he was responsible for the founding of the Kelmscott Press—for, he declared, had he not persuaded the reticent Walker to deliver that lecture, Morris would not have been inspired to action!

Morris's first step was to ask Walker to become a partner with him in a printing business, using Walker's establishment as its workshop. Though he declined the offer, Walker encouraged Morris to proceed and offered his counsel and services, which indeed he gave freely from that point on.

Morris immediately set himself to the task of designing a typeface of his own. He resolved upon a Roman letter-form and, from books in his own collection, chose two as models: Nicholas Jensen's from his *Pliny* of 1476, and one from a book printed the same year in Venice by Jacobus Rubeus. These, photographically enlarged, were studied and experimented with, and in a few months the lowercase letters were ready. Morris engaged a craftsman named Prince to cut them, and decided on a size called "English," comparable to 14 point. When the full font of eighty-one characters, tied letters, punctuation marks and figures was ready for casting, over a year had elapsed since designing had begun.

An Albion handpress was delivered and installed in a nearby cottage, and a retired master printer, William Bowden, was hired as both compositor and pressman. Meanwhile, handmade paper was in the process of production by a friend in Kent named Batchelor. The model was a fifteenth century Italian laid sheet, and Morris insisted it be made of linen and well sized to provide a firm surface. Just after the middle of February, 1891, with ten reams of paper on hand and a goodly supply of type, Bowden's son was engaged as a compositor. The Kelmscott Press was ready to go.

The typeface had been named "Golden," since first plans had envisioned Caxton's translation of *The Golden Legend* as the initial production. It was soon apparent that this was to be a monumental task. Morris can be pardoned for an impatience to produce his first book soon, and he chose his own prose romance, just finished, *The Story of the Glittering Plain*. From first galleys on March 2 to the finished, vellum-bound book on May 8 would indicate intensive efforts, for Morris designed twenty-three wood blocks (engraved by A. Leverett), and perhaps it was this push that caused a month's illness. But in June he was back at work, now designing a blackletter face, to be called "Troy." Its design took three months, and in three months more the full stock of type was delivered from the foundry—on the last day of the year 1891.

A second book had been completed by then, his own *Poems by the Way*, printed in black and red. In the second year, seven books were issued, the first four being in the same small quarto size as those of the first year. The last of these contained a wood engraving designed by E. Burne-Jones, and for the following one he did two designs and one title. These were for the three-volume, 1,286 page *Golden Legend* that had been so long in work that it became known as "The Interminable." It was the first large quarto and the first to be bound in other than vellum, being in boards with linen backs and paper labels. By then a second Albion press had been added and they had moved to larger quarters nearby.

All the books up to now had used the Golden type; but the next work, another large quarto in two volumes, *The Recuyell of the Historyes of Troye*, used the Troy types for its 200,000 words of text, and for its table and glossary employed another face Morris had designed and named Chaucer. It was really a reduced size of the Troy, but with slightly shortened decenders. The binding was vellum.

During the third year, thirteen books were issued; ten in the fourth; six in the fifth; and in the sixth year there were seven, including the 554-page *Chaucer* and the eight volumes of *The Earthly Paradise*. Some of these last were finished after Morris's death in October of 1896 at the age of sixty-two.

Seven more that were in work at this time were completed during 1897 and 1898, when the press was closed. The total for a bit over seven years came to fifty-three books in sixty-seven volumes, including a final one with a history by S. C. Cockerell. The number of copies in each printing varied from 150 to 600, and a few copies of each were also printed on vellum.

Of Morris's designs for initials, borders, ornaments, frames, titles and printer's marks there were a total of 664 during his six Kelmscott years. All of these woodblocks are housed in the British Museum, not to be used before the year 1998.

It seems necessary to give these figures of issues, printings and designs —and the amount of work completed *is* to be marveled at—but to anyone who has handled a single Kelmscott, figures are not needed.

Many great men in our world of the printed word have paid tribute to the one and only William Morris. One of these men was Elbert Hubbard, who wrote:

"The man who could influence the entire housekeeping of half a world, who could paint beautiful pictures, compose music, speak four languages, write sublime verse, address a public assemblage effectively, produce plays, resurrect the lost art of making books—books such as were made only in olden times as a loving religious service—who lived a clean, wholesome, manly life—beloved by those who knew him best— shall we not call him Master?"

Chapter opening from *The Wood Beyond the World*, 1894.

Page from a Kelmscott Press list, showing Morris's three typefaces. *Godefrey of Boloyne* is described in the Troy type, the blackletter first used in 1892, in great primer or 18-point size. *The Order of Chivalry* and *Sir Thomas More's Utopia* are described in the Chaucer type, the same face but in pica or 12-point size. *Cavendish's Life of Wolsey* is listed in Morris's roman-style face, the Golden type, first used in 1892 for *The Golden Legend*.

Books already printed:

The Order of Chivalry. Reprinted from Caxton's Edition of 1484. With L'Ordene de Chevalerie, a French Poem of the 13th Century, translated by William Morris. Small 4to. With a woodcut designed by E. Burne-Jones. February 24, 1893. 225 printed. In red and black. 10 copies on vellum. Published by Reeves and Turner, at Thirty Shillings. Out of print.

Godefrey of Boloyne. Reprinted from Caxton's edition of 1481 . Large 4to. 27th April, 1893 . 300 printed. In black and red. 6 copies on vellum. Published by William Morris at the Kelmscott Press. Six Guineas.

CAVENDISH'S LIFE OF WOLSEY. Reprinted from the author's MS. Octavo. 30th March, 1893. 250 printed. 6 copies on vellum. Published by Reeves & Turner, 5, Wellington Street, Strand, at Two Guineas. Out of print.

Sir Thomas More's Utopia, Englished by Ralph Robinson, with preface by William Morris. 8vo. 4th August, 1893. 300 printed. In black and red. 10 on vellum. Published by Reeves and Turner, at Thirty Shillings. Out of print.

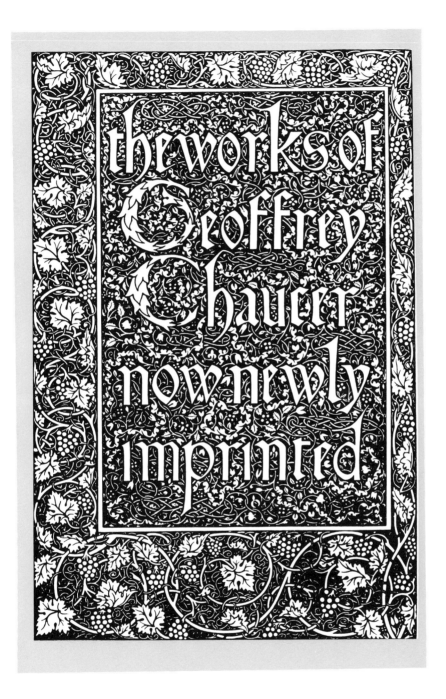

Title page of the Kelmscott Chaucer, with type and decoration by William Morris.

Frederic William Goudy.

FREDERIC WILLIAM GOUDY

by Paul A. Bennett

I SUPPOSE Fred Goudy was a genius, if we've bred any in our times. Certainly the definition fits like a glove: one having ". . . a remarkable aptitude for some special pursuit; a distinguishing natural capacity or tendency. . . ."

Consider briefly the Goudy accomplishments. His first type, Camelot, was designed in 1896. He got ten dollars for it from the Dickinson Type Foundry in Boston. In all, he designed 120-odd types, by his own count—though not all were actually cut. To the end of his eighty-two years, Fred found a naïve pleasure in the knowledge that he had designed more typefaces than any man before him. That not all were good types, he knew full well. Perhaps he cut too many faces, but what does it matter now? Here was one man with the courage to do precisely what he wanted, in the way he wished. If people applauded and bought his types, that was fine. If they didn't, he kept right on—empty pockets or not.

His towering monument will be the sound and enduring types from his fivescore and twenty. And some of these are as fine, to my notion, as any produced anywhere.

Paul A. Bennett was director of typographic promotion for Mergenthaler Linotype, lecturer, teacher, writer, moving spirit of the Typophiles. Lecture given May 13, 1965. Chapter adapted by C.B.G. from Mr. Bennett's lecture notes, including parts of articles in *Publishers' Weekly*, June 7, 1947, March 1, 1965; additional details from *Printing News*, May 29, 1965. Paul Bennett died in 1966.

Goudy (1865–1947) was dean of American type designers. His most prolific years spanned the decades from 1911 to 1932, when he completed sixty-seven designs, and produced at least two dozen good, popular types. Among these were Kennerley, Lanston, Goudy Old Style and New Style; the Forum and Hadriano Titling letters; Goudy Modern and Open, Deepdene, Village No. 2, Medieval, Goudy Text and Deepdene Text; the Garamont and Italian Old Style faces for Monotype; the Cloister Initials for American Type Foundry, and several private faces, including the Franciscan for the Grabhorn Press, and Companion Old Style for *Woman's Home Companion.*

Fred Goudy had a passion for beauty in letters, restless energy and a compulsion for type designing unequalled before or since. Ideas for his faces came from unexpected areas; the Hadriano is one instance. During a visit to the Louvre in 1910, he was particularly attracted to three letters on a tablet with several lines of capitals. When the guard left the room, Fred took out his notebook and made a rubbing of the "P," "E," and "R." Eight years later, the rubbing turned up while he was going through some papers at his shop at Marlboro, and the thought came of adding the missing letters to make a new type. Tracing the letters of the rubbing, and correcting the broken edges, he added the twenty-three new letters in what he conceived was the spirit of the inscription, retaining the same weight and form.

Goudy was born in Bloomington, Indiana, the son of a schoolteacher father who later ran a real estate office. Fred Goudy's interest in type and printing stemmed from his Chicago days. It was at McClurg's bookstore in Chicago that he first saw the finely printed books of the Kelmscott, Vale, Eragny, and Doves presses. William Morris became his inspiration. A type of his own, in that distant day, was an undreamed-of possibility.

He had landed in Chicago in 1890, fresh from Springfield, Illinois, Minneapolis and the Dakota Territory, where he had done office work of one sort or another, as a bookkeeper, cashier in a department store, accountant in a real estate office, and private secretary to a financial broker. In some of these jobs he had come into contact with printers— the need for office stationery, the modest advertising requirements of the firm he was with—all were stepping stones to what became his life's work.

The details of Goudy's career have been related many times, but best, I think, in his autobiography, *A Half-Century of Type Design and Typography*, published in 1946 by the Typophiles.

Many are the Goudy legends, and many the memories of those who knew this friendly man. Whenever the cause of typography and good printing could be helped, Fred was ready to roll up his sleeves, pitch in, and do more than his share.

He talked to printing and advertising groups the country over, unsparing of his strength and time. He had a genuine gift for friendship, and a way with youngsters and students.

I've seen him, dozens of times, greet an acquaintance who was "just passing by and dropped in for a few minutes." Fred would get out specimen after specimen to illustrate some particular point. An hour, even two might pass—no matter. If the interest was genuine, that was sufficient. F.W.G. was a true craftsman and genuinely loved to share his knowledge.

An example of his concern for the student is his book *The Alphabet and Elements of Lettering* (available in paperback facsimile from Dover), which traces the history and characteristics of lettering and type, and arranges the letters of the alphabet, each on a page showing the basic style variations the letter has assumed.

Goudy's first three successful types (Pabst, Powell, and Village) grew out of his advertising lettering. His Village Press—a handcraft experiment begun with enthusiastic support from Will Ransom and Fred's wife, Bertha—was established at Park Ridge, Illinois, in a barn back of the Goudy home, in 1903. Fred and Bertha and their press moved east to Hingham, Massachusetts, in 1904, and two years later to New York, where Fred established a shop and office. Here he developed a more personal style, and his fame grew.

There was a damaging fire at the New York shop in January, 1908, that all but wiped him out. There were trips abroad in 1909 and 1910; the quick success of the Kennerley and Forum types a year later, and subsequent triumphs in designing, writing, typefounding (the Village Letter Foundry), teaching, and lettering. In 1923, the Goudys moved to Marlboro, New York, and established the shop that became famous as Deepdene.

Peter Beilenson's biography, *The Story of Frederic W. Goudy* (Peter Pauper Press, 1935) spells out the details well, and ends with a report of Goudy's second disastrous fire, that of January 26, 1939, when his mill and workshop at Marlboro burned down, and with them all the typographic tools and treasures he had accumulated through the years, about seventy-five designs, and more than a hundred instruments and patterns.

It was typical of Goudy that on the evening of the day the calamitous fire occurred, he kept an engagement in New York at a dinner of the Grolier Club, of which he was a devoted and honored member. Not wishing to cast gloom on the gathering, he let practically the whole evening go by before mentioning what had happened to his shop a few hours earlier.

A short time later, on March 8, 1938, the Distaff Side—the informal organization of women in typography—held a party in honor of Goudy's seventy-fourth birthday. For the occasion they published a remarkable garland of tributes, four or more pages each, set in Goudy types, separately printed and all bound together under the title *Goudy Gaudeamus*. They printed 195 copies.

The story of his early years and dreams was told by Goudy himself at the opening of an exhibition of the work of his Village Press, held by the American Institute of Graphic Arts in October, 1933.

> . . . The things we long for are the things we work for. But how seldom do the dreams of youth come true! I expected to become a great engineer, since I was of pronounced mechanical turn of mind, always working at a small lathe or building things when I should have been at my schoolbooks.
>
> That I was to become a printer of sorts or a designer of printing types, was not among the dreams of my youth. Yet I plainly see now that the winning of a prize for the best pencil drawing at our county fair, in Shelbyville, Illinois, and the decoration of a Sunday-school room there for which I drew and cut out of a solid-color wall-paper some 3,000 letters which I arranged in texts and verses on the walls, embellished with initials and ornaments copied from a type specimen book borrowed from the local newspaper office, and which I enlarged by eye and cut out of gilt paper, were merely preliminary to the work I took up twenty years later.
>
> At thirty, I commenced as proprietor of a modest print shop in Chicago. So modest was the equipment that, when I told my foreman (who was also my compositor, my pressman, and on occasion, my office boy) that we were to print a fortnightly magazine—the now famous *Chap Book*—which was in format an innovation in magazine-making in the Golden Nineties—he exclaimed, "My God, what with, three leads and a quad?"
>
> While operating this short-lived venture, I attempted now and then the designing of the odds and ends of decoration a printer needs, but which in those days were not so easy to secure as now. When the shop closed (with the aid of the sheriff) I went back to

bookkeeping. But the damage was done—printer's ink had entered my blood and I never again was the same.

The few following years were busy ones: bookkeeping, drawing in spare times on the side, study, a humdrum existence, but brightened by occasional commissions on the side.

In the meantime, I had married a girl I had met seven years before, Bertha Sprinks. . . . I remember distinctly that one man (her employer) strongly advised her "not to marry that man as he'd never amount to anything"—maybe he was right.

Even in those early days, she joined in my work. A commission from a Chicago type foundry for a set of initials was accepted (we were living in Detroit) and after I had designed each one and drew the outlines in ink, she filled in the rest of the work.

In 1899 we returned to Chicago and I began seriously working for myself. The work was hard as I had to feel my way with each new job, since my experience was not great. Gradually clients came, and the work became easier. By 1902, I was working for Hart Schaffner and Marx, A. C. McClurg and Company, Kuppenheimer, Marshall Field and Company, Lyon and Healy, and other well-known concerns.

It was then the youngster from the western hinterland, Will Ransom, who was attending classes at the Art Institute, had asked to be allowed to work in my atelier. He was there when I designed the type that was to bring about the birth of the Village Press. . . .

F.W.G. told the story of the Village type in a small book Melbert Cary published the same year as the exhibition, 1933. Goudy recalled that the letter was commissioned by the advertising manager of Kuppenheimer in Chicago as a face for their exclusive use. This was an unheard-of idea in those days, and Goudy welcomed it. He says that he began thinking of the Golden type of William Morris, the Doves type and the Montaigne of Bruce Rogers and the Merrymount, and faces of that ilk. What an ancestry for an advertising type!

The drawings were finished and approved, and the question of the cost of producing matrices in various sizes for casting the face came up. The total cost seemed too great for the Kuppenheimer treasurer, so Goudy was paid a nominal sum for his work, and the drawings returned to him. So ended the first chapter. Goudy reflected later:

"As I look back on the matter, I have serious doubts that the design would have proved an advertising success, except as far as the novelty of the idea was concerned.

"Since the nucleus for a private press was represented by repossession of the design, that fact had much to do with the decision to establish the private press. Many details were discussed before the final step was taken."

The Goudys were living then in the village of Park Ridge, Illinois, a suburb of Chicago. He had recalled the poem "The Village Blacksmith" and the thought came of naming the press the Village. Ransom, who had helped with the Kuppenheimer type and who had some experience in book printing, approved, and the newborn press was christened.

Goudy testified at the AIGA Village Press exhibit opening that the few hundred dollars that Ransom had put into the purchase of matrices and equipment made the face a reality. "A little later," he said, "we were able to return his investment to him and continue along the lines we had first laid out.

"The drawings for the face were made about three-quarters of an inch high. As it was my first attempt at a book face, I did not know the type cutter would find it necessary to make large patterns from my drawings, and that the type might lose somewhat in the reproduction. . . ."

A few slight revisions were made in the drawings and they were turned over to Robert Wiebking for cutting and casting. The first size was 16 point, and 150 pounds were cast.

Printing, An Essay, by William Morris, was the first book printed at the new Village Press, and when it was finished Fred acquired Will Ransom's interest in the Press. Bertha did the binding.

Printing, The Blessed Damozel, and a bound dummy of sheets for *The Hollow Land* were awarded a bronze medal at the Louisiana Purchase Exposition in 1904. The Goudys and their Press moved to Hingham, Massachusetts, the same year. F.W.G. had been attracted to Hingham by an article on village industries in *Handicraft,* published by the Boston Society of Arts and Crafts. He looked over the town, liked it, and moved there.

Impressions of the Goudys' life at Hingham (among other places) are given in a little book called *Bertha Goudy: First Lady of Printing* (200 copies published in 1958 by the Distaff Side). It contains tributes to Mrs. Goudy written and designed by several friends, including Bruce Rogers and Mabel H. (Mrs. W. A.) Dwiggins. Mrs. Dwiggins recalled:

[the Goudys] arrived in the little old New England village [Hing-

ham] in the summer of 1904—bag and baggage—one small boy, two
Blenheim spaniels, a very valuable Persian cat, and their printing
press, to set up shop at Lincoln Street under circumstances that
Bertha herself described as "pure heaven". . . .

When William and I arrived in the autumn of that year we found
a flourishing colony. . . . Bertha had a little reed organ, just acquired . . . which she had taught herself to play, and when her
fingers were sore from typesetting she would change to the ivory
keys, playing and singing for hours. She had a pleasant contralto
voice and knew some charming songs. Their friends would drop in,
and everybody sang, whether they could or not. . . .

The Press was set up in the little front parlor of the cottage (I
wonder if the ink stains ever came out of the old wide pine boards),
the type-case close beside the window on the right of the front door.
My most vivid picture of Bertha is of a little curly-headed brunette
hunched up over her composing stick, as she hugged the window for
light, working away from morning till night, tense and quiet. . . .

On Thanksgiving Day, Bertha cooked a wonderful dinner, and
then worried all the way through the eating of it because there were
no tramps to feed. In the Middle West, where we all came from,
there were always tramps at the back door, for a handout, on
Thanksgiving Day, and she didn't know how to get along without
them. Finally one did appear and she heaped his plate till I don't
know how he walked away. . . .

On a weekend when Fred and Bertha were going to New York,
they asked us to come down and take care of the "menagerie" while
they were gone. The menagerie at that time consisted of the small
boy, the Blenhiem spaniels, the Persian cat, two guinea pigs and a
neighbor's dog, which they were boarding—plus our own small
yellow kitten which we had to take with us. The Persian aristocrat
was made so miserable by the alley kitten's following her about that
she presently disappeared altogether. We were thoroughly fright-
ened, for she had never been outdoors in her life. We searched for
hours and the neighbors helped. William said, "If only it had been
any other member of the menagerie!" Finally, after dark, the beam
of the flash-light caught her, on a high shelf in the farthest corner
of the cellar—the only place the kitten couldn't climb to.

The book in process that winter at the Village Press was, I believe,
Rabbi Ben Ezra, and I remember how Fred and Bertha hovered over
every delicate page as it came off the Press, scarcely breathing for
fear it would have some blemish. The first copy was specially bound
as a wedding present for a neighbor, and was borne across the street
almost prayerfully, in hope that it might be appreciated at its full
worth. The edition was not ready for distribution to their subscription list till the next summer (1905) and was to be sold for two

dollars. I am sure the Goudys must have lived for months on the prospect of what they hoped would be many "two dollars." The going was pretty hard in those days. But posterity might like to know what happened to the very first that came in. It was a blistering hot day, and we lived a mile away, with no telephone. Bertha came panting up the hill, waving the two dollars and shouting "Come on, Mabel, we're going down to Nantasket and have a swim!" And we did!

Bruce Rogers wrote in the Distaff book that Bertha "was the fastest compositor (or compositrix) I have ever known and the most exact. She set for me the first volume of T. E. Lawrence's Letters, most of it in a single day. When we pulled the first proofs there wasn't a single correction to be made, not even of spacing." Rogers continued:

> One summer, when Bertha and Fred were abroad, we took care of Deepdene for them. That care included care of Bertha's twenty-nine birds that lived in a large flying cage, made by screening in one end of the porch. There were also two parrots, two Newfoundland dogs, Bridget and Lassie, a little black terrier, Red, a horse, Patrick Henry, and a cow, Fido. The two latter were, however, looked after by an Irishman who lived across from the mill. Young Fred was supposed to be there, but he spent most of his time visiting his friends and we saw very little of him.
>
> Bertha was also an accomplished pianiste. Tchaikowski seemed to be her favorite—at least she played his compositions oftener than those of other composers. While living in Forest Hills she attended all the important concerts in Carnegie Hall. And even after moving to Marlboro she came down frequently for concerts. I don't think she cared for opera as she didn't like her music diluted with acting.
> . . . Bertha was quick at everything and was also quick-tempered. It was her energy that kept Fred steadily at work and contributed enormously to the success that came to him. . . .

Fred Goudy himself said of his wife, at the Village Press exhibition in 1933:

"Bertha has been my companion and co-worker for over thirty-five years. She has aided me with constant care and devotion. Without her help, I should not have accomplished a tithe of what I have been privileged to perform, and in many of the activities of the Press, her work ranks in actual accomplishment above my own. I could not, probably would not, have attempted the details of type composition for which she

THIS IS GOUDY VILLAGE TYPE, A
Revision of The First Complete Book Face
designed by Frederic W. Goudy. In this
letter Goudy has not sought to duplicate
his first attempt at letter cutting, but out of
ripeness of his experience and developed

*THIS ITALIC FACE WAS DESIGNED
For Use With Goudy Village No. 2, A Revision
of the first complete book face designed by Mr.
Frederic W. Goudy. In this face Goudy has not
tried to duplicate his first attempt at letter cutting, but from the wide range of his experience*

Goudy Village No. 410 and Goudy Village Italic No.
4101. (All type specimens shown courtesy Lanston
Monotype Company.)

ALTHOUGH ESSENTIALLY
A Book Letter, Kennerley Series
has had more use as a publicity
type face by leading advertisers
in campaigns that sell consumers

*REGARDED BY MANY AS
One Of The Finest Of Type Faces
designed by Frederic W. Goudy, it
has enjoyed popularity in $12345*

Kennerley Old Style No. 268 and Kennerley Old Style
Italic No. 2681.

THE PROGRESSIVE PRINTER
Will Find Many Ways To Put The
modern types at the disposal of his
customers for sales promotion. It is
the business of the printer to see that
they are used in ways most effective

THE ITALIC COMPOSES VERY
Delightfully In An Even, Gray Color. The
effect is very regular and well-ordered, and
variety among the letters speeds the eye and
avoids a monotonous effect. Deepdene Italic
agrees admirably with the roman in color

Deepdene No. 315, Deepdene
Italic No. 3151, and Deepdene
Bold Italic No. 3171.

LIKE THE BOLD ROMAN,
It Is Clean-Cut And Of Good
legibility. This face has a pen-
drawn effect which is pleasing.

Hadriano Stone Cut No. 409.

ON THIS PAGE IS AN
OUTLINE FORM OF
HADRIANO, A FACE

Goudy Modern No. 293.

IN DESIGNING GOUDY MODERN FREDERIC
W. Goudy Took For His Model A Letter Used By
French engravers of the 18th century for captions.
In trying to produce a type less mechanical and less

BELOW From page designed by Bruce Rogers, set in Goudy's posthumous Goudy 30 type, printed at the Thistle Press, as a signature in *Bertha S. Goudy, First Lady of Printing* (The Distaff Side, 1958).

BERTHA GOUDY

Bertha Goudy and I first met when the Goudys moved from Chicago to Hingham, Massachusetts, in 1904. Fred had come on a month or so earlier and had spent a night or two at our house in East Lexington. He had chosen Hingham as a residence because a Hingham minister named Park, who was an enthusiast for fine printing had written to him several times, wanting Fred to come East.

The Hingham cottage in which they settled was, I think, owned by Park. It was a picturesque white house separated from the street by is, in fact, celebrated, though in other details of our work we share equally, excepting only in type design and arrangement, which is mine."

Many honors came to Goudy through his long life: honorary doctorates from Syracuse University, Mills College, and the University of California (1939–1942); retrospective exhibits of his work by the American Institute of Graphic Arts and the Grolier Club (1943); and a half-dozen medals through two decades, 1920–1949. The awards were made by the AIGA, the American Institute of Architects, the Ulster Irish Society, the journalism schools at Syracuse and the University of Missouri, and other institutions.

Fred loved these tributes and the applause, "but with a deprecating shyness," as a friend pointed out. "He believed in his work, which is a prime essential for a good life, but his sense of humor saved him from pontificating."

Fred appreciated the birthday luncheons and dinners the Typophiles and the Distaff Side arranged through the years. Particularly was he proud of the festschrift volumes printed to surprise him and delight his friends at these affairs. In each instance, these prized editions were small and copies are hard to come by.

The first and scarcest of these books was *Spinach from Many Gardens* (The Typophiles, New York, 1935, 60 copies). *Goudy Gaudeamus* (The Distaff Side, New York, 1939, 195 copies) was also cooperatively printed, for his seventy-fourth birthday. The third, *A Garland for Goudy*, was a collection of verses, privately printed by Peter Beilenson in an edition of 220 copies, for his eightieth birthday.

Fred was not to write any books after his autobiography of 1946. Of the half-dozen he completed, the most important was *The Alphabet*, published by Mitchell Kennerley in 1918, set in Kennerley type by Mrs. Goudy, and handsomely printed by Rudge. (The Kennerley face was designed for a special edition of H. G. Wells' *The Door in the Wall* published by Kennerley in 1911, and named for the publisher.)

In 1922, Fred wrote *Elements of Lettering* as a sequel. It was also published by Kennerley and printed by Rudge. Twenty years later he amplified and enlarged the two books for republication in one volume by the University of California Press. The new edition was called *The Alphabet and Elements of Lettering*. It appeared in 1942, and was set in the private type Fred designed for the Press, called University of California Old Style. (The face, renamed Californian, is now available from Monotype.) The one-volume edition went through several printings and is now available as a Dover paperback, offset from the 1942 edition—an extraordinary buy at two dollars.

The four remaining Goudy books, long out of print, range in date from 1933 to 1940: *The Story of the Village Type* (Press of the Woolly Whale, New York, 1933); *The Capitals from the Trajan Column at Rome*, with twenty-five plates drawn and engraved by the author (Oxford University Press, New York, 1936); *Bertha M. Goudy: Recollections* (Village Press, Marlboro, N.Y., 1939); *Typologia: Studies in Type Design and Type Making*, illustrated (University of California Press, Berkeley, 1940).

Another important Goudy concept was *Ars Typographica*, a handsome periodical published and printed by the Marchbanks Press, New York (for the first three numbers, 1918–1920) and the Press of the Woolly Whale (No. 4, 1934). Goudy edited the first volume—which, to the dismay of bibliographers, took sixteen years to complete. He sold the periodical in 1925 to Douglas C. McMurtrie, who edited and published five additional numbers in New York, as Volumes 2 and 3.

Milton MacKaye's excellent profile of Goudy, "Glorifier of the Alphabet," appeared in the *New Yorker* January 14, 1933.

George L. McKay in 1946 compiled a valuable bibliography of Goudy's published writings which covered fifty-nine items. It was included in *A Half-Century of Type Design and Typography*. An equally valuable reference source is the *Bibliography of the Village Press*, by Melbert B. Cary, Jr. (Press of the Woolly Whale, New York, 1938, 260 copies).

There are representative Goudy collections in various libraries, including an excellent one at the New York Public Library, another at Vassar College Library (the Kennerley collection), and the best, perhaps, at the Grolier Club, New York (the great Cary Collection). The Library of Congress, Washington, has the Frederic and Bertha Goudy Collection (Fred's working library).

The Coggeshall Collection of Goudy types and memorabilia is housed at the Rochester (New York) Institute of Technology, in the Coggeshall-Goudy Memorial Workshop at the School of Printing.

Will Bradley.

WILL BRADLEY

by Steve L. Watts

IT WAS CONSIDERED desirable, on the occasion honoring the memory of a man who was called the dean of American typographers, that the speaker restrict most of his comments to Will Bradley's artistry as a compositor who taught himself to design with foundry type. I cannot evaluate Will's ability as a writer and illustrator, or as an art director of motion pictures. The best that can be done here is to mention significant events in a long lifetime and refer to published Bradleyana.

Will H. Bradley was born July 10, 1868, at Boston, Massachusetts. His parents resided at Lynn, near Boston, where Will's father worked as cartoonist for the *Daily Item*. It was there Will started his schooling, interrupted when his father's lingering illness, resulting from the Civil War, became terminal. The Bradleys removed to Swampscott, and the boy stayed with his father while his mother went out to work.

Hard lines indeed for a little lad whose heart was set on lettering and drawing. His father said he hadn't long to live. There would be nothing to leave for Willie's art education—nothing but the tiny press bought with money earned as delivery boy, and a capful of old discarded type.

The year 1877 left Mrs. Bradley and her son alone in a world of hard times. Then they left Swampscott for Thompsonville, in Connecticut, where the boy went to school for a short while before they boarded the "steam cars" to resume their journey to Ishpeming, Michigan, home of Mrs. Bradley's sister.

Steve L. Watts was manager of typographic merchandising and design director of American Type Founders. In retirement he operated his own Privateer Press. The lecture, "written in the stick" for his publication, *The Pastime Printer*, was given November 18, 1965.

Will passed his tenth birthday at the mining town of Ishpeming, and went to school there for a full term.

"It is your second year in school. You now have a stepfather. He is a fine man and you like him and he likes you—but of course you can't expect him to pay for your art education. You are having trouble with arithmetic—something in division. Teacher says, 'Take your books and go home, Willie, and remain until you have the correct answer'.

"You don't like arithmetic, anyway.

" 'Mother,' you ask, 'may I go to work and earn money so I can learn to be an artist?'

"Your mother is troubled. Finally she says, 'Perhaps it will be for the best. I hope so'."

It was 1880 when Bradley, then going on twelve, became a printer's devil in the *Iron Agitator* office at Ishpeming. His wages at first were three dollars a week, raised to six before long. Then he switched to an eight-dollar job in another printing office across the street. His first boss hired him back at ten dollars in the exalted capacity of job printer. At fifteen he was foreman of the shop.

His rapid rise in printing didn't distract him from his primary aim. Always his sights were "zeroed in" on the target of his ambition—to learn to be an artist, as his father had been. He thought of printing as being along the *wayside*, on the path to his fond objective.

His drawings on blackboards had sorely tried the indulgence of school teachers. Even while foreman of the printing office at a man's wages, he gratified his compulsion by drawing posters to advertise local events.

"Who is this young artist?"

The question was asked by Frank Bromley, visiting landscape painter. Will told him about his father and his own ambition to study art. Mr. Bromley suggested Chicago instead of Boston for his studies.

Seventeen, with four double eagles in his pocket and sporting a downy pair of mutton-chops (on him they looked good), in the fall of 1885 Will took his departure from Ishpeming and the renamed *Iron Ore*. In Chicago, his friend introduced him at Rand McNally's. He started as a beginner, without pay, cutting tints on wood blocks—under the erroneous impression that illustrators engraved their own blocks.

Will applied himself to his appointed monotonous task until three of his twenty-dollar gold pieces had been used for living expenses, and he was getting nowhere. His supervisor evinced the noncommittal indifference of a cautious pawnbroker. Will returned to Ishpeming.

A letter to him at the *Iron Ore* stated that Rand McNally was prepared to offer him three dollars a week to resume his status as trainee with additional duties as janitor an extra half hour both morning and evening. When he had saved sixty dollars, and was turned eighteen, he found at Rand McNally's a new development that affected his career. The advent of line photoengraving facilitated direct reproduction of all pen drawings. He learned what he could about the new process. His savings running out, he found a job as compositor in the printing plant of Knight & Leonard, where Will's ability at designing with type soon caught the eye of Mr. Leonard.

Mr. Leonard took him out of the composing room and installed him with his drawing materials at a flat-top desk in the office. At nineteen he was a full-time designer, and the wages went in two years to twenty-four dollars. He married his childhood sweetheart from Michigan.

It can be said of Will Bradley that he learned mainly by doing and was alert to targets of opportunity. He did not score a bullseye every time, neither did he pursue forlorn hopes to his own undoing.

There were in those days no art magazines helpful to designers, and examples of printers' art reproduced in trade publications excelled only in marvelous dexterity at rule bending and meticulous presswork, both too time-consuming, and no part of art.

Bradley made friends. He was as lively as a cricket but never pertly critical of his contemporaries. To the end of his days he retained that romantic little-boy-in-a-wonderful-world air about him, but he could be adamant as any captain of horse artillery when he wanted his way.

At the age of twenty-one he left Knight & Leonard to start as freelance designer with his studio in the new Caxton building. He mingled with kindred souls and studied their techniques. Instead of imitating the styles of current favorites he evolved one of his own, predicated upon the pattern employed by quaint Colonial printers, with modern treatment to impart artistic balance, texture, and ornamentation. He was ahead of the trend, however, and prevailing type styles were incompatible with traditional arrangement. For his experimental use he bought a small Golding jobber and minimal equipment which included fonts of the old style letter that was later called Caslon, after its originator, and of Priory Text from the same source. When deferred payments proved burdensome, Bradley turned the press and equipment over to Fred W. Goudy, a bookkeeper, who assumed the conditional purchase agreement.

Meanwhile, Bradley was busy at the drawing board. In 1893, year of the World's Fair, his studio was in the Monadnock building. Specimen reproduction of designs by Bradley had attracted favorable attention, even in Europe. An *Inland Printer* cover, one of eighteen designed by Bradley, showed the publication's name lettered in a romanized black face with tall lowercase. Within ten months afterward, American Type Founders Company announced the Bradley series, patterned after Will's lettering and cut by Herman Ihlenburg at the Philadelphia branch of ATF, with enthusiastic suggestions from the artist. Other type foundries in this country and in Europe soon introduced variant versions of his basic letterform, variously named.

For a short time the Bradleys had a cottage on Fox River at Geneva, Illinois. Will attained full stride as designer. Among other important jobs were cover designs for *Harper's Weekly, Harper's Bazaar, Vogue*, and a run of full-page designs for the *Chicago Sunday Tribune*.

By 1895 typography was overdue for important changes. The stiffness of the spidery body letter called *modern* for nearly a hundred years had been relieved to some degree by diluting with display lines set in ornamented types. Those "period" faces have a retrospective interest for latter-day typewranglers. A rising generation has a reflux that is "hot stuph" for a season. It is fun while it lasts.

Transition in the Gaudy Nineties started with a switch to miscalled Elzevir letterforms. French Old Style and a derivative type family named for Theodore DeVinne changed the looks of things. The bookish smart set, with bandwagon acclaim, copied the impracticable attempts by William Morris to beat fifteenth century prototypos at their own game. This triggered a spread of spurious Jensonian faces, black as the Duke of Hell's boots. The vogue petered out.

There were about as many claimants to the rediscovery of Caslon's types as there used to be pressmen who had worked with Bob Miehle. Live long enough and you become a mythomaniac, believing your inventions. Who is left to gainsay you?

Caslon did not need to be resurrected. It was "common as wheat in a mill" in the composing rooms of Pickering, Chatto & Windus, Joel Munsell and John Wilson & Son, to pick a few. However, Will Bradley was the first to use Caslon in a new and artistic manner, by substituting blocks of type in panel arrangement for monotonous alternation of long and short lines. He used big type heroically instead of screamers and geometric gilhickies to solicit the eye, he took liberties with letterspacing and avoided the obvious in spacing between lines and positioning decorative elements. He created borders and outside ornaments that complemented his romantic whimsy. No matter if his playfulness gagged you, his designs held together like a mosaic pattern and his treatment communicated the message.

In 1895 Bradley came back to the city of Boston. After a close study of Colonial typography at Boston Public Library he settled at Springfield and set up the Wayside Press along with his studio in a new office building. Relying on his income as designer of posters, covers and title pages to carry the expensive burden at the outset, Bradley got ready to start publication of a magazine for artists, giving it the unlikely name, *Bradley: His Book.*

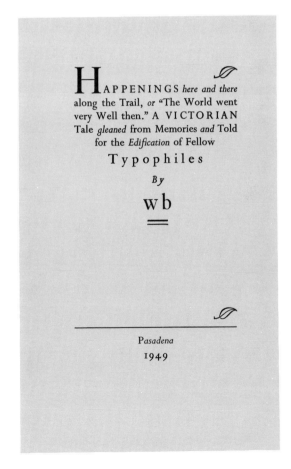

Title page of a brochure of
Mr. Bradley's reminiscences,
printed by Grant Dahlstrom,
The Castle Press, 1949.

To begin with, Wayside Press had a Gally Universal heavy platen and two smaller Gordon snappers. Type dress was chiefly Caslon Old Style replete with quaint characters and tied letters, Caslon Italic and a black of the Colonial era, thus duplicating the types Isaiah Thomas imported from the Caslon letter foundry ere non-intercourse sentiment impeded traffic with Great Britain.

The first important drop-in customer at Wayside Press was Horace A. Moses. He headed Mittineague Paper Company, former name of the present-day Strathmore Paper Company. Samples printed in color, executed in the Bradley style on their splendid deckle-edge text and cover papers, altered merchandising ideas and spread Bradley's fame. Orders for fine printing, on top of editing and supervising production of his publication, overtaxed the physical energy and financial ability of the young man. The business depended on his personal direction and active participation in strenuous work. At last publication of the magazine was discontinued and Wayside Press as a unit—name, goodwill and Will's services—went to University Press at Cambridge. The situation proved so unsatisfactory that Will withdrew.

The Wayside Press story has been told hurriedly. Bradley's work during that period elicited much comment in trade journals—not all of it expressing admiration.

Printer and Bookmaker for June 1897 ran a lengthy article by H. A. Adam, in which he said in part:

"The work now being produced by Will H. Bradley must appeal strongly to the progressive printer, for without doubt he is the first man who has really grasped the full significance of photo-engraving and its relation to printing. Some of Bradley's work must have entailed a great deal of care on his part in the effort to have it printed as he wanted it. He has, it is said, always been loath to entrust any portion of his work to printers not wholly under his control. Unlike many other artists and illustrators Bradley sees his productions through from beginning to end. He supervises everything, sees that the work is properly engraved and printed. His designs are unique and his drawings are made with a definite printing intention.

"That Bradley's work has had a great influence on the conceptions of artistic printers cannot be gainsaid. Would that it had more!"

Compelled to give up his beloved Wayside Press and also abandon his hopes of combining a career as publisher and printer with productive output as creative designer, Bradley proved his mettle in adversity.

P. A. B.

H*is*
Book

Produced *by the* Friends of PAUL A. BENNETT *and* presented
on the evening of Thursday December 3 1953

A typical Will Bradley layout, prepared for the occasion of a testimonial to
Paul A. Bennett, 1953.

While cover designs for *Collier's* were bridging an awkward gap, Edward Bok commissioned the laying out of an editorial prospectus for the *Ladies' Home Journal*. "For this," Bradley said, "I used a special casting of an old face not then on the market, Mr. Phinney of the Boston branch of ATF telling me it was to be called Wayside." Next he created designs for eight full pages of house interiors and a series of house designs for the *Ladies' Home Journal*.

Still striving to regain his health by working every day in the open, a custom he continued for the rest of his life when weather permitted, he built with his own hands a cottage in the White Mountains. In 1903 the fourteen-room residence at Concord was built, using olden time mortise-and-tenon timbers and joists framed by himself and cut by a carpenter on the site, adjacent to Nathaniel Hawthorne's Wayside House.

Meanwhile Bradley wrote and illustrated *Castle Perilous*, which was later published as a three-part serial appearing in *Collier's Weekly*. The demand for poster and cover designs kept him lucratively active while on the side he wrote *Shards of the Silver Sword*, praised by Robert Underwood Johnson but considered too archaic for publication in *Century*.

Now we come to a time in Bradley's career that his admirers today still argue about. His *Memories* are brief on this subject: "Asked by Mr. Robert W. Nelson to undertake an extensive advertising campaign for American Type Founders Company. Promised as many large Miehle presses as might be required. Promise was faithfully kept and two or three big mailings of specimen showings and a little magazine, *American Chap-Book*, went out each month. Designed three type faces and much decorative material."

What type faces did Bradley design in 1904–1905? Not the Wayside series some will ascribe to him. He was co-designer with J. W. Phinney and Morris Benton of the face then called Antique Bold. Bewick Roman was Bradley's, according to E. G. Gress. The third (and fourth) must have been the Bradley Roman and Italic, to be mentioned later as the Peter Poodle types.

The Chap-Book Cuts, some made in sizes up to 10 by 23 picas, were among the largest ever cast typehigh in foundry metal. Post Ornaments, a series in style akin to Bradley's, were not his designs. A font of two-color Mission Toys cuts sold like hotcakes.

Among printers Bradley was remembered for his *American Chap-*

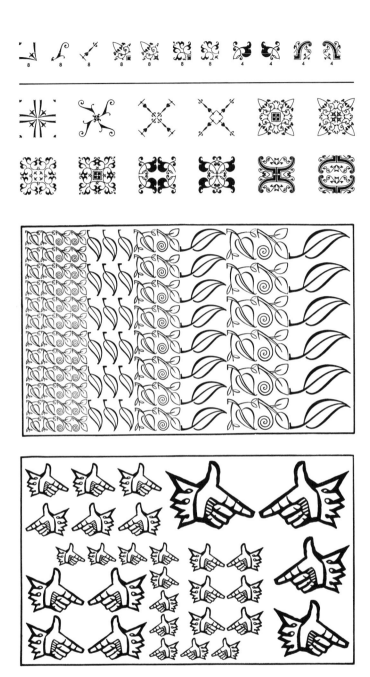

From an American Type Founders catalog, *ATF Typo-graphic Accessories*, June 1957, a showing of Bradley Combination Ornaments, a showing of a "Handipack" font of Bradley Decorators, and a Handipack of Bradley's Chapbook Pointers.

Books. They set the style for years. Many splendid and timely designs by Bradley for ATF have been forgotten because they were made only as electrotypes shown in the *American Cut Book*, issued in 1905 bearing a misleading "1900" copyright date on the title page. His designs carry no credit lines but his touch is apparent. Among other notably successful brochures written and designed for ATF were his *White Book of Cloister*, *Golden Book of Business* and *The Printer Man's Joy*.

These typefaces were drawn when Will wrote *Peter Poodle, Toymaker to the King*, around 1901, and cut by the foundry as private types, on 14-point body, in 1905. A special casting was made for Will's book, which was published October 1906 by Dodd, Mead & Company.

(Matrices for Bradley Roman and Italic were at ATF in 1952, when David Silvé asked about them.)

In 1907 Bradley laid out a new typographic treatment for *Collier's*, so well received that he was retained as art editor. Occupying a studio in the Metropolitan Tower, he handled the art editorship of five or six publications at the same time, including *Good Housekeeping*, *Metropolitan*, and *Century*. He went to Boston to revise the typographic layout of the *Christian Science Monitor*. A series of stories, *Tales of Noodleburg*, commenced in 1906, appeared monthly for a year in *St. Nicholas* and were published as a book, *Wonderbox Stories*, by the Century Company.

Through the years 1910 to 1914 William Randolph Hearst came to be Will Bradley's best customer. He would consult personally with Bradley to get his ideas, then tell him to go ahead—no deadline or estimated cost mentioned, no formal purchase order until Will submitted his bill.

In 1915 he became supervising art director for Hearst publications and motion pictures. Mr. Hearst was at that time making two film serials, *Patria* and *Beatrice Fairfax*. The pictures were made at Ithaca where Will functioned as art supervisor. It turned out to be a full-time job, not entirely to his liking. For two or three years, beginning in 1918, he wrote and directed pictures as an independent venture. *Moongold* was a Pierrot pantomime shot against a background of black velvet.

After forty-two years of chop-and-change activity, Bradley went back to the Hearst publications in 1921, devoting his time to art supervision of magazines and planning the typographic and pictorial publicity for motion pictures. He remained on that job until retirement in 1930.

During this period his *Spoils*, a drama in free verse, was published in

Hearst's International. Also his novel, *Launcelot and the Ladies,* was published by Harpers.

As one of the judges in the "Fifty Books of the Year," on February 3, 1931, Bradley made an address at the opening exhibition in New York Public Library.

When he retired from all active work for the Hearst publications, his declared intention was "to enjoy sunshine and help other people get on with what they have been trying to do."

Steadfast to honor Bradley were former boy printers of my generation. Not many of us then knew his name, because we never saw the *American Printer, Inland Printer,* or *Printing Art* magazines in country newspaper offices. Nevertheless his inspiration got through to us, by induction perhaps. A little chap couldn't reach the uppercase "G" without using a thick specimen book to underlay his form. On reaching manhood's estate he learned about Bradley and sang praises due his *exemplaire.*

Mrs. Bradley and her sun-loving husband lived in California at South Pasadena. He liked to go to Grant Dahlstrom's Castle Press and set a little type now and then.

In July 1948 the Typophiles in New York City hosted a birthday salute to His Elegance, naming him, *in absentia,* Dean of Typographers.

Grant Dahlstrom in 1949 printed as a pamphlet Bradley's *Memories: 1875–1895,* illustrated by "w.b."

The following year Bradley gave a talk before the Zamorano Club of Los Angeles, and became an honorary member.

Huntington Library opened an exhibit of Bradleyana in November 1950. During this exhibition, early in 1951, a visitor was Tom Cleland, who met Bradley for the first time. The Rounce and Coffin Club honored Bradley with an eloquent citation.

Mrs. Bradley died in 1952. Will joined his daughter, Fern, and her husband, Edward Dufner, at Short Hills, New Jersey. There he resumed activity, designing for Strathmore a brochure and portfolio in the series featuring distinguished designers.

David Silvé and Richard McArthur, jointly with the Typophiles, arranged a luncheon for Will in New York on his eighty-fourth birthday.

Strathmore presented his last work at a luncheon honoring him in 1954. Later that year he was the thirtieth recipient of the AIGA medal.

He died January 30, 1962, at La Mesa, California, aged ninety-three.

Bruce Rogers.

BRUCE ROGERS

by James Hendrickson

BRUCE ROGERS, Indiana-born book designer (1870–1957), was by common consent of his contemporaries the supreme artist of the book of his time. Updike, Dwiggins, Rollins, Cleland, Bradley, Goudy, Warde, Ruzicka, Grabhorn, Meynell, Morison, all have readily conceded this.[1] It may be ventured further that, in variety and quantity of performance as well as in general excellence, his record has no parallel in the whole history of printing.

Your reporter therefore could only regard himself as singularly fortunate when, in the summer of 1922, he found himself working as special compositor to Mr. Rogers at the Printing House of William Edwin Rudge in Mount Vernon, New York. The master and man relationship there established was to survive and renew itself in sundry typographical projects over the next thirty-five years.

But let us take the Rogers career in orderly sequence[2]—for it was an orderly career even though it was a varied one. His name was Albert Bruce Rogers, but he promptly divested himself of the "Albert." After he had begun to sign his books with a printer's mark and the initials "B" and "R," he came to be known to friends and admirers simply and affectionately as BR.

He was born of English Yorkshire stock on May 14, 1870, in Linnwood, Indiana, now a suburb of Lafayette. He died eighty-seven years later on May 18, 1957, at his home, October House, in New Fairfield,

James Hendrickson, who worked with William Edwin Rudge and Bruce Rogers, has had a long career in typography, book design and dramatic work. He was the director of the American Institute of Graphic Arts Workshop. Lecture given April 29, 1965.

Connecticut. He thus had a working life of more than sixty-five years, during which he designed upwards of seven hundred books, including two folio Bibles. He had already come into international recognition in his early thirties.

For convenience we will divide the Rogers story into six phases. There was the Indiana, or "incunabula" period, as he himself has labeled it (1870–1895), the Riverside Press period (1895–1911), the Dyke Mill period (1911–1916), the Mount Vernon-Rudge period (1919–1928), the second English sojourn (1928–1932), and the long October House period (1932–1957).

The Indiana period included the usual early schooling. "From his father, Mr. Rogers had learned to develop an inherited talent for drawing and penmanship, so that when he entered Purdue University at sixteen, he was prepared to make the most of advanced courses in drafting and decorative design. He decided to become an illustrator. . . ."[3]

Graduating in 1890, he worked for a time as a newspaper artist for the *Indianapolis News*. Later, while doing free-lance drawing in Indianapolis, "he made the acquaintance of Mr. J. M. Bowles, the founder of a quarterly, *Modern Art*. . . . Mr. Bowles had some of the Kelmscott books and showed them to Mr. Rogers, to whom they came as a revelation. He has said that upon seeing Morris's printing, his whole interest in book production became rationalized and intensified. He abandoned the prevalent idea that a book could be made beautiful through the worth of an illustrator alone, and determined instead to use that curiosity he had always felt as to type and paper toward a study of the physical form of printed books."[4]

In 1895 *Modern Art* was acquired by L. Prang and Company, Boston art publishers. Bowles, its editor, and later Rogers, followed it to Boston. It was natural that Rogers should have gravitated to Boston, which in 1895 was in its late heyday as the "Athens of America." There was still a literary and bookish spirit in the air, and we know that BR took full advantage of the opportunities afforded him for study and self-improvement. There were libraries and art museums and several good workshops, and in nearby Cambridge were a great university and two distinguished old presses, the Riverside Press and the University Press. In Boston itself were the newly established Merrymount Press of D. B. Updike and the Heintzemann Press where Carl Rollins later got his start. There too were the Society of Printers and the Club of Odd

Volumes, of both of which Rogers ultimately became an active member.

After a year of free-lancing for Prang at fifty cents per hour (J. M. Bowles tells how Rogers might "work for a few hours, then go to the cashier, get his money and walk in the beautiful Massachusetts country for one, two or three days . . ."[5], BR went to work for Houghton, Mifflin and Company at the Riverside Press. Here he worked for four years on trade books and the design of book advertisements for *The Atlantic Monthly*. In 1900 a Department of Special Bookmaking for the production of fine limited editions was created and placed under Mr. Rogers' direction. The beginning of this project was not nearly as readily managed as has been suggested. BR has told how he "had to plead for two or three years and ultimately threaten to go elsewhere" before the Riverside Press Editions, as they were called, were finally launched. But according to J. M. Bowles, "they turned out to be, surprisingly, almost a commercial success." The rest is printing history.

Because printing was only then beginning to struggle out of the long eclipse of the arts in the nineteenth century, these Riverside Press Editions came as nothing less than a lovely revelation to those who had to do with books and printing. And, considering the low estate to which printing had fallen, it is still a matter of wonder how Rogers, lacking any respectable criteria, managed to develop a taste so fine and powers of selection and invention so admirable as are shown in these early works. Printed on dampened handmade papers, these Riverside Press Editions possess a charm and a gaiety, a style and a variety—withal a sure-handedness in type arrangement—that is difficult even to suggest. BR's talent for drawing was put to good use in the creation of initial letters, borders, and typographic spots, always of a deft typographic quality. In less than a dozen years sixty notable books were produced. Not all were of equal merit, perhaps, some obviously derivative of earlier historical styles (if that be a vice), and some frankly experimental. But at least a dozen are small masterpeices. BR in his later years never did anything finer than the *Songs and Sonnets of Pierre de Ronsard* (1903), *The Song of Roland* (1906), *The Banquet of Pluto* (1908), or Walton's *The Compleat Angler* (1909).

Rogers left the Riverside Press in 1911. Excepting his four-days-a-week schedule at the Cambridge University Press (England), and the very loose arrangement he had with Rudge, BR was to be a free-lancer henceforth for the rest of his life. In terms of personal comfort and material welfare he and Mrs. Rogers[6] were to pay rather dearly for this freedom, but one also recognizes that it was this very frugality in his personal life that accounts in part for his amazing artistic output.

We may read between the lines and see that this five-year period, 1911 to 1916, must have been a difficult one, for the record shows that few books were produced. Following an unproductive visit to England in 1912, BR returned to New York and, among other assignments, resumed his long, cordial relations with Henry Watson Kent, who was in charge of publications at the Metropolitan Museum of Art and who managed the Museum Press. This was an actual press, which under Kent's direction did some surprisingly fine work. Kent now commissioned Rogers to design for the Museum's use the type later known as Centaur, and for many years the Museum enjoyed the exclusive right to use the capitals while Rogers retained ownership of the lowercase. This type was first used for a book in 1915 when BR printed a translation by George B. Ives of Maurice de Guerin's *The Centaur* at Carl Rollins' Montague Press in the historic old Dyke Mill at Montague, Massachusetts. A slight quarto volume, in an edition of 135 copies, it is now a cherished collector's item. While we have called these years "the Dyke Mill period," we should explain that BR worked at Montague only a part of this time. However, the Dyke Mill days with Rollins were among his happiest memories.

In 1916 Rogers again sailed for England, to join Sir Emery Walker in establishing a press with which they hoped to continue the great tradition of the Kelmscott Press and the Doves Press. Walker, proprietor of a collotype works, had been technical adviser and an important associate in both presses, first with William Morris and then with Cobden-Sanderson. Because of wartime difficulties, the Mall Press, as the new press was named, lasted only long enough for BR to produce laboriously a printing in the new Centaur type of Dürer's *Of the Just Shaping of Letters*, to be published by the Grolier Club.

At the insistence of Sydney Cockerell, Rogers was then retained as typographic adviser to the Cambridge University Press. This proved to be a frustrating experience. Not only was there an extreme shortage of competent workmen because of the war, but also there were almost insuperable obstacles to overcome in the inertia of the work-ways in this old printing house. Rogers prepared a masterly and somewhat devastating report for the Syndics on the typography of the Cambridge University Press, a report which, if not acted upon in Rogers' time, certainly

Autographed title page of *Bruce Rogers, Designer of Books*, Harvard, 1925.

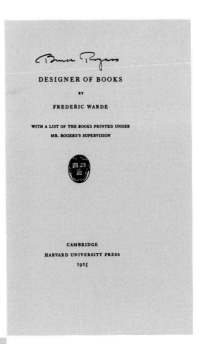

DESIGNER OF BOOKS

BY

FREDERIC WARDE

WITH A LIST OF THE BOOKS PRINTED UNDER
MR. ROGERS'S SUPERVISION

CAMBRIDGE
HARVARD UNIVERSITY PRESS
1925

The Second Epistle General of
PETER

CHAPTER 1

SIMON Peter, a servant and an apostle of Jesus Christ, to them that have obtained like precious faith with us through the righteousness of God and our Saviour Jesus Christ: ¶2 Grace and peace be multiplied unto you through the knowledge of God, and of Jesus our Lord. ¶3 According as his divine power hath given unto us all things that pertain unto life and godliness, through the knowledge of him that hath called us to glory and virtue: ¶4 Whereby are given unto us exceeding great and precious promises: that by these ye might be partakers of the divine nature, having escaped the corruption that is in the world through lust. ¶5 And beside this, giving all diligence, add to your faith virtue; and to virtue knowledge; ¶6 And to knowledge temperance; and to temperance patience; and to patience godliness; ¶7 And to godliness brotherly kindness; and to brotherly kindness charity. ¶8 For if these things be in you, and abound, they make you that ye shall neither be barren nor unfruitful in the knowledge of our Lord Jesus Christ. ¶9 But he that lacketh these things is blind, and cannot see afar off, and hath forgotten that he was purged from his old sins. ¶10 Wherefore the rather, brethren, give diligence to make your calling and election sure: for if ye do these things, ye shall never fall: ¶11 For so an entrance shall be ministered unto you abundantly into the everlasting kingdom of our Lord and Saviour Jesus Christ. ¶12 Wherefore I will not be negligent to put you always in remembrance of these things, though ye know them, and be established in the present truth. ¶13 Yea, I think it meet, as long as I am in this tabernacle, to stir you up by putting you in remembrance; ¶14 Knowing that shortly I must put off this my tabernacle, even as our Lord Jesus Christ hath shewed me. ¶15 Moreover I will endeavour that ye may be able after my decease to have these things always in remembrance. ¶16 For we have not

followed cunningly devised fables, when we made known unto you the power and coming of our Lord Jesus Christ, but were eyewitnesses of his majesty. ¶17 For he received from God the Father honour and glory, when there came such a voice to him from the excellent glory, This is my beloved Son, in whom I am well pleased. ¶18 And this voice which came from heaven we heard, when we were with him in the holy mount. ¶19 We have also a more sure word of prophecy; whereunto ye do well that ye take heed, as unto a light that shineth in a dark place, until the day dawn, and the day star arise in your hearts: ¶20 Knowing this first, that no prophecy of the scripture is of any private interpretation. ¶21 For the prophecy came not in old time by the will of man: but holy men of God spake as they were moved by the Holy Ghost.

CHAPTER 2

BUT there were false prophets also among the people, even as there shall be false teachers among you, who privily shall bring in damnable heresies, even denying the Lord that bought them, and bring upon themselves swift destruction. ¶2 And many shall follow their pernicious ways; by reason of whom the way of truth shall be evil spoken of. ¶3 And through covetousness shall they with feigned words make merchandise of you: whose judgment now of a long time lingereth not, and their damnation slumbereth not. ¶4 For if God spared not the angels that sinned, but cast them down to hell, and delivered them into chains of darkness, to be reserved unto judgment; ¶5 And spared not the old world, but saved Noah the eighth person, a preacher of righteousness, bringing in the flood upon the world of the ungodly; ¶6 And turning the cities of Sodom and Gomorrha into ashes condemned them with an overthrow, making them an ensample unto those that after

1194

Page from the Oxford Lectern Bible, printed at the University Press, Oxford, 1935.

paved the way for his two brilliant successors as typographic adviser to the Press, Stanley Morison and the present incumbent, John Dreyfus. It has always seemed to me an interesting paradox that Bruce Rogers of Indiana (as Emery Walker delighted in introducing him to his friends) should be found directing typography in these famous English presses— for two years at Cambridge, and a dozen years later, with the great *Lectern Bible* and other books, at Oxford.

We now come to a part of the story of which your reporter has personal knowledge, the Mount Vernon-Rudge period. If there seems to be undue emphasis on these phases of the Rogers story in which I participated, I hope the reader will bear with me, for I feel that my best contribution will be to record, even at a little length, some of the more intimate recollections that I have of BR and his work. Moreover, did not BR himself once admonish me, "Never apologize"?

Shortly after BR's return from England in 1919 he met Mr. William Edwin Rudge, who had a printing plant in William Street, almost under the Brooklyn Bridge. The meeting resulted in a few single commissions and later, when Rudge had moved to a fine new stone building in Mount Vernon, Rogers agreed to join him on a three-days-a-week basis.

Your reporter now quotes from an article he prepared for one of the Typophiles Chapbooks.[7]

> The Rudge shops were sequestered in a rock-shouldered parkway near the Columbus Avenue station of the New York, New Haven and Hartford Railroad, and there was a certain monastic quiet and repose about this Printing House of William Edwin Rudge, as it was called. The windows of BR's studio looked out upon a grove of trees and a stone-flagged dooryard where the birds were almost the only visitors. Rudge had seen a vision of creating here the finest printing office in America, and so BR was given a very free hand. The choicest of foundry types, Linotype and Monotype matrices and fine printing papers were unhesitatingly and ungrudgingly provided for BR's use. This combination of happy physical environment and a liberal-handed proprietor resulted, as might be expected, in a prolific, varied, and often highly experimental output.
>
> The Rudge composing room in the early 1920s was much like any other composing room of the day except that its personnel was unusual. There were the regular union journeymen, but in addition there were the young fellows all over the place (and once even a girl from England) each one "a new cloud in the overhead," as the chairman of the union chapel humorously put it. Edgar Wells, perhaps because he was working exclusively on BR's assignments, even

dared to wear a smock, tempting the risibilities of the regular compositors. The name of Bruce Rogers dominated the whole establishment, and it was "Bruce Rogers this" and "Bruce Rogers that." But
there was one itinerant journeyman down from Canada who finally
said in exasperation, "Who is this Bruce Rogers, anyway? I never
heard of him." To which Lambden, the chapel chairman, retorted,
"Oh, yeah? Well I guess he has never heard of you, either."

Edgar Wells decided to move on shortly after my arrival and by
good fortune his job as BR's special compositor was assigned to me.
Then followed exhilarating days, setting stunning-looking type
pages from BR's handsomely sketched layouts, sometimes in unknown and exciting imported types, and where the hours and hours
of time consumed never seemed to be of importance. Wells had
completed the very intricate task of setting the borders for *The
Pierrot of the Minute* and I started with the composition of the
poem itself.

Mr. Rogers' preoccupation with typographic ornament probably
began with the *Pierrot* and with the *Monotype Bulletin* showing the
Scotch Roman types with the new added long descenders initiated
by him, and embellished with many unusual arrangements of type
ornaments. His retention on a yearly basis by J. Mawry Dove, as a
sort of anonymous art adviser to the Lanston Monotype Company
at about this time, no doubt confirmed his dedication to a period of
experimentation with type ornaments. [This was probably BR's best
time financially. In addition to a weekly remittance in three figures
from the Monotype Company, there were retainers from Rudge and
from the Harvard University Press, plus private commissions. The
purchase of October House probably came out of this affluence.]

BR's first studio at Mount Vernon (perhaps because I knew it
better) always seemed to me to have more character than his later
and larger one on the floor above. It was rather frugal in its appointments of a small table with slightly inclined drawingboard top by
one window; a longer table on horses, strewn with paper samples,
by the other; a chest of drawers containing broadsides and large
books along one side wall; in the corner a small type cabinet containing special imported borders; and, on top of the cabinet, a 6″ × 9″
Albion hand-press actually used only once in seven years. The back
wall was largely covered by an enormous wardrobe surmounted by
a ship model, while the remaining side of the room was lined with
long, low book-shelves. Twin Chinese jars stood on the chest and a
type broadside or two hung on the walls. There was always an
atmosphere of English cigarette smoke faintly evident upon coming
into the room, and also an atmosphere of polite and mild disorder
in the disarray of work-desk and table.

Rudge had his own handsome library to the right of the front

entrance and also his fine offices in New York, but this [BR's] room
was really the inner sanctum of the Rudge printing plant; and here
a compositor or occasionally a pressman might come with proofs of
BR's work for his approval, always assured of a pleasant, if reserved,
reception. We younger workers approached his door with a certain
amount of awe, and when going to him for help with some knotty
problem arising in some of my own little commercial jobs, the ease
with which he would encompass the problems and then tentatively
suggest a most admirable solution, would send me back to the composing room to announce to the first person I encountered: "The
man is a magician!" This is not to imply that BR always had an immediate answer to any typographic problem. His attitude, towards
his own work as well, was rather, "Perhaps if you would do this,
well, no, or yes, perhaps that would look better." And his often
ruthless rejection in his own designs of what to my less cultivated
eye seemed a beautiful and finished effect was at times most discon-
certing.

A multitude of random impressions of BR during those days
crowds my memory. He has always insisted that he is no printer,
saying, "If 'printer' be the word, then I am afraid I can't claim to be
one, either by birth, inclination, training, or practice"; but his astonishing knowledge of types, their peculiarities and special possibilities, and their application to paper, will immediately confound
him in his own statement. I have seen him stand alongside a press at
Mount Vernon and offer suggestions which, however dubiously accepted by the pressman, would result in a solution of some thereto-
fore insurmountable technical problems. . . . There was *The Green
Hat* title-page where our designer tried to avoid the too obvious by
ordering trial proofs in black and brown on the green-tinted paper,
but ultimately succumbing to a blue-green tint instead of the brown.
. . . There was the cover to the *Venetian Printers* pamphlet showing the then new Goudy Italian Old Style type, where the compositor was instructed to insert thin spaces between some of the
triangular units of the border to avoid a geometric rigidity in the
resulting pattern. . . . Or the time when your recorder had lifted an
arrangement of typographic flowers from an Updike page, to be
mildly reprimanded with "Don't borrow contemporary work—you
are sure to be found out". . . . Or when Scribner's production man
complained in the galley proofs for *Ethan Frome* that "This is not
according to Hoyle," BR turned to me and remarked, evenly,
"We're Hoyle."

The list of distinguished and significant Rogers items done at
Mount Vernon is a matter of record, but in addition to the im-
portant books produced, it can be stated that BR's presence in the
Rudge printing house gave a great prestige value to the commercial

F E B R U A R Y

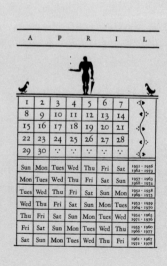

IT IS NOW FEBRUARY, and the Sun is gotten up a
Cocke-stride of his climbing, the Valleyes now are
painted white, and the Brookes are full of water : the
Frog goes to seeke out the Paddocke, and the Crow and
the Rooke begin to mislike their old Makes : forward
Connies begin now to kindle, & the fat grounds are not
without Lambes : the Gardiner fals to sorting of his
seeds, and the Husbandman falls afresh to scowring of
his Ploughshare: the Terme travellers make the Shooe-
makers Harvest, and the Chaundlers cheese makes the
chalke walke apace : The Fishmonger sorts his ware
against Lent : and a Lambe-skinne is good for a lame
arme: the waters now alter the nature of their softnes,

A P R I L

1	2	3	4	5	6	7	
8	9	10	11	12	13	14	
15	16	17	18	19	20	21	
22	23	24	25	26	27	28	
29	30						
Sun	Mon	Tues	Wed	Thu	Fri	Sat	1951 · 1956 1962 · 1973
Mon	Tues	Wed	Thu	Fri	Sat	Sun	1957 · 1963 1968 · 1974
Tues	Wed	Thu	Fri	Sat	Sun	Mon	1952 · 1958 1969 · 1975
Wed	Thu	Fri	Sat	Sun	Mon	Tues	1953 · 1959 1964 · 1970
Thu	Fri	Sat	Sun	Mon	Tues	Wed	1954 · 1965 1971 · 1976
Fri	Sat	Sun	Mon	Tues	Wed	Thu	1955 · 1960 1966 · 1977
Sat	Sun	Mon	Tues	Wed	Thu	Fri	1961 · 1967 1972 · 1978

BELOW   Atlantic Charter, printed
at William E. Rudge's Sons, New
York, 1943.

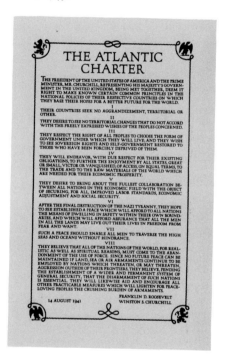

LEFT   Pages from *The Twelve
Moneths and Christmas Day from
"Fantastics" by Nicholas Breton*
[1626] printed by Clarke & Way,
New York, 1951.

printing output of the plant. In fact, there were not a few of the commercial jobs in which he had an actual hand. Also, his example was a continuous inspiration to the younger workers, particularly those in the composing room, many of whom would turn in typographical arrangements with something like BR's own standard of craftsmanship.

In all fairness it must be added that, in return for the Rogers contribution to the Rudge reputation, Rudge contributed very considerably to the building of the Rogers tradition. At a critical and somewhat fallow period in BR's development Rudge provided him with a new and enthusiastic environment in which to work and experiment. Also, Rudge's masterly salesmanship (assisted, it must be admitted, by the lush financial period of the twenties) brought BR books for the first time securely into the auction rooms as valuable collector's items, catalogued under his name instead of the authors'.

The Rogers-Rudge relationship was severed in 1928 with BR's departure for his second sojourn in England, although the *Boswell Papers* and several other items were carried on at Mount Vernon under his guidance by cable or correspondence during his stay abroad. Mr. Rudge's death occurred in 1931 while BR was still in London, but the Printing House of William Edwin Rudge continued operations some five years longer. The Rogers *Utopia* for the Limited Editions Club was produced during this later period.

The Harvard University Press association runs parallel to the Rudge connection. Mr. Rogers was retained as typographic adviser to the Press in 1920 and continued until 1936, during which time there were produced some thirty books which he cared to claim.

Another venture of this period, to which BR was more or less a godfather, was your reporter's June House Press in the country back of Stamford, Connecticut, on the property later purchased by Frank Altschul, where he now has his Overbrook Press. The June House, so called for the June family, one of the earlier owners, was a small frame dwelling dating back probably to the close of the eighteenth century. It had a big fireplace with built-in Dutch oven. BR produced more than one excellent omelet before this fireplace, commenting as he did so, "Some of these days we will look back upon this as the happiest time of our lives." James Raye Wells[8] and I, on Rogers' advice, had purchased a handpress from the maker, one Schneidlwind, in Chicago, and with meager type equipment (Monotype Fournier, also on BR's advice) we managed to produce and sell two Walt Whitman items and several others from 1925 to 1927. But the June House Press was never much more than a weekend plaything.

BR took a lease on a water-mill on an adjoining property which he named Cuckoo Mill with the hope, never realized, of one day having a press there. Somewhere there must be copies of a New Year's greeting card with a charming drawing by BR of the Cuckoo Mill in winter. The implication of the name was BR's playful reminder that, like the cuckoo bird which is known for its custom of laying its eggs in the nest of other birds for them to hatch, he had never had a press of his own and his books were always produced in other men's printing houses . . . . The June house was later destroyed by fire.

BR once spoke to me of the desirability of perhaps "leaving one's mark," and I imagine he had something of this in mind when he departed for England in the fall of 1928 to do a printing of Homer's *Odyssey*, in a new translation by the famed Lawrence of Arabia. Let us have it as told by Rogers himself: "It was in 1927, while reading Lawrence's *Seven Pillars of Wisdom* for the first time, that it occurred to me that its author was the very man to translate the *Odyssey* anew. It was a book that I had long wanted to print in a style fitting its splendor as a story, but I had never read any of the existing translations with complete satisfaction: they all lacked something vital. Here, at last, was a man who could make Homer live again—a man of action who was also a scholar and who could write swift and graphic English. But where was he? At that time he was to me a half-legendary person and I knew only that somewhere out east of Suez was an air craftsman who had legally changed his name to Shaw. I casually mentioned my project and my perplexity to Col. Ralph Isham, who startled me by exclaiming, 'The very thing for Shaw to do! I'll write him tomorrow. He's in Karachi.' "9

After extended negotiations, largely because of a genuinely modest demur on Shaw's part at the thought of tackling Homer, he embarked on the translation. During the four years required to complete the *Odyssey* project Rogers and Lawrence (or Shaw) became fast friends, though a more unlikely combination of personalities is difficult to imagine. The book was painstakingly printed in the Centaur types on a gray handmade paper and bound in full black Niger leather. As the making of this book is discussed in detail by Mr. Rogers in *Paragraphs on Printing*, I will comment only that the *Odyssey* is one of the more magnificent of Rogers' books, as well as one of the most expensive!

The Monotype Corporation of London, under Mr. Rogers' super-vision, was at this time cutting a full series, for general use, of the Centaur types with Frederic Warde's Arrighi for the italic. Out of this activity came a tender from the Oxford University Press for BR to do a folio Bible, utilizing his Centaur types. The resultant Oxford Lectern Bible required six years for completion. It has been called by Joseph Blumenthal "the most important and notable typographic achievement of the twentieth century."

Another world's classic produced by BR at the Oxford University Press during this period was a handsome printing, in the original Fell types, of Coleridge's *The Rime of the Ancient Mariner,* with an intro-duction by "Q" (Sir Arthur Quiller-Couch). Also in the Fell types was a printing of the Croxall translation of *Aesop's Fables* for The Limited Editions Club.

In 1932 Mr. Rogers returned to the United States, and although he made yearly visits to England and the Continent until 1939, he was to live and work henceforth at October House, a fine old brick dwelling in New Fairfield, Connecticut, which he had purchased back in 1925. The house was ostensibly named for a cornerstone which bore the date "October ye 17 AD 1771," but I have suspected that BR was also indulging in a bit of fancy: This was to be a house for the October of his days. (And had not the Henricksons had a June House?) Here the many Limited Editions Club items, *The Bruce Rogers World Bible, The Catalogue of the Frick Collection,* etc., were planned and executed, and here in the later years came an annual pilgrimage of graphic arts folk to pay admiring tribute to BR at a garden party on his birthday.

Midway in this October House period were two notable extratypo-graphic projects—the one a figurehead for the sailing ship *Joseph Conrad,* which BR carved in the wood, working for the most part in a small hotel room in West Forty-fifth Street. The other project, more nearly typographic, was the design of that handsome lettering for the quotation from Emerson which is cut in the stone at the south wall of Hunter College. BR climbed the workman's scaffolding, in good weather and bad, to oversee the carving.

In the spring of 1942 Louis Ansbacher conceived of the idea that his then employer, Fred Rudge, should print and publish a book dealing with BR's work as book designer, and *Paragraphs on Printing* was the outcome. I was retained as amanuensis and after a half-year of fairly strenuous editorial work and another half-year of production the book was published, receiving considerable acclaim not only for the beautiful examples shown of BR's work but also for the modesty and uncompromising integrity of BR's approach to the subject of book design. The extract which follows is from my "Induction" to another one of Paul Bennett's Typophiles Chapbooks.[10]

This "play on BRinting" reflects, not altogether inaccurately, the processes by which the text of *Paragraphs on Printing* came into being. The old proverb, "Many a true word is spoken in jest," applies here, and those who know the protagonist will recognize that he speaks, for the most part, "in character." The title, *Through the Mill with BR*, is the author's salute to Mr. Rogers' lifelong attachment to water mills, and at the same time it hints at the rigors attending the garnering of the text of *Paragraphs on Printing*.

Meetings were arranged once or twice a week between Mr. Rogers, my wife and myself. These meetings would be wherever convenience permitted, in BR's hotel, our own hotel, or perhaps in A. Colish's printing shop, or in the Duschnes bookshop. (There were the occasional jollier get-togethers at dinner or tavern.)

The procedure, in theory, was for J. H. [James Hendrickson] to engage BR in discussion of typographic matters, and for C.B. [Claire Bruce] to make a short-hand record of these conversations. However, when the notes were translated, the resulting copy all too often was found to be confused and repetitious. (I submit that a literal transcript of any conversation might astonish and embarrass the participants.) The "elicitor" would then edit material as necessary, and mail the corrected draft to New Fairfield for the author to approve or rewrite as he might see fit.

This went on for some months with the elicitor treading a delicate path wherein he was swayed between a duty to the publisher to obtain as many words of text as possible and a determination not to lose a highly valued friendship in the process. Periodically BR would put his foot down, as it were, and announce that he was through—"not another word!" Then would come a period of jockeying for more copy until the author's interest could be again aroused. Thus the daily tally of words in hand became an increasingly anxious game. It was a great day when BR lighted upon the word "elicited" for the title-page. His author's eye regained its lustre and the project immediately took a strong tack to windward.

It need hardly be pointed out that the title of *Paragraphs on Printing* came of our artist's seemingly infallible knack of making the most of his materials—in this case a mass of fragmentary and somewhat compromising copy.

Time and present space permit only a cursory concluding comment by your reporter. As to personality, BR was exacting but fair, proud and a little reticent but innately modest, frugal in his ways but generous in his dealings, and essentially kind, but candid and honestly spoken to a fault.

His most impressive quality was his timelessness. Today, tomorrow, next year seemed ever the same to him. He may, on occasion, have made haste, but I never saw him in a hurry at his work. If pressed unduly for his approval of a press sheet, he might say, "They can't hurry me," and put on his hat and coat and leave for the day.

He once said at the beginning of an interview for publication, "Now the first thing that you can say of me is that I am a pessimist." I am sure that he meant this as indicating his attitude toward his work. Years of experience had taught him to anticipate a hundred difficulties. It will always remain a mystery to anyone cognizant of printing house hazards how it was possible for BR to surmount these difficulties, working as he did in many different printing environments, his instructions and corrections often being handled by correspondence. He had never had a printing establishment of his own because he had always chosen to spare himself from management details for the more important work of designing books. I myself know of two instances where patrons would have made it possible for him to have his own press. BR's lifelong predicament, it seems to me, was that he had refined a craft into an art, more truly into a fine art, with the inevitable economic and professional contradictions which this entailed.

The young designer may do well to study the Rogers books in their original formats. He can learn much from a master working in the grand manner—or shall we use Meyer Wagman's[11] designation, "the classical manner"? The so-called contemporary or "modern" school of typography was far from BR's thoughts. Asymmetrical arrangements and sans serif types, for the most part, were strange to him. The anemic and repetitious and sometimes downright illegible type arrangements of the "modern" boys stand in strange contrast to his suave or gay, or even noble, but always eminently readable pages.

What will the future say of Mr. Rogers' place as a book designer? With the advent of computer typesetting and photographic printing, can one even foresee a future for book design as we have known it? Carl Rollins wrote in a review of *Paragraphs on Printing*, "One cannot say how these examples will survive the future, but, for the years of eclecticism which gave Mr. Rogers his opportunity, they stand unrivalled."[12] And Louis Ansbacher once said something to the same point, if perhaps in more colloquial terms. I later quoted his words to BR, who only smiled, but not in protest, "Some day perhaps there may come a book designer to equal BR, but there will never be a better."

Your reporter has never recorded just how he first "met up" with BR and wherefore he appears in and out of the Rogers story from the Rudge days onward. An explanatory note may therefore be in order.

I had been a "boy wonder" printer in Kansas City, with a press in the corner of my mother's big, old-fashioned kitchen. I had heard of Bruce Rogers and had seen reproductions of his work in the trade journals and in Edmund Gress's admirable book, *The Art and Practice of Typography*, but had never expected to meet such a noted figure. My family had hopes for me as a coming printer businessman, until one day I announced that my ambitions lay in the direction of the stage. Family consternation! A wartime turn in the Navy did not change matters, and in 1920 I was off to New York and the American Academy of Dramatic Arts.

Various theatrical engagements followed, but then, as now, the theatrical profession always had more vacation time than work periods. I had become a full journeyman printer and my trade proved to be a very practical help to an impecunious actor. In the summer of 1922 I called on Hal Marchbanks, then the best-known printer in America, and while he had no work for me he did advise my trying Rudge, who was having difficulty in obtaining suitable help after he had moved his plant out of the city.

At Mr. Rudge's invitation I visited the plant in Mount Vernon. After Rudge had shown me through the establishment, which was an impressive one, he announced that whenever I could make up my mind to spend the next five years of my life there he believed they "could make a niche" for me. Which offer well-nigh sent me on my way at once! His complaint was that the young fellows would come to work for him, "soak up all they could learn," and then go elsewhere. As I was leaving a dignified personage came down the hall and Mr. Rudge asked, "Do you know who that is?" When I replied in the negative he informed me that it was Bruce Rogers and that he was working here. I could see Rudge observing me to see whether the information registered, which of course it did with considerable impact. As my intentions were for a summertime job only, here was an unexpected complication. I sensed immediately the unique opportunity which presented itself, merely to work in the same environment with Mr. Rogers. So, in spite of a tentative theatrical engagement for the fall, I decided to take the job, but with some private reservations. When, after only a few weeks, I was assigned to be BR's special workman, the question as to whether to stay with the job was aggravated ten-fold. And to render my personal problems even more acute, I had already fallen in love with a dancer and actress by the name of Claire Bruce.

I stayed on at Rudge's, and it was several years before I could get my dramatic career back in the track. It was my mother, a real pioneer woman with practical answers for everything, who finally solved my ever-present dilemma, whether to be printer or actor, by asking, "Why not do both?" So there were two seasons with the company of Robert B. Mantell, preeminent classical actor of the day. The lady before mentioned, now my wife, and I then formed our own Shakespearean repertory company, presenting plays throughout the United States. This continued for fourteen seasons until the war called a halt in 1942. During this time, in the holiday seasons between tours, I operated Crosby Gage's private press at his Watch Hill Farm near Peekskill. (The Watch Hill Press was established in 1927 by Crosby Gage, Broadway theatrical producer, and Frederick Warde. I succeeded Warde in 1931.)

In the intervals between BR's repeated trips abroad in the thirties we had the usual contacts, and he gave me one or two small printing commissions which I processed at the Watch Hill Press. This free-lancing period culminated in the *Paragraphs on Printing* project with Mr. Rogers in 1942.

Three more BR books with which I had but an incidental connection are *Poems of Alcuin, Sappho and Ibycus*, Alfred A. Knopf, New York 1945 (printed by A. Colish); *David Ross, Modern Pioneer*, Alfred A. Knopf, New York 1946; and *The Happy Hypocrite*, by Max Beerbohm, published by Bruce Rogers, October House, New Fairfield 1955 (printed by the Stinehour Press from type composed by William E. Rudge's Sons).

Notes

1. "Rogers . . . the most exquisitely sensitive designer of books that this country, or perhaps any country, possesses." *The Work of Bruce Rogers*, D. B. Updike (New York: Oxford University Press, 1939).
2. "The first requisite of all book design is orderliness." *Paragraphs on Printing*, Elicited from Bruce Rogers in Talks with James Hendrickson on the Functions of the Book Designer (New York: William E. Rudge's Sons, 1943).
3. Frederic Warde, *Bruce Rogers: Designer of Books* (Cambridge: Harvard University Press, 1925). This is one of the best and most appreciatively written of BR reference books. It is especially valuable as the statements made were undoubtedly edited by BR himself.
4. *Ibid.*
5. J. M. Bowles, "On the Early Work of Bruce Rogers," *The Colophon*, Part Eleven.
6. Anna Embree Baker, whom Mr. Rogers married in 1900. Mrs. Rogers died in 1936. One of the best collections of BR's books is that at Purdue University, the Anna Embree Rogers Collection.
7. The Typophiles, *BR Marks and Remarks* (New York: The Typophiles, 1946).
8. My partner in crime in this adventure. At least two of the items printed were deliberate piracies. Wells was Rudge's publishers' man. He later promoted lists of finely printed limited editions of English and American authors with Crosby Gage, and subsequently with Elbridge Adams under the imprint of the Fountain Press. James Raye Wells, who later went to live in Spain, is not to be confused with James M. Wells of the Newberry Library.
9. Bruce Rogers, *Letters from T. E. Shaw to Bruce Rogers* (New York: privately printed, 1933). Col. Isham was the owner of the then recently discovered Boswell papers which Rogers was starting through the press at Mount Vernon.
10. Claire Bruce, *Through the Mill with BR, A Play on BRinting* (New York: The Typophiles, 1950).
11. Art director for Kurt H. Volk, Inc., a graduate of Marchbanks Press and himself one of the best typographers in America.
12. Carl Purington Rollins, *Off the Dead Bank* (New York: The Typophiles, 1949).

Edward Johnston.

Portrait by Will Rothenstein, 1922; from the collection of Mrs. Hubert Wellington

EDWARD JOHNSTON

by Alan M. Fern

My first knowledge of the work of Edward Johnston (1872–1944) came from my high school days, when I was fortunate enough to be studying the graphic arts. We learned lettering and calligraphy from Miss Dorothy Skewis, who had studied with Ernst Detterer in Chicago and who meticulously taught us how to distinguish between lettering (in which the shapes and weights of letters are designed and then drawn in) and calligraphy (in which the pen creates forms and gradations in weight as the letters are written). Detterer had been a disciple of Johnston, although I did not know this at the time, and so it was natural for Miss Skewis to use Johnston's book, *Writing and Illuminating, and Lettering*. I enjoyed the course, and perhaps I even learned something, but I am sorry to say that I took Mr. Johnston for granted. I supposed he was just another writer of excellent textbooks, and thought no more about it. Rereading the book now, I cannot imagine how I failed to notice the remarkable character of the author which is evident in every chapter.

At least the name remained in my mind, and in the university my interest in calligraphy continued. Therefore, when I was in England a few years later and was asked by Mrs. Hubert Wellington (one of the kindest and best calligraphers in the world) whether I wished to meet a daughter of Edward Johnston, I agreed at once. Priscilla Johnston and I became friends, and soon I was invited to visit her sister, Barbara, who was living with her son at "Cleves," the family house at Ditchling,

Alan Fern, historian and teacher, is assistant chief of the prints and photography division (formerly curator of fine prints) at the Library of Congress. Lecture given May 20, 1965.

Sussex. Although, when I stayed at Ditchling, Mr. and Mrs. Johnston and their oldest daughter were no longer alive, the house was. After my visits there I felt I had come to know Edward Johnston quite well, and I began to understand why and how he had made such an impact on his friends and students.

Priscilla Johnston has written the definitive biography of her father, and since I cannot separate what I learned for myself from what she has written, I shall here acknowledge her excellent portrait as a source for much of what follows.

Before turning to his work, I should like to sketch a few salient facts about Edward Johnston. He was born in South America of Scottish parents in 1872. With his family, he crossed the Atlantic three times before he was three years old, and finally came to live in Britain. Young Edward never attended school. His family was most unconventional: the mother was a hypochondriac, the children were tutored at home. Some of this concern for health seems to have been transmitted to young Edward, who later remarked, "I was born tired." Yet he was never really ill until after his sixty-fourth year; his weariness showed itself primarily in his slow and deliberate manner.

From his seventeenth year, Edward made fancy illuminations as a pastime, but as it was his intention to become a physician, he enrolled at the University of Edinburgh and graduated there. In 1898, at the age of twenty-six, he went to London and, instead of going into the practice of medicine, began to accept commissions for decorated writing from family and friends. Almost at once he met W. R. Lethaby, then principal of the Central School of Arts and Crafts, and revealed to him that he intended to "go in for art." Lethaby persuaded young Johnston to specialize in lettering since he had an interest in it and an aptitude for it and since this was a sadly neglected field (as Lethaby was sensitive enough to know). Johnston soon learned that the profession was totally unformed, and that he would have to make his own course of study.

Lethaby showed his confidence in Johnston by immediately appointing him to take charge of writing and lettering classes at the Central School, much to Johnston's dismay. Along with Johnston's habitual lassitude was a streak of determined thoroughness, and now this came into play. Lethaby introduced his new writing master to Sydney C. Cockerell, who during William Morris's lifetime had been secretary of the Kelmscott Press, and Cockerell in turn introduced Johnston to some of the most important manuscripts in the British Museum. He began to

Trial sheets written by Edward Johnston on vellum, about 1902.

hac dips the rocky highland
f Slauth Wood in the lake,
There lies a leafy island ⸺
What flapping herons wake
The drowsy water rats; ⸺
That we've hid our fairy vats
Full of berries
And of reddest stolen cherries

seeketh NOT
her own, is ·
NOT EASILY pro=
voked, Thinketh
NO evIL; RE=
JOICETH NOT IN
INIQUITY, BUT
REJOICETH IN
The TRUTH

Trial sheet, on vellum, of Greek writing by Edward Johnston, about 1911.

COI ΔE ΘEOI TOCAΔOIENOCAΦPECICHCIΙΙENOINAC
ANΔPATEKΛIOIKONKAIOΙIOΦPOCYNHNOΠACEIAN
ECΘΛIINOYΙIENΓAPTOYΓEKPEICCONKAIAPEION
H OO OΙIOΦPONEONTE NOIΙIACINOIKONEXHTON
ANΔPAHAEΓYNHΠOΛΛΛΛΓEΛΔYCΙIENEECCI
XAPΙIATA ΔEYΙIENETHCIΙIAΛICTAΔETEKΛYONAYTOI.

Colophon of a manuscript book, 1912, written by Johnston.

This book, consisting of 22 leaves of vellum, was
in part written in November—(and presented together—
with the accompanying book of letters to Mr. Stopford
Brooke on the 14th. of that month)—and was finish'd
in December following by me Edward Johnston at
Ditchling in Sussex (note: the monogram on leaf 19.
was put in for a finish by me, without permission).
20.

FEAR no more the heat o' the sun,
Nor the furious winter's rages;
Thou thy worldly task hast done,
Home art gone, and ta'en thy wages:
Golden lads and girls all must,
As chimney-sweepers, come to dust.

FEAR no more the frown o' the great,
Thou art past the tyrant's stroke;
Care no more to clothe and eat;
To thee the reed is as the oak:
The sceptre, learning, physic, must
All follow this, and come to dust.

FEAR no more the lightning-flash,
Nor th' all-dreaded thunder-stone;
Fear not slander, censure rash;
Thou hast finish'd joy and moan:
All lovers young, all lovers must
Consign to thee, and come to dust.

G. No exorciser harm thee! A. Nor no witchcraft charm thee! G. Ghost unlaid forbear thee!
A. Nothing ill come near thee!
Both. Quiet consummation have, And renowned be thy grave!

The Song in Shakespeare's CYMBELINE. Sung by Guiderius and Arviragus

Song from Shakespeare's *Cymbeline*, written by Johnston 1911–1912 in red with gold initial; from facsimile published by the Chiswick Book Shop, New York.

guide Johnston's aesthetic development as well. From discussions with his mentors, from the manuscripts he pored over, and from his own dedication to art, Johnston formulated his ideal: "To make *living letters* with a formal pen." He used these terms in a letter to Cockerell late in his life, recalling the role his friend had played in shaping the concept and helping him to attain it, and even if his words in 1898 might have been different, the intention was still there.

Johnston took rooms in Lincoln's Inn, not far from the Central School. A photograph of him there, taken in 1902, shows a serious young man, handsomely moustached, seated before a desk constructed of hinged boards supported on a cannister for proper slope (this is illustrated in his book), writing with a quill. Into this room moved a student of his, Eric Gill, who was to remain his closest friend for sixteen years, and here Johnston developed his style of calligraphy and wrote his book.

Almost thirty years later, another photograph shows Johnston with his wife in the garden at Ditchling. The moustache is grayer and the hair thinner, but the gaze of quiet concentration is still there. One can also discern the bulging jacket pockets, filled with the tools of his craft and with objects concerned with his endeavors in the natural sciences (for which he never lost his love).

The house itself was filled with many indications of Johnston's involvement with letter-forms. Two stones with magnificent inscriptions cut by Eric Gill were on the mantel, furniture given to the daughters bore Johnston's inscriptions carved on the legs, and even toys and a perpetual calendar included handsome lettering and calligraphy.

Johnston had died in 1944; but when I visited Ditchling ten years later, his workroom still contained many samples of his writing, for he rarely discarded anything. One could find pieces of paper and vellum that traced his entire development. Some lines of experimental half-uncial must go back to 1899. They remind us that he copied tenth-century English manuscripts when Cockerell was guiding him through the British Museum, and we can see how Johnston slowly came to make these letter forms his own, and from them evolved the bold "foundational" hand that was his first achievement.

A proof sheet from the Doves Press must date from around 1908; and, along with some charming drawings, it shows that Johnston was able to write a creditable chancery script, although he did not commonly use that form. One page is a trial sheet of flourishes which Johnston was commissioned to put in Doves Press books—the direct outcome of his teaching Cobden-Sanderson at the Central School.

Elsewhere in his workroom were proofs of the half-titles lettered by Johnston for the Insel Verlag, the first results of his meeting with Harry, Graf (Count) Kessler, in 1904.

In these bits of paper, fruits of his first decade in a new profession, we see Johnston at work in writing, illuminating, and lettering—the three elements of the book he wrote to put into more widely available form the discoveries he had been imparting to his classes.

Over the next few years his skill as a calligrapher developed incredibly. About 1906, he abandoned the half-uncial forever, and perfected the swelling, round foundational hand. He began to teach at the Royal College of Art in 1901, and began to receive commissions of many kinds.

He did not rejoice in his achievement, though he took great pride in his work. Johnston was forever pointing to the imperfections in his own work (as well as in the work of others) not to belittle, but to teach. It was as if he were saying, "anything that can be done at all can be done better"; and so he pointed to a place where the vellum was not perfectly prepared, where the spacing could have been improved, or where an unnecessary flourish had been used.

Johnston never remained content with one achievement, and any chance to explore a new facet of calligraphy tempted him despite his continual weariness and his doubts about ever reaching perfection. Around 1911, Count Kessler asked him to write an inscription in Greek, and Johnston began to search for the simplest, most direct Greek letter forms. Twenty-three years later he was still searching, for another client, and produced a noble passage from Plato's *Symposium*.

In 1923 and 1924, Johnston evolved his pointed italic hand. This major change in his style also marked the period of his greatest activity. Scrolls for the livery companies of the City of London, wedding presentations, passages for private patrons—requests of all kinds came to him and were sometimes finished. Johnston must have infuriated many an impatient client, for he gave equal concentration to all things. A toy for his daughters, the mending of a favorite knife, the preparation of vellum for writing, each demanded his undivided attention, and the calligraphy itself required an almost mystic harmony between hand and materials. Moreover, a small private income provided the basis of a living for the Johnstons; the family could always live simply, and thus starvation was never an energizing spectre.

Another distraction was his teaching. After moving to the Sussex Downs in 1920, an appearance in the classroom required a trip to London. One might think that an hour on the train would be a minor consideration for a person who had crossed the ocean so often; but, in fact, Johnston found the trip a hardship and returned home as quickly as was practical.

As a teacher he must have been unparalleled. A photograph by E. O. Hoppé shows him standing before a blackboard which is covered with alphabets, letters, and demonstration strokes, all drawn with a squared block of chalk. His students remember his unfailing courtesy, his unexpected flashes of wit, his deeply perceptive comments, and his ability to invest the microcosm of letters with the concerns of the larger world.

Edward Johnston's ability to communicate his ideas about quality in lettering and calligraphy led him into another area which is far less familiar to students of his work, but which was to extend his influence even farther than Lethaby or Cockerell could have foreseen.

I have mentioned the meeting between Johnston and Kessler in 1904, and a brief allusion was made to the lettering Johnston designed for the Insel Verlag on Kessler's recommendation. I did not mention that Johnston had serious reservations about doing work so far from his normal interests—the creation of letters directly with the pen—but Kessler was the kind of man who, by his enthusiasm, knowledge, and persuasiveness, could override even the most deeply felt objections. Born into a German banking family, Count Kessler was sent to school in England, joined in editing *Pan* and was a champion of avant-garde art and literature, entered the diplomatic service, and was finally banished by Hitler. Since his youth, he had been fascinated by printing, and a few years after meeting Johnston he founded the Cranach Press in Weimar. The Cranach Press embodied the ideals of the English private press movement, and even used English talent. E. Gordon Craig, Eric Gill, Emery Walker, J. H. Mason, and the punch-cutters E. H. Prince and George Friend all produced work for Kessler's press. From France came the sculptor Aristide Maillol to make wood engravings, and his brother who made paper.

Count Kessler was a fascinating character in many respects. Unfortunately space does not allow him the full treatment he deserves, but suffice it to say that his wealth and profession allowed him to travel widely and frequently, so he was able to visit his artists often and spur them on to new achievement.

For his press, Kessler had commissioned from Emery Walker a roman type similar to the one Walker and Cobden-Sanderson had used at the Doves Press. Now an italic was needed, and Walker's first efforts did not fully please Kessler. He went to Johnston to discuss the shortcomings of the typeface, and after hearing a lucid discourse on the construction of italics (with illustrations in chalk on colored paper), he engaged Johnston to redesign the type. Walker and Mr. Prince (who was cutting the punches) were a trifle annoyed with Kessler; sensing this, Johnston was even more reluctant to take on a job for which he felt he had so little aptitude.

However, once committed, Johnston threw himself into the task with all the scientific and artistic knowledge at his command. Drawings were enlarged and the sheets covered with mathematical computations in three colors (and striking calligraphy). The lowercase alphabet was soon finished, but not quickly enough for Kessler, and capital letters were now required.

Meanwhile, the reluctant type designer had been entangled in another job. In 1912, Gerard Meynell approached Johnston with an idea for a new magazine to be devoted to typography and related matters, and persuaded him to design the cover and inside titles. Again Johnston had conscientious objections, this time to writing for reproduction, and again a persuasive patron overcame them by persistent argument. Meynell and J. H. Mason were working on a typeface for the journal, particularly designed for machine composition (the first face ever conceived solely for this purpose), and Johnston joined in this venture. The first issue of *The Imprint* appeared in 1913, with lettering and borders reproduced from Johnston's writing, with a typeface designed with Johnston's collaboration, and with articles by Johnston, Lethaby, Mason, Meynell, Joseph Pennell, and others, on typography, page design, illustration, printers' marks, and presswork.

The italic capitals for Kessler were still giving trouble, but Johnston may have consoled himself with the thought that once they were finished he would be able to channel his limited energies into his calligraphic commissions and teaching. No sooner had *The Imprint* appeared, however, than a new problem faced him: Frank Pick, an executive of the London Passenger Transport Board, wanted to have a

Types designed by
Johnston for Graf
Kessler's Cranach Press:
a blackletter based in
part on type of the
Mainz Psalter, 1457;
an italic based on
Arrighi; a Greek type,
unfinished design.

Bevor wir mit dem Schneiden beginnen, wollen wir uns klar machen, dass
die auf diese Weise entstandenen Stempel und Platten zum Drucke die-
nen sollen. Alle hier behandelten Verfahren sind Arten des Hochdruckes
d. h. die Erhöhungen drucken, die Vertiefungen bleiben frei. Wir wollen
ferner daran denken, dass die beim Drucken aufgewendete Kraft unsere
Stempel und Platten belastet und die Gefahr des Wegbrechens und Breit-
quetschens der stehengebliebenen Erhöhungen, wenn auch bei dem einen

και πολλοι εκ γαλα Δε ποΔε ιολκε ειϊτολε
αιεΔ λακο γε ποιελοπιΔε απο Δε καιλεπο
οι πιλοποι καλοι Δαποι Δε γαλε: και :Δοι
ελεκοπιΔα αλλα ιελκιΔα απο λιΔοπα λοι
ποΔε αλλοι εκ οΔοι κιολα εποΔα λοιπα
γλικο και ποικ απο ΔιαΛα αγγελοι ϊαλαιοι

Trial page for Cranach Press of an unpublished *Odes of Horace*, prepared by
Johnston about 1930; woodcut by Aristide Maillol.

Q. HORATI FLACCI CARMINUM

LIBER PRIMUS CARMEN I

Maecenas atavis edite regibus,
O et praesidium et dulce decus meum!
Sunt quos curriculo pulverem Olympicum
Collegisse iuvat, metaque fervidis

Evitata rotis palmaque nobilis
Terrarum dominos evehit ad deos;
Hunc, si mobilium turba Quiritium
Certat tergeminis tollere honoribus;
Illum, si proprio condidit horreo,
Quidquid de Libycis verritur areis.
Gaudentem patrios findere sarculo
Agros Attalicis condicionibus
Numquam demoveas, ut trabe Cypria
Myrtoum pavidus nauta secet mare;
Luctantem Icariis fluctibus Africum
Mercator metuens otium et oppidi
Laudat rura sui: mox reficit rates
Quassas, indocilis pauperiem pati.
Est qui nec veteris pocula Massici
Nec partem solido demere de die
Spernit, nunc viridi membra sub arbuto

1   2

new letter-form designed for the Underground Railways, as part of a total modernization of the system. Pick wanted an alphabet with "the bold simplicity of the authentic lettering of the finest periods and yet belong[ing] unmistakably to the XX century." Gerard Meynell approached Johnston, who agreed to think about it only if Eric Gill would join him. Gill later dropped out of the project, but judging from his later type designs, the preliminary conversations on the project shaped the ideas of both artists.

Johnston now found himself faced with a totally new challenge. In his previous type designs he had been able to base his work on earlier models, refining and redrawing them for a different function, to be sure, but always keeping within a clearly defined tradition. The Underground type was different. As with his first explorations into calligraphy, Johnston had to formulate the problem and arrive at its solution himself.

To one who knows only Johnston's calligraphy, the Underground type must come as a shock. Finished in 1916, it is the very first modern sans serif face, the direct ancestor of Gill Sans, Futura, and their kin; and it is still as strikingly alive in the 1960s as it was when it was designed fifty years ago. Johnston always asserted that the Underground type was based on the proportions of letters used in classical Roman inscriptions. Taking these proportions, he arrived at a standard form for each character and numeral, rendered them in lines of uniform width, and elegantly squared the ends of each stroke. At the same time, he redesigned in simplified form the symbol still in use by London Transport.

Of all his work, Edward Johnston's work for the London Underground has had the greatest impact on the contemporary world. He and Frank Pick showed how graphic design could affect industry, improving function while improving appearance, and giving a sense of corporate identity in modern terms—all before the Bauhaus was founded.

You will recall that this took place before the First World War, and that only after the war was Johnston to be really busy with calligraphic commissions. He was never quite finished with his work for Count Kessler; in the 1920s he redrew a blackletter for the Cranach Press and was fascinated to find that "Schoeffer's typefaces [which were his models] must have been almost perfect copies of the formal penmanship of the time, altered only *in what was necessary to suit metal types.* . . ." This kind of observation was characteristic for Johnston. Others had discussed this fact, but Johnston arrived at it himself by knowing how letters were written and types engraved.

Perhaps the greatest importance of Edward Johnston's work lies here. He bridged the gulf between the revival of craftsmanship that was England's contribution to the late nineteenth century and the knowledge of basic form which underlies twentieth-century design. He was evidently a delightful man. He was difficult, as only a genius can be. He was an inspired teacher, whose students have carried a love for fine letter-forms (and the ability to create them) to every part of the world. He was a brilliant craftsman, blessed with the ability to derive the entire basis of his art from his own observation and manual skill. And he provided the twentieth century with part of its culture of letter-forms, both written and typographic.

Bibliography

Johnston, Edward. *Writing and Illuminating, and Lettering* . . . with diagrams and illustrations by the author and Noel Rooke. London, Sir Isaac Pitman Sons, Ltd., 1906 (still in print).

Tributes to Edward Johnston, Calligrapher. Privately printed by kind permission of The Society of Scribes and Illuminators at the Maidstone College of Art in the County of Kent, 1948.

Johnston, Priscilla. *Edward Johnston.* London, Faber and Faber, 1959.

Fern, Alan. "The Count and the Calligrapher." *Apollo* (London), March, 1964, pp. 214–220.

Dreyfus, John. "Emery Walker: A Victorian Champion of Chancery Italic." *Calligraphy and Palaeography. Essays presented to Alfred Fairbank* . . . (A. S. Osley, editor). New York, October House, Inc., 1966 (London ed. 1965), pp. 207–211.

Rudolf Koch.

RUDOLF KOCH

by Fritz Kredel

RUDOLF KOCH was born in Nuremberg in 1876. His father was a Museum Inspector (Supervisor of the Guards) at the Bavarian Arts and Crafts Museum, with a very meager salary. To make ends meet, he had to find as much additional work as he could as a sculptor. He died in 1886 at the untimely age of forty-one. His widow was forced to take young Rudolf out of the Gymnasium, which she could no longer afford, and send him to a "Realschule." Higher education was not for Rudolf and in 1892, a friend of his deceased father took him into a metal factory in Hanau where he was to learn the trade of a chaser. He had to work eleven hours a day; in addition, he went twice a week in the evenings, for two hours, to art school. But before he had ended his apprenticeship, he returned to Nuremberg, disappointed and unhappy, convinced that the profession of a chaser was not for him. He then visited the art school in his home town of Nuremberg, but the school seemed to be more a sinecure for meritorious old professors than a place where young people could get an education. After three semesters there, he decided that he wanted to become an art teacher. He went to Munich to prepare himself for the exam at the technical high school. It ended in catastrophe; because he had received part of his education outside Bavaria in the foreign state of Prussia, he was not admitted to the exam.

Koch now began looking for a job as a designer and painter, though as he writes in his autobiography, he could neither draw nor paint. To

Fritz Kredel, once a pupil of Koch, is a noted artist, graphic designer, author and teacher who has illustrated volumes of The Limited Editions Club and may other examples of fine bookmaking. Lecture given June 10, 1965.

his own surprise, he found a job at a firm, Wenzel and Neumann, in Leipzig. It was the time of art nouveau, in Germany called *Jugendstil*, of which Koch was a devoted disciple. After a few weeks he was sent to London to work for Raphael Tuck and Sons, the main customer of the firm. He was supposed to design calendars, but his work was not satisfactory, and he came back to Leipzig with "sawed-off pants," as the saying goes. Here he made his boss very happy, because, conscious of his inability to do satisfactory work, he gave up his job. Still, he kept on running around with a portfolio full of mediocre drawings, looking for any sort of work, but rarely finding any, and heartbroken by repeated rejections.

At Christmas he went home, with the last of his money. The family regarded him as a dismal failure, and his mother, who like all mothers had nourished the highest hopes for her gifted son, silently buried her dreams. He returned to Leipzig with new drawings, of water lilies in art nouveau style, and found another job, this time at a book bindery. Here he finally succeeded in becoming a free-lance artist again. Feeling that the worst was over, he did what most young people do when they have scarcely gotten their noses above water—he got married. His bride, Rosa, was the daughter of a printer of copper plates; her maiden name was also Koch, but there was no blood relationship.

For four years Rudolf worked in Leipzig as a book designer. The turning point in his career came when one evening he tried to do some lettering, or rather, tried to imitate printed letter-forms with a broad pen. So far, he had not had the slightest idea what calligraphy or type were, but as he says in his autobiography, the character was always there at the first stroke. Now he worked for himself in this manner whenever he found the time, and when he submitted his products to publishers, they immediately gave him jobs. The dream of his youth had come true; he had become a book artist.

In 1906, he read in a newspaper that the Rudhardsche Foundry in Offenbach, at that time owned by the brothers Klingspor, was looking for a designer. Koch applied and was accepted. He moved to Offenbach, near Frankfurt, and stayed there for the rest of his life. In 1908 the cutting of his first typeface was begun, and at the same time the art school in Offenbach gave him an opportunity to teach lettering in the so-called special class for lettering and calligraphy, *Fachklasse für Schrift*. I must point out this was not the "Werkstatt," about which we will hear later.

In those peaceful years before World War I, Koch led the quiet life of a law-abiding citizen, with a good income, friends who respected him, a wife and four children, and all of the ups and downs of a bourgeois existence. His first typeface was an enormous success, and he created many other fine typefaces during that period, aside from all the work he did privately at home whenever he found the time. He was first of all a calligrapher. All his typefaces, with one exception, were developed from calligraphy or lettering.

"Lettering," he once wrote, "gives me the purest and greatest pleasure, and on countless occasions in my life it has been to me what song is to the singer, painting to the painter, a cheer to the joyous and a sigh to the afflicted. To me it is the happiest and most perfect expression of my life."

He wrote many beautiful manuscripts at this time. A handwritten book seemed to him the pinnacle of achievement.

"No serious calligrapher can ignore the handwritten book," he wrote. "Here, finally, all important questions come up. Here he can show if he is a real artist. Not before he has mastered this task can he call himself more than an apprentice."

"It is not necessary, however," he added, "to write volumes with hundreds of pages. Six to eight pages are enough and in two to three hours the work can be done, including the folding of the pages and sewing them into a cover, just as long as one remains fresh, and the last touch of the hand is done with the same joy as the first one." This remark may seem to indicate that he worked very fast, but this was never so. In fact, it is typical of him that he always worked with the greatest concentration and calm. Even those pages which seemed to be done in the greatest excitement were not written in a hurry.

This comfortable and peaceful situation was shattered by the outbreak of World War I. Koch, in spite of the fact that he was close to forty and had a wife and four children, was called to the colors. He served as an infantryman, and never rose even to the rank of private first class. He was in the thick of battle, first in Serbia and later in France. The agonies of war were not spared him. He described his experiences in his diary, which was later published by the Insel Publishing House in Leipzig.

One episode, more on the amusing side, I remember—he was once in a rear area and was ordered to paint street signs. A young soldier who helped with the job disclosed that his father was the owner of a printing shop. Koch asked him if he also knew something about modern type-faces, and when the soldier emphatically said that he did, Koch showed him a newspaper, printed in his own type. The young man was disturbed because he could not name the face. Koch told him that this was "Kochschrift" and that he himself was the designer, but the young man shook his head and declared that maybe Koch had done the retouching, but those fine typefaces were done exclusively by famous professors. Koch became so embarrassed that he did not know what to answer, and on his way home he had serious doubts that he had really created that type. "This was my only triumph as a type designer," he wrote, "and it ended miserably enough."

In 1918, after having been in a military hospital for several months, he was finally discharged and could return home. He began to work again at Klingspor. He taught at the art school and worked at home as he had done before, but he was a changed man.

The horrors of war and the nearness of death had shaken him to the bottom of his soul. Many things that he had regarded as important before seemed to have no value anymore. From then on he strove for what is called in German *das Wesentliche*, a word hard to translate. "The essential," I might say, though this does not quite give the full meaning.

In addition, through his experiences with simple people, farmhands, craftsmen, and ordinary workmen, Koch had developed an almost Tolstoyan desire never to be anything more than *primus inter pares*. The haughty, condescending attitude of the great artist in the ivory tower seemed to him ridiculous and disgusting. The invisible line that separates artists from craftsmen did not exist for him. He respected everyone at Klingspor as a valuable member of the factory—all concerned with doing their work as best they could. How much he felt obliged to the type cutter may be illustrated by his own words: "We are nothing one without the other. The designer with the greater freedom of his hand and broader knowledge of the forms gives to the type cutter only a kind of guide. He has to anticipate the work of the engraver and he opens the way for it. The drawing itself is nothing. It is done only in view of the type cutter's work. The type cutter, on the other hand, feels the intentions of the designer and the laws of harmony of the design. His tools, his steady and firm hand give every movement its final form. His work is at least as important as that of the designer."

This unselfish attitude, however, did not prevent Koch from one day taking the tools of the engraver into his own hands. He had the desire to create a type out of the material itself. He was, of course, guided by his own written letters, but there was no transmission, photographic or otherwise, on the metal.

"Seven years were necessary," he writes, "before I had the courage to do this." He called his creation "Neuland" (Newland). When he showed the first proofs to Dr. Klingspor, the latter cried, "abominable, horrible, unbearably ugly, but by all means go ahead." Four of his typefaces were created in this way: Neuland, Jessen, Marathon, and Claudius. The last one was cut under his supervision by his son, Paul, who had in the meantime become an excellent type cutter.

In 1920, the so-called Werkstatt was founded. Koch had long felt that little could be achieved in the crowded, highly regimented art schools of his day. "I feel sorry for the poor art students," he wrote to a friend. "I am certainly no organizer, but if I had a workshop I know that I could help at least a few of them. I have thought of giving up Klingspor and having my own working place at school, but that may not be necessary. I would like to do that as a free man, without being a state employee. To be surrounded by just a few honest and serious students, to be their helper and leader, that would please me more than anything else."

Finally he got what he desired. The school offered him a corridor-shaped room right under the roof, with slanted walls and windows on only one side. One had to climb on a table to look outside. In summertime it was often unbearably hot, but in winter it was nice and cool. At the beginning, there were only three or four students working with Koch in the workshop. One was Friedl Heinrichsen, who called Koch "Uncle," though they were not related; their families had been friends for generations. Then Carl Vollmer and I, and later Berthold-Wolpe and Richard Bender, joined the group. There was also Dorothee Freise and her sister, Kathrine, and the unforgettable Ernst Kellner, who later worked for the Insel-Verlag and became director of Haag-Drugulin, the great printing firm in Leipzig.

I have never forgotten that one of the first things I noticed when I met Koch was a sheet of paper which he had pasted behind the glass of his bookcase. On it in large letters he had written, *Trachte ich denn nach Glücke? Ich trachte nach meinem Werke!* (Do I strive for happiness? I strive for my work!) This line from Nietzsche could well be called the theme of Koch's whole life. A dedicated and serious worker he was indeed.

Koch was a very unusual man, even in appearance. The shortness of

Maximilian-Antiqua (Koch) 1914	ABCDEFGHIJKLMNOPQRSTUVWX YZ1234567890
Magere Kochschrift 1921	ABCDEFGHIJKLMNOPQRSTUVWX YZ abcdefghijklmnopqrstuvwxyzchckfchffffifltff
Deutsche Zierschrift (Rudolf Koch) 1921	ABCDEFGHIJKLMNOPQRSTUV WXYZ abcdefghijklmnopqrstuvwxyzchfch
Frühling (Rudolf Koch) 1914	ABCDEFGHIJKLMNOPQRSTUV WXYZ abcdefghijklmnopqrstuvwxyzchfchffffiffltfltkfn
Koch-Antiqua 1922	ABCDEFGHIJKLMNOPQRSTUVWX YZÆŒ abcdefghijklmnopqrstuvwxyzchdckchffffifflf
Koch-Antiqua-Kursiv 1922	ABCDEFGHIJKLMNOPQRSTUVW XYZÆŒ abcdefghijklmnopqrstuvwxyzchckfch
Grobe Koch-Antiqua 1924	ABCDEFGHIJKLMNOPQRSTUVWXY ZÆŒabcdefghijklmnopqrstuvwxyzchckfchffflfiflle
Neuland (Rudolf Koch) 1923	ABCDEFGHIJKLMNOPQRSTUVW XYZÄÖÜ+1234567890
Tiemann-Mediäval 1909	ABCDEFGHIJKLMNOPQuRSTUV WXYZ ŒŒ abcdefghijklmnopqrsstuvwxyz
Tiemann-Kursiv 1912	ABCDEFGHIJKLMNOPQuRSTUV WXYZŒŒ abcdefghijklmnopqrsstuvwxyz

Die Kunst ist ein ernsthaftes Geschäft, am ernsthaftesten, wenn sie sich mit edlen heiligen Gegenständen beschäftigt; der Künstler aber steht über der Kunst und dem Gegenstande: über jener, da er sie zu seinen Zwecken braucht, über diesem, weil er ihn nach eigner Weise behandelt.

ABOVE LEFT   Some typefaces designed by Koch for Klingspor, 1914–1922. (From *The Fleuron*, No. 5, 1926; courtesy Cambridge University Press.)

ABOVE RIGHT   Koch's Wilhelm Klingspor Schrift, a typeface completed in 1927. (From *The Fleuron*, No. 6, 1928; courtesy Cambridge University Press.)

BELOW   Two pages from Koch's festschrift volume for the machine manufacturers, Faber & Schleicher, A.G. (From *The Fleuron*, No. 6, 1928; courtesy Cambridge University Press.)

his body was made up by overlong legs, so when standing he was of normal height; when sitting he had to use cushions and he had a special chair in the workshop. His face looked like a badly drawn picture by Van Gogh. A somewhat underdeveloped chin with a frayed goatee was topped by an overly broad and prominent underlip. The nose, potato-shaped, was stark red, though Koch was a very modest drinker. But one saw nothing of all this when he addressed one and talked in his deep, resonant voice. When he looked at one with his wonderful dark blue eyes under a nobly shaped forehead, one felt that this was an unusual personality.

Though he was a very earnest and sincere man, he had a great sense of humor. There was no stuffy atmosphere in the workshop and quite often it was a place of youthful abandon. Of course there was no room for vulgar or cheap jokes or silly jabber, and an offender would have soon regretted his mistake, because Koch could be very outspoken.

What Koch wanted most was to be an educator. He wrote to a friend, "I am nothing but an educator. Of course I want to educate not calligraphers, but human beings." The human relation was almost more important to him than the work itself. His first and foremost concern was to help his students to improve themselves and to bring out their best qualities. To achieve this, he himself had to give the best example and indeed, he was qualified like no one else. His reliability, loyalty, and noble character were *sans reproche*.

During the nearly fourteen years that I worked with him, never did we need more than a verbal agreement or a handshake in financial matters. But there was nothing weak or sentimental about him. He was smart and knew well how to protect his own interests.

In 1922, Victor Hammer came from Vienna to Offenbach to have his Uncial cut at Klingspor. Koch and he became friends right away, for though there could hardly be a greater contrast, they understood each other in one respect—they were both eager to do their work as per-fectly as possible. Hammer brought Koch's attention to the fact that lettering or calligraphy did not necessarily have to be done on paper or vellum alone; there are other materials which allow the artist to work on a much larger scale, such as embroidering and weaving. Koch became enthusiastic about this idea. He even traveled with Hammer to Vienna to see some of the outstanding tapestries in the museums there.

I happen to have a photo of this trip. There are three important men in the picture. In the background, on horseback, is Prince Eugène, one of the greatest generals the Austrians ever had. (Unfortunately, he was a Frenchman, not an Austrian!) In the foreground stand Victor Hammer, rather smartly dressed with overcoat and umbrella, and Rudolf Koch with a valuable Panama hat, but otherwise somewhat relaxed and not exactly a Beau Brummel. His pose, the way he arranges his legs and stands with one hand on his hip, confirms, in my opinion, the old saying that an artist always portrays himself. I think his *Ex Libris* looks surprisingly as he himself does in the picture.

When Koch returned, he immediately started to embroider a small tapestry himself. But he was not satisfied. The material, which of course was machine-made, seemed to him lifeless and cold. He decided that he had to start from scratch. He bought spinning wheels and a loom, and the workshop became a bit crowded. The work was done by two sisters, one of Koch's daughters and a woman who came now to the workshop to do the spinning and embroidery. When dyeing also had to be done, the workshop space was simply too small, so Koch rented a room in a nearby school and later had another workshop built at his own expense, next to the old one, also under the roof of the school.

The first five tapestries were embroidered without any commercial purpose. In an exhibition, however, they made deep impressions on many people. The first person to give Koch a commission for embroideries was his long-time friend and benefactor, Dr. Guggenheim. He had already bought many of Koch's manuscripts in the early years and also had given jobs to us students. With his usual, unusual generosity he ordered no fewer than four large tapestries. Two of them were always hanging in his living room. The other two came out on the holidays, especially the Seder evenings. Later he ordered a smaller one showing the insigne of the house of Guggenheim. It was not embroidered, however, but woven. They all are now in the Klingspor Museum in Offenbach, together with the manuscripts, except one which is here in the Jewish Museum and the smaller one which still belongs to Mrs. Guggenheim.

Finally, the church became interested. In Helmstedt, now often mentioned in the papers as a border point between East and West Germany, there existed a cloister where the sisters, aside from holding school, also embroidered paraments—the decorative dressings for the altar and pulpit. In 1929, there was a meeting at the cloister of church dignitaries and laymen to discuss new possibilities, and Koch and I were invited. Koch brought samples of his work and gave a lecture and, while

38   Arnika   Heckenrose   39

ABOVE   A spread from *Das Kleine Blumenbuch*, drawn by Koch, woodcuts made by Fritz Kredel, printed in color (Insel Verlag, 1958).

BELOW   A page set by Koch in his Gothic type, 1926, for *The Four Gospels*, with an alphabet of the type. (From *The Fleuron*, No. 6, 1928; courtesy Cambridge University Press.)

ABOVE   In this photo, taken on a trip to Vienna with Victor Hammer, Koch (hand on hip) stands at an angle that resembles the angle in the design of his bookplate. (Courtesy Fritz Kredel.)

not all agreed with his viewpoints, he impressed many of the churchmen and was commissioned by several churches to do paraments for them. Later some of the sisters from the cloister came to work with us in Offenbach.

Soon after we had returned to Offenbach, there came a time when I not only worked with Koch, but was also living in his house as a kind of boarder. In these years, the workshop flourished as never before or after, and visitors came to see us from many parts of the world. From nearby Switzerland came Eugene Kuhn, Willi Baus, Imre Reiner and others. From the New World we received Edna and Peter Beilenson, Philip Hofer, Frederic Warde, Joseph Blumenthal and George Macy. Lydia and Warren Chappell worked for eight months with us, he studying calligraphy with Koch and typecutting with Paul, while Lydia embroidered in the tapestry workshop and learned bookbinding in the bookbinders' class. From England came Stanley Morison and Francis Meynell.

Quite a number of our large works were created at that time, often without a patron or a publisher. They came later. Koch's income was substantial, but he used most of his money to pay for the work that he wanted to do. There were, aside from the tapestries, the book of signs, the flower book, a collection of Christian symbols in twelve folders, an ABC book, a large decorative map of Germany, and numerous others.

Many of these things were community work. Quite often a number of members worked together. The map of Germany, for instance, was drawn by myself, while Koch wrote the poetry around the border. Bender pasted my drawings together and Berthold Wolpe contributed the compass. In the case of the flower book, Koch gave me his sketchbooks and I had not only to do the woodcutting, but also had to design some of the flowers; for the dandelion, for instance, I had five different sketches to work from.

Koch remained, in spite of all the other things in which he was involved, first of all a calligrapher. Having acquired the most perfectly disciplined, well-trained hand, he could afford to go far beyond the usual. He cast off the shackles of convention and tradition and, by doing so, created some outstanding pieces of art—unique, unheard-of, never done before in this manner. He succeeded in expressing, with letter forms only, the deepest emotions, the strongest feelings. Nobody, to my knowledge, has ever done anything better.

Being a deeply religious and pious man, he took many of his inspirations from the Holy Scriptures. And yet if any other text only had enough weight, he wrote it with the same sincerity, conviction, and strength. I did the woodcuts for many of these pages, and I have often been asked why Koch insisted on having them done that way. The answer is rather simple. First of all, I believe that no other method of reproduction brings out the character of this kind of calligraphy better than woodcut; second, there is a certain crispness and sharpness which cannot be achieved by any other medium.

I have sometimes heard people say that Koch's work was too Teutonic, too German. Well, as we say, "From an ox, you cannot expect more than a piece of beef." One might say with the same right that Raphael was too Italian or Rembrandt too Dutch. It is the quality, I think, that counts, not the national or provincial character. He sometimes has been described, too, as a super-patriot and as a religious hypocrite. Some of his writings, taken out of context, may seem strange enough, and anyone who wished to show him in the wrong light could easily find opportunities to do so.

A strong personality—Koch undoubtedly was one—is never uncontroversial in itself. But nobody was more ready than Koch to accept a different opinion or convince himself of his own errors. For him, as I have mentioned, the human relations always seemed more important than anything else. Warm-hearted and loyal, helpful and dependable, he was what I call a real man.

Will Ransom.

Portrait by Appleton, Buffalo, 1937

WILL RANSOM

by James M. Wells

ONE'S NON-ACQUAINTANCE (if I may coin a useful word) can be divided into two categories—the people one never knew, but would like to have known; and those one is delighted to have been spared. Will Ransom (1878–1955) emphatically belongs in the former group. Alas, I never met him. We exchanged a half-dozen letters, and once spoke by telephone—that was all. Yet, after ten years of living with his self-portrait on my office wall—and a very pleasant piece of painting it is—I feel that we have become close friends. I also feel that I suffered a considerable loss when he died just before he was to come to the Newberry for a month or two, as he had promised to do, for he was a man I should very much have liked to know—a man of infinite kindness and warmth, great integrity, and a true genius for friendship. This I know from having skimmed thousands of letters written by him or to him; from the youthful diaries and journals he left behind; and from the testimony of many who did have the good fortune to know him. I spent almost six months sorting and arranging the vast accumulation of papers which constitute the Will Ransom Archives, and from that experience there emerged a portrait of a man who was not only kind but who was good company, a man not above gossip, thanks be, but whose gossip was never malicious. Even though he had more than his fair share of

James M. Wells, writer and scholar in the fields of bibliography, calligraphy and the history of printing, is associate director and custodian of the John M. Wing Foundation, Newberry Library, Chicago. Lecture given February 3, 1966, based on Wells's unsigned article, "Will Ransom: A Biographical Portrait" (*The Newberry Library Bulletin*, November 1955).

bad luck, he rarely complained—and he always, no matter how pressing his own problems, managed to find a way of sympathizing with those who brought their problems to him, as they frequently did.

Will Ransom was born in Saint Louis, Michigan, in 1878. Both his parents were schoolteachers, interested in music and the other arts, and they strongly influenced the boy. The family moved west to Snohomish, Washington, when he was a child; it was here that Will grew up. He was first taught at home by his mother, who in addition to reading and the other essentials gave him lessons on the cello and piano. She encouraged him to join a number of local music groups, for which he designed and printed tickets, programs, and posters—his first commissions.

Like so many of his generation, he was bowled over by the life and work of William Morris—his juvenilia are a mélange of Morris (often filtered through the Elbert Hubbard imitations of Morris), Beardsley, and the other current vogues; his youthful drawings are a wild and wonderful combination of Aubrey Beardsley and Charles Dana Gibson, with Morris borders thrown in—the whole tastefully bound in Roycrofters ooze leather. He not only printed and bound but tried his hand at calligraphy and illumination, writing out Tennyson and his own essays with a quill and decorating them with art nouveau borders and initials—usually for presentation to his family or his current girl friend. More ambitious were hectograph limited editions of his short stories, touched up with gold and color, a few copies of which were bought by loyal friends and relatives. It was all very high-minded, very derivative, very harmless, and fairly awful.

Ransom's first printing job was in the office of the Vancouver, Washington, *Columbian;* the pay, one dollar a week, he spent mostly on books. Ransom was a born collector who, unfortunately, never quite had the means to indulge his natural bent. He went on to a job with the Snohomish *Weekly Tribune,* where he was a triple-threat man: reporter, bookkeeper, and printer's devil. He also kept up his music, playing in a trio which performed for church socials and private parties, and occasionally got a job filling in with a theater orchestra for extra pocket money, since the family budget—they *were* schoolteachers—could not stretch very far. When he had any free time—and he can't have had much—he hung around the *Tribune* office, setting type and running off various things he had written—the proprietors were apparently fond of him and gave him the run of the place. He must have been, as in later life, extremely conscientious—neat, tidy, precise—a lad who didn't leave the presses dirty or too much type tied up.

During this time he began a journal, which came with the remainder of his papers to the Library. It bears the revealing and characteristic title, "Troubles." It is filled with youthful aspiration, high thought, and frequent changes of course, as one would expect—but through it occur the twin leitmotivs of printing and art. He had decided early in life, and never changed his mind, that his future lay in the graphic arts. He was constantly trying his hand at new skills; wood engraving, leather binding, and writing on vellum were among them.

Eventually he decided to combine all his talents in a single work which would represent his own conception of the Ideal Book. A close friend, John Bird, talked him out of making this a manuscript, suggesting that instead he print and publish a small edition aimed at the Christmas gift market—at once enhancing his reputation, spreading the gospel, and even picking up a bit of spare cash. On the latter score he discovered, like so many printer-publishers, that it is easier to design and print a book, hard work though that may be, than to market it, once one's friends and family have had their free copies! Bird not only volunteered advice, but advanced a small sum to make possible the establishment of the Handicraft Shop, and its first *édition de luxe*, in September 1901.

The first title—royalty free, since the author was English—was Tennyson's *The Lady of Shallott*, of which Ransom was enamored, having already written out the poem as a manuscript. The edition was limited to one hundred copies. In order to get the book out by Christmas it was necessary to sacrifice some of the things that the publisher wanted: photoengravings took the place of woodcuts, and the hand coloring was farmed out to an assembly line consisting of a fond aunt and a loyal girl friend. Ninety-five copies were actually completed, sewn and bound in various bindings, and announced in the press of Snohomish, Seattle, Chicago, and other leading metropolitan centers. Even better, seventy-five were sold for cash, and a few others swapped with other private-press printers, establishing contacts for his future life's work and implanting the germ from which he never recovered. A special copy, with a warm dedication, was dispatched to Elbert Hubbard at East Aurora; Fra Elbertus replied with a friendly note and a signed photograph. There was enough money for a second volume, Wilde's *Ave Imperatrix* (chosen as one of his safer works), illustrated

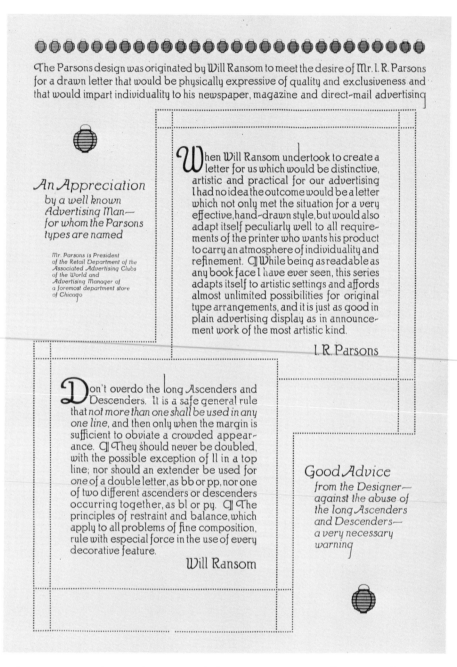

The Parsons design was originated by Will Ransom to meet the desire of Mr. I. R. Parsons for a drawn letter that would be physically expressive of quality and exclusiveness and that would impart individuality to his newspaper, magazine and direct-mail advertising

An Appreciation
by a well known
Advertising Man—
for whom the Parsons
types are named

Mr. Parsons is President
of the Retail Department of the
Associated Advertising Clubs
of the World and
Advertising Manager of
a foremost department store
of Chicago

When Will Ransom undertook to create a letter for us which would be distinctive, artistic and practical for our advertising I had no idea the outcome would be a letter which not only met the situation for a very effective, hand-drawn style, but would also adapt itself peculiarly well to all requirements of the printer who wants his product to carry an atmosphere of individuality and refinement. ¶ While being as readable as any book face I have ever seen, this series adapts itself to artistic settings and affords almost unlimited possibilities for original type arrangements, and it is just as good in plain advertising display as in announcement work of the most artistic kind.

I. R. Parsons

Don't overdo the long Ascenders and Descenders. It is a safe general rule that *not more than one shall be used in any one line*, and then only when the margin is sufficient to obviate a crowded appearance. ¶ They should never be doubled, with the possible exception of ll in a top line; nor should an extender be used for one of a double letter, as bb or pp, nor one of two different ascenders or descenders occurring together, as bl or py. ¶ The principles of restraint and balance, which apply to all problems of fine composition, rule with especial force in the use of every decorative feature.

Will Ransom

Good Advice
from the Designer—
against the abuse of
the long Ascenders
and Descenders—
a very necessary
warning

The Parsons typeface, designed by Will Ransom for Barnhart Brothers and Spindler, Chicago, about 1920.

by another friend, John Clancy. The run was increased to 150 copies of the regular edition, plus ten on japan vellum for private distribution. There were a number of favorable reviews, pasted dutifully in a scrapbook. The best one bears the laconic inscription, in Ransom's hand, "Wrote it myself." Again, most of the edition sold out.

By 1903 Ransom had saved enough money to feel he could afford art school; moreover, he had persuaded his family that he probably could support himself as an artist. Irving Way, a Chicago bookseller whom he met in Seattle, had told him about the new school at the Art Institute and about the tremendous vitality and excitement of the city, then experiencing one of its periodic renaissances. Way also offered Ransom an introduction to a printer friend who had settled in a Chicago suburb, a bright young chap called Fred Goudy. Chicago seemed a logical place—not too far from home and comparatively cheap, with a good school and a few people to help him get started. Accordingly, in March 1903, he registered as a first-year design student in the School of the Art Institute, found a room at the corner of Oak and La Salle which was small but reasonable, and began exploring the city. Many of his evenings were spent at the Newberry, which had opened about ten years before and which had a small museum of the book as well as an evening lecture series. Others were spent at the theater and concerts, or on long walks about the city. His days at the School were filled with excitement, and he did well—at the end of the year he had won several firsts, and three of his pieces were reproduced in the yearbook.

As soon as Ransom got to town he went to call on Way, who shared space with Goudy in the Fine Arts Building. Way was out, but Goudy remembered having heard about "the young man from Snohomish" and gave him a warm welcome. Ransom took to dropping in at the Fine Arts Building at odd hours to watch Goudy at work and shoot the breeze with him, and often went out to Park Ridge to visit him and his wife. In Goudy's studio he made a number of congenial friends: Oz Cooper, who taught lettering at Frank Holme's Correspondence School; Holme himself; Ralph Fletcher Seymour, another earnest young Morrisite; and W. A. Dwiggins. By the end of the year Ransom had just about decided to quit school and start earning some money—Chicago was more expensive than he'd anticipated—and was overjoyed when Goudy suggested he move out to Park Ridge and the Goudys to start a small press and printing shop in their barn.

They chose Village Press as their imprint; like all proper private presses it would have its own typeface, a reworking of one which Goudy had designed on commission for B. Kuppenheimer's clothing plant and which had been turned down when the patron learned how much matrix-engraving and casting would cost. At first these costs seemed prohibitive to the Village Press as well, but Ransom secured backing from his old friend, John Bird, who endorsed Goudy's notes. When that money ran out, he got an additional loan of $250 from an Iowa banker (the brother of an old school friend), using two life-insurance policies as security. Robert Wiebking did the engraving, and American Type Founders cast the type—the latter job being COD, perhaps a result of the firm's experience with aspiring new private presses.

The story of the Village Press has been told often and well, so I shall skip over it in my account of Ransom's career, important as it was in his development. After an exciting but unprofitable year, he accepted his parents' advice to give up art and find a more secure calling. For the next nine years he was a bookkeeper in Chicago. There is little documentation for that period—it is almost as though he had deliberately tried to blot it out. In general he was the kind of man who threw little away, whether paid bills or old laundry lists—his daughter, when faced with the problem of getting his papers to the Newberry, described him as the world's greatest pack rat, a title for which he certainly deserved consideration. I myself can think of a few rivals, including a prominent American writer whose papers, no longer at the Newberry, included the x-rays of his ulcers.

In 1911 things looked up. Ransom married Helen Ruhman, a piano teacher, who shared his love of music, who was willing to gamble on the future, and who encouraged his return to art. When the going got rough—and it often did—she took in piano pupils to help tide the family over. When a new opportunity beckoned, and he moved in order to better himself—as he often did—she gave up her established clientele and packed the books and dishes. She encouraged him both in his work and his avocation, the private press bibliography, helping to file the constantly increasing volume of records. The rest of the family was also drafted. Their only child, Frances Rose, remembers filing hundreds of $3'' \times 5''$s at the age of ten, with far less cheerfulness about it than her mother showed.

Will set up shop as a free-lance artist and lettering man in the Steger Building, in the south end of the Loop, on Wabash Avenue. His sample book shows a wide range of accounts: Fields, Carsons, the Rock Island, a half-dozen music groups—the latter probably free jobs. There were also a number of publishers and booksellers among his customers, including the Morris Bookstore and the Brothers of the Book. The latter, which at first glance seems a bibliophile's club, complete with yearbook, officers, an ambitious publishing program stressing Chicago writers, and nearly a thousand members, was actually an early limited-editions club run almost singlehandedly by Lawrence Woodworth, a banker by day and a bookman by night; he made all the decisions and ran the whole show, even designing most of the books until Ransom's arrival. Woodworth quickly realized his good fortune, gave Ransom the grandiloquent title of "Artificer," and turned design and production over to him, retaining sales and editorial decisions for himself.

In 1918 Ransom, who had tried his hand at several typefaces, designed Parsons, which had a considerable success; it was named for the advertising manager of Carson's, an old friend and a good customer. Like most advertising faces, it had a brief life-span—aside from Carson's ads, its most frequent use was in movie titles and captions.

In 1921 Ransom decided to try his hand at publishing again. Woodworth had died in 1918, and with him the Brothers of the Book. As usual, Ransom had great hopes (expectations would not have been quite the *mot juste*) and too little capital. Most of his publications, even though they were subsidized by their authors, did not quite pay their way. Chicago had then, as now, a great many writers—including a fair number who could pay to see their work in print—and a shortage of publishers. But there was not enough local trade to support a publisher, and not enough money to pay for travelers, so that the shelves were soon glutted with unsold copies. The first volume issued by "Will Ransom, Maker of Books," appeared in February 1922, the initial work in a series of seven "First Writers." They were set and printed by hand by the publisher, on paper made by Dard Hunter—only the binding was sent out. Ransom drew special borders and initials for his books, and lettered title pages and decoration for some. In general, they are pleasant but not really first-rate little books; they are neither fish nor flesh, neither quite typographic nor quite calligraphic, combining the two elements a bit awkwardly. Ransom had had little opportunity to design books, and lacked assurance—prelims and decoration are often a bit forced. When compared with the work of such contemporaries as Updike or Meynell, these attempts seem amateurish.

In addition to his own publications, Ransom took in outside commissions, usually catalogs and other advertising pieces. His most ambitious book during this period was an American edition, for copyright purposes, of Richard Hughes' *Gipsy Night and Other Poems*, earlier issued in England by the Golden Cockerel Press. This led to a long friendship with the author, who later made his reputation with *The Innocent Voyage*. But sales were slow and costs high, and in 1925, Will had to sell his equipment and go back to commercial art. He spent a few months free-lancing, then got a job as director of typography for the Faithorn Company. Here he had an occasional chance at a book, but mostly he executed or commissioned a wide variety of commercial jobbing and advertising.

All this time he continued to collect bits and pieces of printing which struck his fancy—the occasional book, when he could afford it, the prospectus if the book was beyond his means. He had done this ever since the Snohomish days, neatly docketing each piece as to where and when he had gotten it—a boon to the bibliographer, who can sometimes date a piece whose printer and publisher were too careless or unthinking to provide that information. Even as a boy he had begun to write letters of thanks and appreciation for things he had seen and liked, asking questions about their design and printing, and to compile records of his discoveries. He was accurate, tidy, and loath to throw away anything which struck his fancy.

In 1927 this stood him in good stead, when he was asked to write for *Publishers' Weekly* a series on private presses. In this series he traced the history of the private press movement, a task which had until then been performed for only a few of the English and European presses; cited his own experience as a proprietor of such a press, including the financial hazards involved; and praised some of the recently established presses whose work he admired. The articles were so well received that Bowker commissioned him to turn them into a book, a monograph to be accompanied by detailed bibliographies. This was the period during which limited editions and private presses were very much *à la mode*, and there was both a need and a market for the book. All his spare time for the next two years was devoted to *Private Presses and Their Books* —examining and describing the work of some 300 private presses (after he had established in his own mind what constituted a private press); writing to libraries, dealers, collectors, and printers for information about the books; and organizing a vast amount of material with remark-

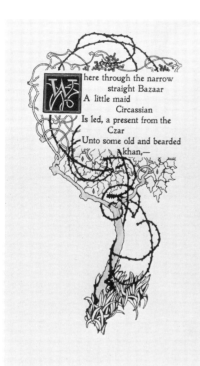

here through the narrow
straight Bazaar
A little maid
Circassian
Is led, a present from the
Czar
Unto some old and bearded
Akhan,—

VENUS AND ADONIS

BY WILLIAM SHAKESPEARE
ILLUSTRATED BY ROCKWELL KENT

ROCHESTER · THE PRINTING HOUSE OF LEO HART · MCMXXXI

ABOVE LEFT Page from Oscar Wilde's *Ave Imperatrix*, printed by Ransom at his Handicraft Shop, Snohomish, Washington, 1902.

ABOVE RIGHT Title page of a book designed by Ransom for Leo Hart, 1931.

RIGHT Chapter opening from F. W. Von Hagen's *Maya Explorer*, 1947, designed by Ransom for the University of Oklahoma Press.

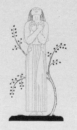

Chapter 1 The innkeeper of Shrewsbury Towne, Josiah Halstead, dispensing his week-gathered gossip, some old, some new, along with his hot buttered rums, had two items to re-late to the Monmouth County farmers of New Jersey who gath-ered in his tavern: the destruction of the French fleet at Trafalgar by Lord Nelson, and the birth of a son to Clemence Stephens on November 28, 1805.

This Shrewsbury, where every personal event was warp and woof of the social fabric, had more than superficial interest in the matter of its latest addition, for this new "Stephens" was, on his mother's side, a Lloyd, and the Lloyds had been associated with New Jersey ever since settlers had come to Monmouth. In 1743 John Lloyd, who was to provide name and ancestry to his famous grandson, was born in Imlaystown. When the Revolutionary War came, he quickly espoused the rebel cause and, exhibiting superior attainments, was commissioned a captain in Waddell's Company. At first these Loyalists, led by Governor William Franklin, the affable, engaging bastard son of Benjamin Franklin, had the uppermost hand, until the leader was arrested in the name of the Continental Congress and packed off, amidst insult, to im-prisonment. All imperial authority now dissolved, and local revo-lutionary committees took over. Then, in July, 1776, General Howe arrived with a hundred sail, dropped off Sandy Hook, landed his troops on Staten Island, and not long after occupied the best lands of Sussex and Monmouth counties. Washington appeared to oppose the British, but with his raw troops he was able to offer only guerrilla warfare, and was forced to retreat deeper into Jersey.

For two years Captain John Lloyd fought the discouraging guerrilla fights of George Washington's strategy. Then when the rebels took the offensive in January, 1777, he resigned his com-

3

able clarity and accuracy. The result, although with a few inevitable mistakes which mortified the author, was an admirable job, useful enough to be reprinted some thirty years later.

The year 1929 marked the beginnings of many things still with us, and the end of others—among which was the craze for limited editions and private presses, which have never regained the esteem they once had. Book collecting has continued, and a few hardy perennials have survived, but today's collector is more apt to pursue a shabby first edition of an important text in science or literature than a sumptuous reprint on handmade paper, no matter how beautifully bound or printed. Only in France has this sort of bibliomania really survived, and there it is more of an adjunct to the picture market than to book collecting.

The next ten years were tough ones for Ransom, as for many other designers and printers. Early in 1930 he left Faithorn, once more to start the struggle of free-lancing. His letters from this period make discouraging reading, although he was a man who always tried not to complain— he had too much pride and too great a reluctance to trouble others to do so. There was no money for books, scarcely enough to pay the postage on his enormous correspondence, now augmented by his fame as a bibliographer.

Late that year—1930—he left Chicago for Rochester, to become director of a newly-established book department at the Printing House of Leo Hart, a venture in which the senior Hart was encouraged by his son Horace, who had been bitten by the fine printing bug as a Harvard undergraduate. The post seemed to offer just what Ransom was looking for—an opportunity to make the kind of fine books he admired, supported by the regular run of commercial printing which the firm already had in considerable volume. During the five years he was there Ransom produced a number of limited editions of high distinction, among them some of his best work, together with a regular dependable amount of trade book and commercial printing. Among the former were Shakespeare's *Venus and Adonis*, illustrated by Rockwell Kent; Cooper's *Last of the Mohicans*, for The Limited Editions Club; and Dwiggins's edition of *The Travels of Marco Polo*, a charming and thoroughly satisfying book. These show far greater assurance and maturity than the books of his handpress period, partly because of experience, partly because his eye and taste had been improved by the opportunity to see much fine work as a bibliographer. Moreover, like Meynell, Updike, Dwiggins, Morison, and others of his generation, he had realized that, used intelligently, machines could do first-rate printing; what was required to get such work from them were high standards of design and craftsmanship. But temperamental difficulties as well as economic ones (work of the quality Ransom wanted is not always as profitable as less careful work) dictated another move, this time to Buffalo, where he worked briefly for a printer and then again as a free-lance. These were days when many talented and experienced men had trouble keeping jobs—Ransom was not by any means alone in his difficulties. But, one senses both from the man and from his letters, part of his problem was a rugged integrity, an insistence upon putting quality above profit, which did not always sit well with employers who were finding it hard to survive, much less make a profit.

There were few books, and little time for bookshops, during these years—the gap had to be filled by post. Will exchanged letters regularly with old friends like Goudy, Dwiggins, and Rollins, as well as with a host of strangers: printers both professional and amateur; collectors; bibliographers; librarians; booksellers; all of whom had used his book, admired his knowledge and taste, and wanted help or advice. It is in these letters to perfect strangers that the man's sterling worth and unfailing kindness shine through. No matter how poor the samples sent for advice and comment—and some were very poor indeed—Ransom found some kind word of appreciation and encouragement, whether for the printing, the text, the paper or binding, the humor or dignity of the design. Every recipient of a letter from Will Ransom, and there were thousands of them, felt that a human being, not an automaton, had read his letter, looked at his work, and thought about what he was going to say before he said it. A twelve-year-old would be told of the difficulties Ransom's daughter, Frances, had with makeready or spelling; a professional printer with no access to libraries or competent advice would have recommended to him some comparatively inexpensive book which might help solve his problems. A struggling poet, printing his own verse in the basement, would hear about Richard Hughes' success after years of earlier neglect. Some of these friendships with people he never met lasted for many years. About this time, in 1937, Will began a series of monthly articles for *Bookbinding and Book Production* which continued until 1945; in them he epitomized his philosophy of book design and production. Like the man, the articles are sound, clear, and solid.

In 1939 preparations began, despite the war, for the celebration of the 500th anniversary of printing—a date picked arbitrarily, since no one really knows when or where Gutenberg made his invention, or even exactly what he invented. Obviously special pomp and circumstance were called for on the half-millennium, and with unusual foresight someone decided a coordinator ought to be appointed early to try to keep straight all the events and publications the year would bring forth and to eliminate duplication as much as possible. The American Institute of Graphic Arts organized a supervisory committee and its president, Melbert Cary, Jr., proprietor of the Press of the Woolly Whale and a longtime friend and admirer of Ransom's, got him the job of executive secretary. He thoroughly enjoyed the job, which gave him ample opportunity to exercise his talent for organization, his meticulous mastery of detail, and his prodigious memory for people and their work. He also enjoyed living in New York, which he had never done before, meeting and working with new and stimulating people and being at the center of activity.

At the end of the year, when the Anniversary Committee was dissolved, Ransom spent a brief interim with The Limited Editions Club, for which he designed a number of books over the years, and then went on to a job with Little and Ives. He got on well with George Macy, but realized that there was no place in the Macy organization for a man with strong convictions of his own about the way the books should be chosen, designed, and printed; they parted amicably, which was not always the case with Macy alumni.

In 1941 Ransom began the last, most fruitful, and most satisfying period of his professional career, as art director of the University of Oklahoma Press, with the rank of Associate Professor at the University. Here, almost for the first time in his life, he found peace, quiet, and security, together with the challenge of designing books whose content as well as production intrigued him. He enjoyed working with Savoie Lottinville, director of the Press, and his staff, and took immediately and happily to life in a university community.

Even though he supervised the design and production of several hundred books during his years at the Press, he also had ample leisure to keep up his correspondence and records of press books, which resulted in the publication, from 1945 to 1960, of a series of *Selective Check Lists of Press Books*, originally issued by Phillip Duschnes and recently reprinted. These extended the range of his earlier book to the end of the Second World War. He also had time during these years to write an extremely sensitive and perceptive essay on Frederic Warde, that odd and enigmatic man whose work and personality have fascinated many others, and to write his charming little book on the Kelmscott, Ashendene, and Doves presses for the Typophiles and a group of associated publishers. He was still working almost to the day of his death, May 24, 1955—still compiling records, still planning to extend further his bibliographies and check lists—still a remarkably young and vigorous man, despite his seventy-seven years.

Will Ransom was a man of high courage, warm heart, and great integrity, who devoted far more of his life to helping others than to looking after himself. He had the instincts of scholarship, and taught himself its apparatus. His work as a bibliographer of the private press has stood up remarkably well, and will probably continue to do so. The books he designed, although not among the greatest of their period, are, like their designer, solid and honest. In short, as I said at the beginning of this piece, Will Ransom is a man I never knew, but wish I had.

T. M. Cleland.

T. M. CLELAND

by Max M. Stein

WHEN DR. LESLIE announced that I was to give a talk on Thomas Maitland Cleland (1880–1964), an episode flashed into my mind which I think is worth telling about.

In 1957, The Limited Editions Club produced an edition of *Mont Saint-Michel and Chartres*. This was, as far as I know, the only book which Tom Cleland designed but did not illustrate for the Club, and the colophon reads in part as follows:

> Designed and Printed under the Supervision of Thomas Maitland Cleland at the Press of A. Colish.

Strange as it may seem, Tom somehow did not see the colophon page before it was printed. Unaware of this, I proudly took a finished copy up to his home in Danbury to let him see what we had wrought. He slowly leafed through the pages with very little comment until he got to the colophon page, when suddenly he thundered "My name is not Thomas Maitland Cleland—no one ever heard of Thomas Maitland Cleland—my name is T. M. Cleland! That's the name that people associate with my work. Please never, never print it in any other way." Needless to say, we never did print it in any other way.

I first met Tom in 1934. I had just been engaged to teach printing in a

Max M. Stein is the longtime production manager of the George Macy Companies, publishers of The Limited Editions Club and the Heritage Club. Lecture given April 15, 1965.

private school for boys. The founder of this school, an extremely wealthy woman, felt very strongly the need to instill in young people an appreciation of, as she put it, "craftsmanship as applied to the fine art of printing—particularly the printing of books." I soon discovered that in addition to teaching, I was expected to produce privately printed books and pamphlets. It was in connection with one of these books that Tom entered the scene. My employer told me that through Belle Green, who was then curator of books at the Morgan Library, she had heard of a wonderful designer by the name of T. M. Cleland who was so exclusive that he refused to take telephone calls. (Little did she know, as I learned later, that Tom was slightly hard of hearing and hated phone calls for the simple reason that he just couldn't hear on the phone.) She got in touch with him and arranged for a meeting at her home. It was to be a "tea."

At this point, I must confess that I was all of twenty-two years old, had never heard of Tom Cleland and had never attended a "tea" of any kind, let alone one in such opulent surroundings.

At the appointed time, Tom drove up in grand style and we soon found ourselves up to our ears in footmen in knee breeches, tiny sandwiches, napkins, sugar, cream, and tea. After some discussion, Tom undertook to design the book, which I was to set by hand (about 100 pages 8½″ × 11″) and print on a Washington hand press on dampened paper. Tom recommended that we use the Stempel Janson type, and with the help of Melbert Cary, we imported the whole series from Germany.

The project started off in great shape. I set specimen pages which were supposed to go to Tom for approval, after which I was to proceed with printing. (Incidentally, I had only enough of the 14 point to set eight pages at a time.)

You will note that I said, "pages were supposed to go to Tom." It seems that each time I had specimen pages ready, my "boss" would ask to see them. As soon as she saw them, she proceeded to change them. I then had the unhappy task of taking these altered proofs to Tom who had a conniption each time he saw them. It all came to a head one rainy night in Tom's studio in the Danbury hills. He delivered one of the most eloquent swear speeches I ever heard, with very little repetition. He then wrote my employer a very rude letter, but so beautifully worded that it went completely over her head. Her only remark was,

"It is too bad he cannot finish the job—he is such a gentleman."

And this brings to mind one of Tom's quotations which Eleanor Steiner-Prag mentioned to me: "A gentleman is never rude except by intention."

How did Tom Cleland get into the graphic arts? Who or what inspired him? A few short weeks before Frank Fortney's death, Paul Bennett, Frank and I spent a wonderful weekend in Vermont with Bob Dothard. At some point, Bob asked Frank the same question—who or what inspired him to become a bookbinder. Frank's answer was, "I wanted to quit school, and my father said I could do so if I continued in night school and got myself a job. A friend of mine worked in a bindery so I got a job in the bindery with him." That's how Frank Fortney started and we all know he became a great binder.

As far as I know, Tom Cleland was not inspired by anyone in particular either. His father was a doctor in New York and had hopes that Tom would follow in his footsteps, but Tom quit school at the age of fifteen and enrolled in a course in applied ornament at The Artist-Artisan Institute. He attended for only a few months and in the following year, 1896, began his career as a free-lance artist. He acquired a small press which he set up in his father's house and proceeded to experiment, for Tom believed even then that one learned by doing. He soon moved his small operation to Boston and while there established a contact with D. B. Updike, beginning a friendship which continued for forty-two years.

There is no doubt that Updike's interest helped greatly to inspire him, but it is obvious that he was a "natural." He had an inborn talent—the equivalent of what in the musical world is called "perfect pitch." He just couldn't design anything in bad taste. He knew instinctively the proper relationship of typefaces, type sizes and ornaments. If he couldn't find the ornament he needed, he drew one, and it was always just right. This is why, very early in his career, he became so impatient with mediocre designers. Just as the musician with "perfect pitch" cannot understand how a musician can play a wrong note, so Tom could not understand how a designer could design anything in bad taste.

We must remember that he had no formal art training to speak of and no formal training in the craft of printing. He was completely self-taught. Yet at the age of nineteen, he was commissioned by Bruce Son and Company Type Foundry to design a typeface, which he named "Della

ABOVE Cleland's title spread and illustration, from The Limited Editions Club's
She Stoops to Conquer, 1964; courtesy George Macy Companies, Max M. Stein.

BELOW Title spread designed by Cleland, from The Limited Editions Club's
The History of Tom Jones, 1952; courtesy George Macy Companies, Max M.
Stein.

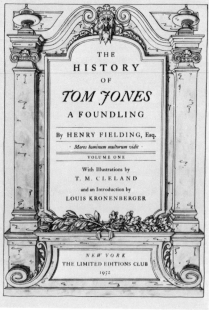

Robbia." Even though this typeface had quite a wide sale, Tom considered it the worst thing he had ever done. Here are his words on the subject:

"It is true that I committed an atrocious error in my early youth which is still sold by typefounders and used by printers who do not know any better; but considering that I was only nineteen at the time, I have hoped that it might be overlooked and forgotten by now. . . . I cannot afford to buy the evidence—the existing types and matrices—and destroy them, so they yet may destroy me."

At the age of twenty-four, Tom became art director of *McClure's Magazine* and in a short time completely redesigned its format. This brought his talent into great demand, and his career was well on its way.

In the years just preceding the First World War, the automotive industry was beginning to boom. There was a great need for catalogs and brochures of all kinds, and there were no well-organized advertising agencies such as we have today to produce this material. Tom fitted ideally into this situation. He produced catalogs and brochures for such firms as Locomobile, Cadillac and Rolls Royce. He did not just design these items, but also illustrated them and printed most of them in his own establishment. Unfortunately I could find very few examples of these catalogs, but he did show them to me on several occasions, and I was awed by the detailed drawings which he made of the chassis, motors, exteriors and interiors, and other parts.

In 1921, Tom produced for the Strathmore Paper Company *A Grammar of Color*, a tremendous undertaking which demonstrates his versatility. He wrote the explanatory text, illustrated it with diagrams, composed the type, mixed all the inks and did all the presswork. Color experts today still consider this book an outstanding model of design and printing.

In the late twenties, Tom became art director for *Fortune* magazine. He created the typographic style which is still in use today and made the now famous Wheel of Fortune drawing which was used for the cover of the first issue. Tom also designed or had a hand in the design of such diverse publications as *Engineering News-Record* and *Newsweek*.

Probably one of the most interesting and exciting opportunities that came his way was his assignment to design the newspaper *P.M.* He summed up his feelings in undertaking this task in these words: "I want, above all, to restore order to what is now a typographic turmoil—piling emphasis upon emphasis—until nothing can be seen or read. Typography should not attract attention to itself and away from what it is used for—it should be a discreet servant of text and not a showman with delirium tremens."

Later in criticism he wrote:

". . . In any case there is no excuse for the still worse—the worst of all—'If You Ask Me' heading on page 10. To letterspace any lowercase is bad enough, and I have given definite instructions to the composing room on this subject over and over again. But to letterspace italics is the one unforgivable typographic sin, and such italics!"

P.M. won the Ayer award for the outstanding tabloid in the country.

Up until this time, Tom had concerned himself with what might be called commercial design and illustration. He expressed his dissatisfaction to W. A. Kittredge, who had suggested that Tom design and illustrate a book, in these words: "The idea of illustrating a book is indeed thrilling just at the moment when I am most disheartened over the thought of everything I do going into the paper bale. But it also frightens me a little. Presumably you think I could do it, or you would not ask me. . . . The one thing I am sure of is that I want to do it, and I want to do it so much that I am willing to break my neck in the attempt— if breaking my neck will help me to draw any better."

Tom's opportunity to design and illustrate a book actually came a few years later when George Macy, head of The Limited Editions Club, offered him the opportunity to do *The Life and Opinions of Tristram Shandy, Gentleman.* The book was a great success in both design and illustration, and in addition, Tom perfected a method for actually marbling a page of the book while still maintaining the margins of a normal type page. In order to explain why this was necessary and to give some idea of the prodigious task Tom undertook, I quote from our September 1935 issue of *The Monthly Letter.*

> Toward the end of Chapter XXXVI, exactly at page 269 in the first volume of our edition, the author suddenly challenged the reader "to penetrate the moral of the next marbled page (motley emblem of my work!)," and proceeded (in the first edition) to place a marbled page immediately thereafter. This page was actually marbled. Within the measurements of the space which would be taken by the block of type printed upon the paper, a colored marbled design was placed. In succeeding editions, the publishers were content simply to cut a piece of marbled paper out of a large

sheet and at this point in the text, to insert a whole marbled leaf. In even more recent editions, as in the edition included among the Oxford World's Classics, a blank page is placed, and the legend printed: "In the early editions a marbled leaf was inserted here." But T. M. Cleland is not that kind of a man; he is meticulous and painstaking. Since Laurence Sterne said that the next would be a marbled page, Mr. Cleland insisted that our edition must have, not a blank page, not a marbled leaf, but a marbled page. And he proceeded to marble the page with his own hands.

The process of making a marbled leaf is difficult enough. To marble a sheet of white paper so that the marbling occurs only within the measurements of the space of the page of type, is an imposing task indeed. It took Mr. Cleland almost one month of solid labor to achieve this task for you. It is probable that this is the first time, in nearly two centuries, that any craftsman has essayed so meticulous and painstaking and difficult a task. In order that you might understand why we dub it with so many adjectives, we asked Mr. Cleland to attempt briefly to explain how he built the contraption with which he performed the task:

"Marbling of paper and book edges, as not everyone is aware, is done by spattering colors which float upon a liquid surface composed of gum and water where they may be manipulated in an infinity of patterns. The sheet of paper is gently laid upon this surface and taken up again with the colors adhering to it. In this manner the art has been practiced for several centuries.

"Obviously this problem called for some form of mat which would mask out the margins of the page and permit the color to touch only the rectangle of the page itself. To repeat this operation successfully some fifteen hundred times presented practical difficulties of a kind which I promise not to tell you about. It is enough to say that after many futile attempts to find the right thing, I finally constructed an affair of wood, with a mat of very flat sheet metal which holds the signatures of the book to guides for correct register, exposing a blank page through the opening mat. The whole thing is laid very carefully—to avoid air pockets which would cause blank spaces—upon the surface of floating color in a tank especially made for the purpose. It is taken up again with the color film adhering to its entire surface, but reaching the paper only through the opening in the mat. The excess liquid is drained off, the sheets removed, blotted, and then placed between blotters for drying. The surface of the tank must be wiped clean of remaining color by sliding strips of absorbent paper over it, a new pattern of color spattered on with small brooms made for the purpose, and the whole process repeated for another page."

The marbled paper sides for the binding of the two-volume set were also made by Tom.

George Macy in commenting later in the *Quarto Millenary* said, "It seems curious that Mr. Cleland should have been so famous as a book-artist despite the fact that this was his first completely-illustrated book. And what a beauty it is!"

Tom Cleland went on to do seven other books for The Limited Editions Club. The titles are, in addition to *Tristram Shandy: Jonathan Wild; The Essays of Montaigne; The History of Tom Jones; Mont-Saint-Michel and Chartres; The Way of the World; Monsieur Beaucaire;* and *She Stoops to Conquer.*

Tom was a perfectionist with infinite patience, but this made him a trial to his clients. George Macy complained in 1942 about delays in receiving the finished work for *Jonathan Wild:*

"The history books will of course refer to you as a sensitive and conscientious artist; and those adjectives will look wonderful after you and I have departed this earth. But just think how much simpler your life would be, not only your life in the past, but your life in the future, if you were a trifle less sensitive and a trifle less conscientious!"

I don't suppose any artist who has any sensitivity or any conscience is ever completely satisfied with any drawing he has made; the moment he looks at the finished drawing he can see how it could have been improved. But since he is never satisfied, redrawing the drawing then becomes an endless occupation.

Tom's patience is evident in his undertaking the monumental job of producing *Manon Lescaut* for Mr. Altschul. He executed the illustrations by silk screen, but not in the usual manner of working the colors over a key drawing. Rather, he literally painted by the silk screen method. This meant that for a single illustration he made as many as fifteen or twenty applications of color—in some cases just an eyebrow or a spot of color in the hair. In order to obtain perfect register he built all of the silk screen frames himself. Of course, he mixed all of the colors himself and made many tests to be sure that the colors were permanent. This book occupied him for six long years, and he was close to eighty years old when he undertook the job.

At this point, I must make special note of his knowledge of color and the mixing of inks. He was thoroughly familiar with every phase of this highly specialized field. An example is the last book Tom did for us, *She Stoops to Conquer.* He made twenty-one illustrations, each in five colors. He made separate black and white drawings for each color over a "blue" key, and visualized the final result when the colors would overprint. When we were ready for proofing, he went down to Clarke & Way and

Advertisement by Cleland for the
Locomobile Company, 1917; from
*The Decorative Work of T. M.
Cleland*, The Pynson Printers, 1929.

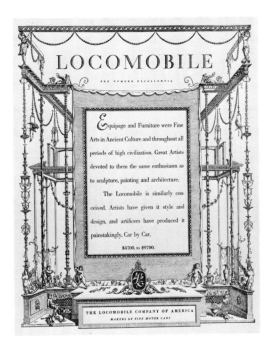

Advertisement by Cleland for Cadillac;
from *The Decorative Work of T. M.
Cleland*, The Pynson Printers, 1929.

Diagram from *A Grammar of Color*,
written and illustrated by Cleland for
Strathmore Paper Company, 1921.

instructed the men in the plant on exactly how to mix the colors, the proper trapping of the ink, etc. Needless to say, the final printing had practically no changes from this first proofing. He knew just what he wanted and how to get it.

To further illustrate his knowledge of color, I quote from a letter which he wrote to George Macy in 1943 in reference to the application of color by pochoir for the illustrations in *Jonathan Wild*. The problem had to do with the permanence of the colors, and he lectured Mr. Macy in his own inimitable style:

> . . . As a publisher you have had to learn something about the materials involved in your trade—paper, type, presswork, binding etc.—and especially so as a publisher of classics or uncopyrighted works in which the superiority of these material elements was the principal thing you had to offer. It will do you no harm to learn more; and since books with pictures colored by stenciling is one of the things you sell, you should know something about the materials used in that process. The present case of your argument about the cost of this job is a perfect instance and example of *why* it would be to your advantage to know about them. (I don't care a damn if you're bored or not, George, or how long it takes me to write this letter, I'm going to tell you something about pigments, so you will be armed for any dispute on that subject when it comes again, just as you are now armed to deal with paper makers, photo-engravers and other such industrial white trash.)
>
> I'll be decent enough to make it very brief and sketchy however, though that's as far as I am prepared to go in decency. Like nearly everything else including people, there are, broadly speaking, two sorts of coloring materials: genuine and synthetic. In the case of pigments, however, it is only fair to say that there are some instances in which the synthetics are actually an improvement upon the natural products. But in the paints with which we are concerned here, there are natural pigments, combinations of chemical elements made in the laboratory, i.e., sulphide of cadmium, or found ready-made in the earth, i.e. iron oxide. These are all solids which, when ground to a powder and mixed to a paste with oil or water and gum, become paints suitable for artistic purposes. Most of these, though not all of them, are far too expensive to be used in great quantities for industrial purposes—house paints, printing inks, etc.
>
> On the other hand there are dyes, which when dissolved in water or some other liquid medium form powerful coloring matter which is *not* solid. Some of these dyes are permanent, i.e. fast to light, but most of them are not. Pigments—that is, solid coloring matter which will form paint or ink—are made from these dyes by precipitating

them on some white or colorless powdered material such as chalk. These are synthetic pigments which are only as permanent as the dyes with which they are dyed. They are suitable for most industrial purposes but, with only a few notable exceptions, entirely unsuitable to any artistic purpose where permanency and reliability are important. The colored illustrations for a fine book seem to me definitely to be such a purpose. Illustrations to be colored by hand stenciling are not *re*productions of a colored original, in the best sense, but are productions of a particular water color technique. They demand the same sort of material that the artist would use in coloring one of them. The water colors known as "Poster" colors are decidedly not fit for coloring the illustrations to a fine book because they are nothing more than precipitated dyes, liable both to fading on exposure to light and "bleeding" through the paper and discoloring its other side. Not all of them have either of these faults, but since they are sold under a variety of fantastic names which give no indication of their composition there is no way of knowing what they will do.

It might be contended that fastness to light was not a requisite of illustrations in a book which is kept closed. But sometimes books are opened or exhibited in a shop window or elsewhere. I noted in the office at Marchbanks some of the plates from "A Man Without A Country" hung on the wall from which nearly all of the yellow and red had faded out completely. The natural pigments, being much more concentrated and more finely ground will, in consequence, go much farther—cover more ground. Miss Brakely, being unfamiliar with the use of these natural pigments, has, I believe, an exaggerated fear of the quantity that will be required. I can't tell exactly how much of each she will need for this edition, and since it is an unknown factor, it might have been better for both parties to make that a separate item in her charge.

(Yes Georgie? I see your hand raised, what do you want? Oh, you want to go to the bathroom. Very well, but don't stay too long, and that will be all of school for you today.)

In reviewing Tom's life, I realize that in such a short space of time I can give only a sketchy presentation, and I have tried to mention a few of the highlights. However, I feel that I would be very remiss if I did not point out his accomplishments in fields other than the graphic arts.

Anyone who ever visited Tom in his studio will remember that in one corner stood a lathe and other pieces of woodworking equipment. On one wall was a large cabinet which contained the most beautiful set of wood chisels I have ever seen. Of every size and variety, each chisel was perfectly sharp and devoid of even the tiniest speck of rust. He had built the cabinet, of course, and each tool was perfectly fitted into a specially made rack. He was an excellent cabinetmaker and was very proud of the things which he had made, from furniture to a tobacco canister and pipe rack.

Speaking of pipes (he was an inveterate pipe smoker) and being something of an inveterate pipe smoker myself, I noticed that his rack contained about twenty pipes. The curious thing was not the number of pipes but the fact that they were all exactly alike. I remarked on this and asked why they were all the same. For asking this foolish question, I was rewarded with a lecture on pipe smoking which lasted about as long as this whole lecture. The gist of the story was that he had made a scientific study of pipes and found that for perfect draw, etc., etc., the size of the bowl and length of stem had to be to exact dimensions, and he had these pipes made especially to these specifications.

Not content with being an expert craftsman in wood, he was also an expert in metal, and another cabinet on the opposite wall contained a set of metalworking tools just as beautifully kept as the woodworking ones.

In whatever he undertook, he learned the craft thoroughly and had the infinite patience to learn every phase of it. He was, in my opinion, the ultimate craftsman. But the enigma of this man was that he was even more than the ultimate craftsman. He loved life and involved himself in every facet of it.

A gourmet, he collected a number of friends to lend financial support and established a restaurant on lower Fifth Avenue called 68, and ran it for a considerable period of time. It is still operating under this name, although under new management and across the street from the original establishment.

With little formal education, he mastered French as well as English, and he wrote articles dealing with the graphic arts world which have become classics.

Here is a typical excerpt from "Harsh Words," an address delivered at the eighteenth annual Fifty Books of the Year exhibition of the American Institute of Graphic Arts in 1940:

> I refuse to bore you or myself by enumerating all the tiresome stock-in-trade eccentricities of the typographic expert in search of something new—the epileptic fits he throws to attract attention to himself at the expense of the words he is printing. You see enough of them every day to know what I mean. Nearly every magazine and newspaper page, not to mention a good many books, present the

same revolting spectacle—the order of the day it seems, is disorder.

And speaking of magazines, it has fallen to my lot from time to time in the past thirty-five years to design and redesign a number of periodicals of one kind and another. Such jobs require really very little actual work—it's by endless argument and conference that they can wear you to the bone. My simple purpose with these things has always been to bring any measure of order the case will permit out of the disorder in which I generally find it. My mission, if I have any, is to suppress typography, not to encourage it—to put it in its place and make it behave like a decently trained servant. I find magazines rolling in the gutter covered with the accumulated mud of years of dissipation. I pick them up and brush them off, give them a cup of black coffee and a new suit of clothes and start them off on respectable typographic careers. But like other missionaries, more often than not, I find them a year or so later, back in the same gutter, drunk and disorderly and remorselessly happy about it.

There is a great temptation to go on lifting passages from Tom's utterances on the graphic arts scene, *ad infinitum*, but the above will serve as an illustration.

It saddens me to say that Tom became quite bitter in the last few years of his life. He felt that the world was passing him by and had already all but forgotten him. I pointed out to him on several occasions that his remarks made over a generation ago were still as pertinent today, but it did little to lift him out of his gloom.

He expostulated endlessly on the political scene and was forever aiming an accusing finger at either the New York *Times* or the New York *Herald Tribune;* when I asked him why he read these papers since they upset him so much, his answer, tinged with bitter humor, was, "I read both papers thoroughly every morning and they make me so mad that all of the poisons come out of my system and I feel fine for the rest of the day."

Just recently I attended the funeral services for a man quite prominent in the graphic arts field. The attendance was unusually large and I was very much impressed. When it came time for the eulogy, the Rabbi said, "The fact that there are so many people here to pay their last respects to this man speaks more for him than the words which I have prepared for this occasion. Therefore, I will let this be his eulogy."

I feel very much the same about Tom Cleland. His work in the final analysis stands as his heritage, and mere words are inadequate.

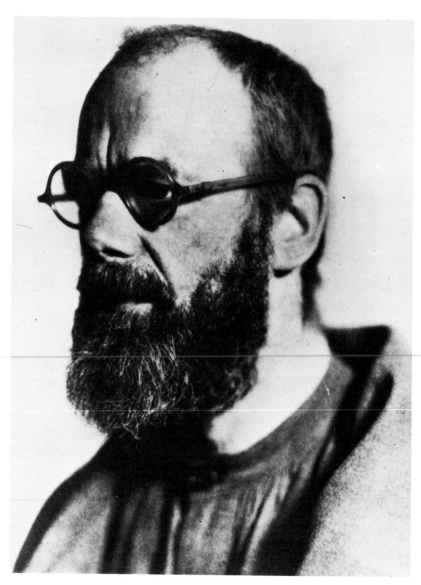
Eric Gill.

ERIC GILL

by Peter Oldenburg

ERIC GILL, the English artist (1882–1940) who started to cut inscriptions into stone, then became an engraver of wood blocks, a sculptor, type designer, essayist, printer, and philosopher, is so well known to most readers of this book that I hardly need to recount the details of his life. In any case, his autobiography (Cape), and *The Life of Eric Gill* by Robert Speaight (P. J. Kennedy & Sons, New York) will give the interested readers excellent accounts of his life. To expound his ideas on the many subjects he was interested in would be presumptuous since Eric Gill himself wrote extensively and well, and much of this material is still in print.

The illustrations in this chapter may give the reader an idea of Gill's contribution to today's design of printed materials—the role he played in helping to change the approach to book design in England. From looking backward to what had been done in the past, and applying the teachings of Edward Johnston to cutting simple and beautiful inscriptions into stone, he developed logically to engraving letters on wood, then to illustrations with lettering for fine books. He also designed typefaces for the Monotype Corporation. Again his work developed naturally from the relief decorations of his stone inscriptions to the more ambitious carving of stone in the full round and relief.

What I would like to attempt here is to give the reader a glimpse of Eric Gill and Pigotts—Pigotts, the working community of craftsmen

Peter Oldenburg began his career as an apprentice to Eric Gill. He is an independent book designer and typographer and is design consultant to the publications department, The Metropolitan Museum of Art. Lecture given May 6, 1965.

grouped around Gill, attracted by his artistic genius as well as his unconventional Catholic philosophy.

I came to Pigotts one afternoon in September of 1933, a refugee from the stifling atmosphere of Hitler's Germany. My English was atrocious, and I was young and certainly not brilliant. But at Pigotts I was welcomed warmly by everyone. René Hague, who ran the print shop, and Denis Tegetmeier, who was and is a very gifted painter and illustrator, both sons-in-law of Eric Gill, invited me to come down to North Dean, to the "pub," for a glass of beer that very evening so that I could hear about the trip from which Denis had just returned. I was made to feel like one of the group, and though I had no notion what was being talked about I felt happy.

Pigotts was a complex of buildings on top of a hill near High Wycombe, just about thirty miles out of London. These buildings were dwellings and old barns as well as some converted and built-out sheds, grouped in a regular square around a central green space. The center of the green was occupied by a solid brick stable with a pig that would provide some of the winter's meat.

The print shop was in a converted shed—long and narrow, forming one entire side of the quadrangle. It was headed by René, who was the chief compositor and pressman, and Bill was second in command, then Gordian Gill, Eric's son, and lastly myself. My duties were lowly and included lighting the potbellied stove in the morning and scrubbing the type with lye after long runs (perhaps 1,000 copies) for George Macy's Limited Editions Club.

The workday started early, 7:30 A.M. or 8, and the tasks were varied. We all took turns at setting type, locking up, making ready, and running the presses. René would give the signal when a form was sufficiently made ready to run, would test the paper to see if it was properly dampened, and usually would perform the delicate task of inking the type. And then Eric Gill would come over from the stone shop either to see if a type page was properly spaced and leaded, or an engraving which he might have been working on was properly printing; and his cheerful "Jolly good, René" would end the brief visit.

Tea time, around ten o'clock, was presided over by Joan, René's wife, in front of the open fire at the house, with delicious home-baked scones and butter, probably made from the milk of the two or three cows that were kept by Joan with the help of the handyman about the place.

At lunch time I would take my sandwich—I didn't live at Pigotts, but in "digs" in Speen a couple of miles away by footpath—and join the stonecutters in their shop diagonally across from the print shop. The other members of the print shop would join their families for lunch.

In this shop was a lively group of young people. Laurie Cribb, Eric Gill's long associate, was the senior member here. There was Donald Potter, a young sculptor, and Anthony Foster, an ex-monk and now a stonemason. David Kindersley and a young man who did carving in wood and was also a violin maker completed the group.

In the barn-like room everyone had his task and place for work. The inscriptions on the stones that had been commissioned from Gill were cut only by Laurie, but preparatory work, such as shaping and polishing the stones, was done by all the others, and everyone had his "own" projects as well. Donald was carving a huge totem pole; Anthony, a statue of the Virgin; and David Kindersley, his first inscriptions, already showing the skill and imagination that make him famous today.

And then the arguments, usually starting with Eric Gill's philosophy—his belief in simple Christian poverty, his bitterness about industrial England, his stand against war. The discussions were frank and lively, because by no means were all of us either religious or subscribed to Gill's ideas. And in the midst of all the shouting Eric would come over here, too, to see how work was going.

An inscription was to be sketched out on the new stone that Donald had just shaped and polished. Eric came with a tiny thumbnail sketch and proceeded to draw in the letters firmly and beautifully spaced—going from left to right, and each line accurately centered! I don't recall that he had ever to go back to do a word or a line over; the stone was ready to be cut.

He would look at everyone's project with interest and enthusiasm, but I do not think that he ever criticized the work. He might show you how to improve your workmanship and technique. "Look after goodness and truth, and beauty will take care of herself."

Directly across from the stone shop was Eric's own workshop adjoining the "big house" and forming a large "L" and thus making the other two sides of the square. Eric's shop was partly used for his sculpture, contained the table for his wood engravings, and further had a room where he would write essays, letters and articles. This was holy territory, and Mary Gill would see that Eric was not disturbed because he was busy with so many varied tasks and had such a lively interest in things and people that he did need a shield from the outside world.

Occasionally, when Eric was away, I would venture into the shop and marvel at the multitude of tasks being worked on: the sketch for a wood engraving on the table and a block just beginning to take shape; the room for writing with stacks of letters, the manuscripts in a hard-to-read but nevertheless beautiful, almost formal italic script. And in the stone shop there was a new relief panel on a huge, sturdy easel—the tools very orderly and very perfectly arranged on the simple wooden table next to the carving. Yet it was not sterile order for order's sake; the place was actually bursting with life and therefore with a certain superficial disorder. But the tools and the things were all exactly where they might be needed, beautifully kept in readiness for whatever task had to be accomplished next. "The good workman *never* complains about his tools, because the good workman has no bad tools." And Eric thought of himself not as an artist but as a good workman.

Six o'clock would come, and the workday in Pigotts would end—but not before Father Bernard would hold an evening service in the little chapel located at the corner where Eric's workshop joined the "big house," Eric's and Mary's dwelling. Father Bernard was a resident priest, a scholarly man who lived above and presided in the little chapel at Pigotts. The tiny, simple chapel had perhaps a dozen seats and looked very much Eric Gill's creation.

His carvings were around the walls, and simple, yet colorful and beautiful, necessary objects provided the decoration for the service. Services were attended by those who wanted to come, those who needed the period of ritual shared with others and were refreshed by the prayer. Never was anyone urged to come; the services must never become an empty formality.

My account of Pigotts would not be complete without mentioning children and Sunday's high tea. Children were around everywhere. Both the Hagues and the Tegetmeiers had little children. Michael, René's son, would spend hours in the print shop sitting on the floor, drawing. The housekeeper had a child, and there were always visitors, often with children. But what a place for children! There were thousands of things to do, workshops and stables to explore, trees to climb, flowers to pick, and no cars or machinery to be any danger.

High tea on Sunday, in the big house around the big table: Eric, Mary, René and Joan, the Tegetmeiers, Father Bernard, perhaps Anthony Foster and two or three distinguished visitors—say, Robert Gibbings and possibly an editor of a progressive Catholic weekly, perhaps Beatrice Warde; the table filled with marvelous food, mostly home-baked and cooked, vegetables from the garden, jams from berries picked by the children in the woods around.

More marvelous than the food was the conversation. Eric Gill was never without lively controversy in the very best sense. He might have disagreed with the traditional Catholic viewpoint. He might have written a letter to *The Times* or to a critic regarding a trend in the London art world. And these subjects would naturally be discussed, expounded and sometimes heatedly debated. But always brilliantly, or so it seemed to me. Eric would generally hold the center of the floor, and never would he lose his good-humored warmth even in the frankest and sharpest exchanges.

That was Pigotts in 1933–1935—the lively extension of Eric Gill's many activities: a group of people, family, students as well as friends, all attracted by the man and the place, though many were not uncritical of both, and yet they came, stayed, worked and produced.

while that the technical & mechanical good quality is increasing the de-humanizing of the workman is also increasing. As we become more and more able to print finer and more elaborate & delicate types of letter it becomes more and more intellectually imperative to standardize all forms and obliterate all elaborations and fancifulness. It becomes easier and easier to print any kind of thing, but more and more imperative to print only one kind. ¶ On the other hand, those who use humane methods can never achieve mechanical perfection, because the slaveries and the standardizations of Industrialism are incompatible with the nature of men. Humane Typography will often be comparatively rough and even uncouth; but while a certain uncouthness does not seriously matter in humane works, lack of un-couthness is the only possible excuse for the pro-ductions of the machine. So while in an industrial-ist society it is technically easy to print any kind of thing, in a humane society only one kind of thing is easy to print, but there is every scope for variety & experiment in the work itself. The more elaborate

¶ Illa tamen gravior, quae cum discumbere coepit
laudat Vergilium, periturae ignoscit Elissae,
committit vates et comparat, inde Maronem
atque alia parte in trutina suspendit Homerum.
cedunt grammatici, vincuntur rhetores, omnis
turba tacet, nec causidicus nec praeco loquetur,
altera nec mulier. verborum tanta cadit vis,
tot pariter pelves ac tintinnabula dicas
pulsari. iam nemo tubas, nemo aera fatiget;
una laboranti poterit succurrere Lunae.
inponit finem sapiens et rebus honestis;
nam quae docta nimis cupit et facunda videri,
crure tenus medio tunicas succingere debet,
caedere Silvano porcum, quadrante lavari.
non habeat matrona, tibi quae iuncta recumbit,
dicendi genus, aut curvum sermone rotato
torqueat enthymema, nec historias sciat omnes,
sed quaedam ex libris et non intellegat. odi
hanc ego quae repetit volvitque Palaemonis artem
servata semper lege et ratione loquendi
ignotosque mihi tenet antiquaria versus
nec curanda viris opicae castigat amicae

Joanna roman and italic. Eric Gill designed a number of typefaces—Gill Sans, Perpetua, Bunyan, Solus, and Joanna. The last was reserved for many years for use at Hague & Gill in Pigotts. It is, to my mind, a very successful face with an extraordinarily interesting and beautiful italic. Its relatively modest differences of thicks and thins make it suitable for smooth papers and for offset reproduction.

Eric Gill's development from stonemason and letter cutter to sculptor: BELOW A simple inscription. RIGHT A typical memorial plaque, but with quite ambitious relief carving. BELOW MIDDLE One of the Stations at Westminster Cathedral—the inscription is secondary. BOTTOM A free-standing relief. BOTTOM RIGHT A small full round sculpture.

Eric Gill illustrated—or perhaps I should say decorated—many books with his wood engravings, done in an entirely new spirit and style. ABOVE LEFT One of the simplest engravings showing Gill's sensuous qualities, from a very late book of engraved nudes. ABOVE RIGHT A border from *Troilus and Criseyde* is rather typical of his work. ABOVE The Four Gospels were adorned by many of the most moving of Gill's engravings. The figures are beautifully entwined with noble letters.

Stanley Morison.

STANLEY MORISON

by F. Ronald Mansbridge

MOST PEOPLE think of Stanley Morison (1889–1968) as an expert
on typography and printing design. This he certainly is—probably the
most influential authority on printing in this century. He was responsible for the design of the outstanding new typeface of our era,
Times Roman; he devised the present-day typography of *The Times*
newspaper; he was typographic director of the Monotype Corporation
and for the Cambridge University Press.

But in addition to being such an active and influential practitioner, he
has been a scholar and historian of type design, of the printed book and
of handwriting. His far-reaching work in these fields alone would be
enough to make a full life; but over and above these things he was
the editor for three years of *The Times Literary Supplement*, the author
of an impressive four-volume *History of The Times*—the work is
anonymous but was largely Morison's—and that is a book which tells
not only the internal history of *The Times* newspaper, exposing its
"skeletons, glories and stupidities with unsparing candor," to use the
words of *Time* magazine, but also throws remarkable light on the
diplomatic history of Europe and especially the relations between England and Germany over the last century. He has written on Anglo-
American relations and the American doctine of the Freedom of the
Seas. He has written on kingship and Christianity. He has made and
published an outstanding study of the *Portraiture of Thomas More* by

F. Ronald Mansbridge, now in charge of the Yale University Press
office in London, was manager of the Cambridge University Press
American office in New York for many years until his retirement at the
end of 1970. Lecture given October 7, 1965.

Holbein and his successors over four centuries. He has not only an interest but first-hand knowledge and first-rate judgment in matters of politics, religion, and art; he has sound business sense, though he has often not followed it himself. He is an ascetic who for nearly half a century has uniformly worn black—black suit, black hat, black shoes, black socks—an ascetic who is a connoisseur of wine and food and never so happy as when enjoying champagne for lunch. He is a deeply religious man who will overcome or override physical pain by a power of will that has been strengthened by faith. He has consorted with millionaires, with lords of the press, and with at least one king, but will spend three quarters of an hour teaching an anonymous secretary why an *F* should look like an *F* and a *J* look like a *J*.

That is the man who was born in 1889—eleven years old at the turn of the century. As a boy he was an invalid, and perhaps we owe a great deal to that simple fact. Because he was saved from the bad conformity of English school teaching he was forced to develop an independent point of view, and he learned to think things through to their rational basis. This is the secret behind so much of his work, and this in the end is what has made him something else over and above all the other things we have listed. It has made him a great teacher, because he in turn has encouraged others and would encourage you and me not to accept things *ex cathedra*, but to think things out for ourselves until we came up with the rational answer.

In his early twenties Morison had a job as a bank clerk in London, but he already had an interest in printing, and he answered an advertisement which appeared in Volume 1, No. 1 of *The Imprint*, a journal founded and edited by Gerard Meynell. This led to an association with Gerard Meynell's uncle, Wilfrid Meynell, director of Burns & Oates, the Roman Catholic publishers; Morison had become a Roman Catholic in his twentieth year. Morison was encouraged to learn and to write about typography and also to write advertising copy and to make layouts. Then followed the Pelican Press and the Cloister Press, and anyone interested in further details can get them from the *Newberry Library Bulletin*, Volume 5, No. 5, August 1960, which contains an admirable article on the work of Stanley Morison by James M. Wells.

The first great landmark among Morison's productions in printing and typography is *The Fleuron*, which appeared in seven numbers between 1923 and 1930. The first four numbers were edited by Oliver Simon and the last three by Morison, but Morison was to a large extent

Examples of Morison's typography, from *The Monotype Recorder*, Volume 43, No. 3; courtesy the Monotype Corporation, Ltd.
RIGHT   Specimen of the first showing of Monotype Baskerville, 1926.
BELOW   Jacket design, red and black on yellow, for Victor Gollancz.

A SPECIMEN
OF
PRINTING LETTER
DESIGNED BY

John Baskerville

ABOUT THE YEAR MDCCLVII

RECUT BY
THE LANSTON
MONOTYPE CORPORATION
LIMITED FOR USE ON THE
"MONOTYPE"

❁❖❁❖❁❖❁❖❁❖❁❖❁❖❁❖❁❖❁❖❁❖❁

LONDON
43 AND 44 FETTER LANE E.C.4
MCMXXVI

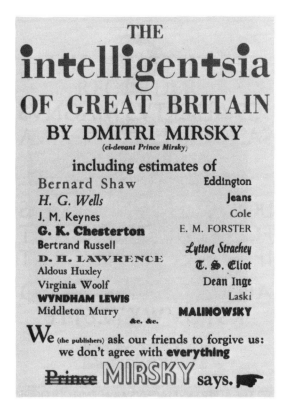

THE
intelligentsia
OF GREAT BRITAIN
BY DMITRI MIRSKY
(ci-devant Prince Mirsky)

including estimates of

Bernard Shaw	Eddington
H. G. Wells	Jeans
J. M. Keynes	Cole
G. K. Chesterton	E. M. FORSTER
Bertrand Russell	*Lytton Strachey*
D. H. LAWRENCE	T. S. Eliot
Aldous Huxley	
Virginia Woolf	Dean Inge
WYNDHAM LEWIS	Laski
Middleton Murry	MALINOWSKY

&c. &c.

We (the publishers) ask our friends to forgive us: we don't agree with **everything**
~~Prince~~ MIRSKY says. ☞

the editor from the beginning. The successive volumes of *The Fleuron* were handsome, even lavish, appallingly low-priced (I speak from the publisher point of view; a guinea a volume!), incisive and often critical. In those days Morison was referred to by some of the die-hards in printing as a "typographical Bolshevik," but *The Fleuron* won recognition and quickly became influential—not only in England but in the United States, in Germany, in France and elsewhere. When the seventh volume was published, and Morison received pleas from many quarters to continue the publication, he decided that the main job had been done for which the journal had been founded, and that his work could be continued more effectively in other media. His decision was communicated to a number of interested parties through an engraving by Denis Tegetmeier entitled "No Reprieve."

In the production of the seven volumes of *The Fleuron* Morison insisted on the highest standards of production. His aim was nothing short of perfection. Any of us today could get a liberal education in the typographic art by spending seven months carefully reading the seven volumes of *The Fleuron,* absorbing what was said in them, and being inspired by the manner in which they were produced. Morison's insistence on perfection was at a heavy cost to his own pocket. He personally provided a large subsidy which was probably a drain on his finances for some years.

It was during the twenties that Morison was appointed typographical adviser to three institutions: in 1922 to the Monotype Corporation in London, in 1925 to Cambridge University Press, and in 1929 to *The Times* newspaper. These appointments were to continue for thirty or forty years. Morison's connection with Monotype and with Cambridge was particularly fortunate and valuable in its effect on book typography. Under Morison's guidance and inspiration, Monotype undertook the programme of cutting newly designed typefaces as well as the recutting of old designs, and it is these designs which are at the heart of the British contribution to the typographical renaissance of this period, while at the same time in America the Mergenthaler Linotype Company was to go forward with its own program of faces designed by such men as Dwiggins and Ruzicka. The Monotype faces include Centaur, Bembo, Poliphilus, Fournier, Baskerville, Bell, Gill, Perpetua, and Times. Each of these new faces was used at Cambridge by the University Printer Walter Lewis, Morison's friend and colleague, and there was consequently a good deal of what today would be called "feedback" from Cambridge to Monotype. One of my early recollections during my first months at Cambridge in 1930 was the feeling of excitement shared by those on the publishing side, as well as on the printing side, in the use of these new faces—some of them being used almost for the first time—in a spring or fall list, for example, and then later in a book. These new faces were described by Morison in *Tally of Types*, printed for private distribution by the Cambridge University Printer in 1953. An unbound set of sheets is displayed in one of the cases here tonight, and you will see that each section on the seventeen types is set in the type-face which it is describing.

Incidentally, in the preface to *Tally of Types*, the present Cambridge Printer, Brooke Crutchley, tells a characteristic story of Morison's appointment at Cambridge. Bruce Rogers had been typographical ad-viser to the Press from 1917 to 1919, and had made a recommendation that after his departure someone should be appointed permanently to the position. Walter Lewis, who had become University Printer in 1923, had recommended Morison, and the Syndics of the University Press had asked him to call for an interview.

"I understand, Mr. Morison," said the Chairman by way of opening the interview, "I understand that you would like to join us." "Only if you are interested in good printing," Morison replied, with what Crutchley describes as "that aggressiveness under examination which has never failed to obtain results."

In the seventh and final volume of *The Fleuron* there appeared an article by Morison, "First Principles of Typography." It was subse-quently reprinted as a small book in America, in England, in Germany, Holland, Spain, Denmark and Australia: Morison's bibliographers com-ment that it has been everything so far but turned into a musical. Those of us who have read it could do worse than read it again, and again, and again. Like many great statements—religious, philosophical, scientific—it is amazingly simple. Here are a couple of extracts:

> Typography may be defined as the art of rightly disposing print-ing material in accordance with specific purpose; of so arranging the letters, distributing the space and controlling the type as to aid to the maximum the reader's comprehension of the text. Typography is the efficient means to an essentially utilitarian and only accidentally aesthetic end, for enjoyment of patterns is rarely the reader's chief aim. Therefore, any disposition of printing material which, whatever the intention, has the effect of coming between author and reader is

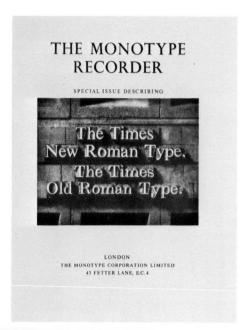

THE MONOTYPE
RECORDER

SPECIAL ISSUE DESCRIBING

The Times
New Roman Type.
The Times
Old Roman Type.

LONDON
THE MONOTYPE CORPORATION LIMITED
43 FETTER LANE, E.C. 4

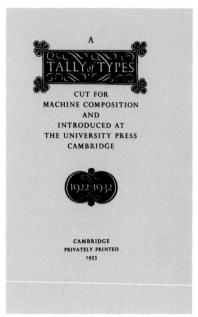

A
TALLY *of* TYPES

CUT FOR
MACHINE COMPOSITION
AND
INTRODUCED AT
THE UNIVERSITY PRESS
CAMBRIDGE

1922–1932

CAMBRIDGE
PRIVATELY PRINTED
1953

CAMBRIDGE AUTHORS' AND PRINTERS'
GUIDES
I

FIRST PRINCIPLES OF
TYPOGRAPHY

BY
STANLEY MORISON

CAMBRIDGE
AT THE UNIVERSITY PRESS
1951

ABOVE LEFT   Cover of the issue of *The Monotype Recorder*, 1932, describing Morison's Times New Roman typeface.

ABOVE RIGHT   Title page of Cambridge University Press list of machine faces, 1953. By permission of the Printer of the University of Cambridge.

LEFT   Title page of pamphlet, Morison's *First Principles of Typography*, Cambridge University Press, 1951, set in Bell types.

wrong. It follows that in the printing of books meant to be read there is little room for "bright" typography. Even dullness and monotony in the typesetting are far less vicious to a reader than typographical eccentricity or pleasantry. Cunning of this sort is desirable, even essential in the typography of propaganda, whether for commerce, politics, or religion, because in such printing only the freshest survives inattention. But the typography of books, apart from the category of narrowly limited editions, requires an obedience to convention which is almost absolute—and with reason.

Type design moves at the pace of the most conservative reader. The good type-designer therefore realizes that, for a new fount to be successful, it has to be so good that only very few people recognize its novelty. If readers do not notice the consummate reticence and rare discipline of a new type, it is probably a good letter. But if my friends think that the tail of my lowercase *r* or the lip of my lowercase *e* is rather jolly, you may know that the fount would have been better had neither been made. A type which is to have anything like a present, let alone a future, will neither be very "different" nor very "jolly."

In his postscript to *The Fleuron*, Morison made the same point in other words: "There is need for obedience to the simplest possible conventions. . . . Such business as letterpress has with the eye should be discharged purely in the role of trained servant—the greatest of whose virtues is self-effacement. The body is more than the raiment; it is not the business of the printer to costume his text."

In saying these things, Morison is of course referring to the typography of book printing. It is less well known that he also practised and wrote on advertising typography and such things as jacket design. For Doubleday he designed a standard format for the Crime Club mysteries, and for Gollancz in London he developed the famous yellow jacket with bold purple lettering: this was to become a hallmark of Gollancz books over many years. Those who work in advertising and display know how hard it is to combine a strong impact with the dignity that may be needed with, for example, a university press. Sixteen years ago I was struggling in my office one day to lay out a cover for the Cambridge University Press American Branch catalogue. Morison dropped in unannounced, as he so often does, and literally inside five minutes gave me a design which I, at least, think so satisfactory that I have continued it ever since with nothing but a change of colour each year.

In the thirties, after the demise of *The Fleuron*, Oliver Simon started a magazine called *Signature*, described as a "quadrimestrial of typography and graphic arts." I am sure many of you know it. It has some notable articles and illustrations. In the third number, Morison contributed an article on advertisement settings. Here again, he shows the same rational common-sense approach that runs through *First Principles.* He protested against what was common at the time, in England at least: many advertisements would attract the reader's eye with a forceful illustration, below which would appear an even, gray panel of copy, looking very much like something out of a history textbook. He pointed out that the reader of an advertisement was often lazy, tired or indifferent. Morison wrote, "Legibility is not enough. We want Readability. The problem is to turn the spectator into a reader, and the reader into a buyer. It is the layout man's job to turn the idle spectator into a reader. It is the copywriter's job to turn the reader into a buyer." Well, what to do? Morison makes some practical suggestions, of which the first is an extremely simple one—that in setting advertising copy, you put more space between sentences, say a pica and a half after every full point. He writes, "The junior typographer of the last decade always used to put in a paragraph mark instead of a space. His successors today put a large circular spot (sometimes called a bullet). William Morris used to put laurel leaves or other foliage. The reason for cutting out all these decorations is that white space is the essential element of display, and the most valuable. In a panel it is the most precious of all things. We must make all the use we can of it and all the time use it with the greatest economy." You may think this is one of the simplest possible instructions, and yet today you will see one advertisement after another in the daily papers and the weekly papers, first-rate advertisements from first-rate agencies, many of which would be improved by this simple device.

Many are familiar with the style of handwriting known as Chancery Cursive. It is so called because it is based on the kind of handwriting known as Cancelleresca, adopted by the Vatican Chancery in the first half of the fifteenth century for the use of the department concerned with the inditing of briefs. Morison didn't start the great vogue that this style of writing has had—especially in England, which needs handwriting reform more than most countries—but he gave it tremendous impetus by his research, by the publication of a number of facsimilies of writing books, and by the inspiration he has given to a great many teachers of this style of handwriting, including our own Paul Standard.

Morison wrote a most interesting article in the special issue of the

THE

FORM AND ORDER

OF THE SERVICE

THAT IS TO BE

PERFORMED

AND

THE CEREMONIES

THAT ARE TO BE

OBSERVED

IN THE

CORONATION

OF HER MAJESTY

QUEEN

ELIZABETH II

IN THE

Abbey Church of S. Peter
Westminster

ON TUESDAY
THE SECOND DAY OF JUNE
MCMLIII

DIEU 𝔢𝔱 DROIT

ET MON

Opening pages of Morison's design for the Coronation Service, Cambridge University Press, 1953. Cambridge illustrations by permission of the Printer of the University of Cambridge.

Penrose Annual published in 1956 to celebrate its fiftieth number. He described the conflict in journalism between word printing and picture printing, tracing it from the early newspapers down to television. He pointed out that a hundred years ago, type still was the dominant feature in newspapers, and then in the 1880s came the *New York Daily Graphic*, followed by the *London Daily Graphic*, printing photographs by the halftone process. Today, in many publications the position is reversed. The aggression of the picture on the word has resulted in the picture being dominant. I should like to quote a characteristic bit of Morisonian writing on television:

"At the moment of writing (22 September 1955), the newspapers report the first impact of commercial television, with standards distinctly bourgeois. The question remains whether, if its costs exceed those estimated, the ITA, like the *Daily Mirror*, will suffer a board-room revolution and change from bourgeois to petty-bourgeois. To do so will certainly increase its number of viewers. Whether this is good or bad is not our business to determine. All we need to perceive is that the uninhibited picture is the irresistible and the paramount attraction of the time. The more pictures we have today, the more pictures we shall have tomorrow. That pictures become better as they become more numerous is obviously false. But this is not our point. Only to realise that the picture is the thing."

That will give you a bit of the flavour of Morison's writing on a subject of this sort. He writes with punch.

Morison has produced a number of great works—the four-volume *History of The Times*, the big folio *History of the English Newspaper*, *The Portraiture of Thomas More*, and so on. He has also produced an immense number—a staggering number—of small pieces, which he calls his "sawdust"—small things that somehow or other come into being as he proceeds with his work. We could spend hours, we could spend days touching on one or other of them—a piece on Richard Austen, the engraver of John Bell's founts; a piece on the history of Black-letter; an outstanding small book on English prayer books; a paper on learned presses, showing that by his definition, the University Presses of Oxford and Cambridge are not as old as they claim to be. But I think that instead of trying to touch even a tenth of all these pieces—I suppose there are nearly 200 of them—I would refer to John Carter's *Handlist of the Writings of Stanley Morison* produced in 1950, supplemented in 1959 by a second *Handlist*, the work of Miss P. M. Handover.

I should like to close by concentrating on just two things: first, Morison's *First Principles of Typography*, which Bruce Rogers described as the "pocket testament of the craft." I hope that everyone who has been sufficiently interested in the subject to listen to me will do something much more rewarding, and that is read *First Principles*, and read it again and again.

Second, I should like to pass on what I think Morison himself would consider more important than following any instruction, even from him—the injunction to think things out for ourselves. To order our printing and our layouts and our designs not because of what some fashion or some fad dictates, not because of what some teacher will tell us, but because of the dictates of reason itself. What is the rational answer? Is there a *reason* for this?

Sir Francis Meynell.

GENTLEMEN OF A TYPOGRAPHIC TURN

by Sir Francis Meynell

IN 1912, when I was twenty-one, I was offered a job in the publishing house of Burns & Oates, of which my father was managing director. I thought it would be a good plan first to learn something of the trade in a firm of a more general kind, so I applied to the late Arthur Waugh (father of Evelyn Waugh), head of the publishing house of Chapman & Hall. He was willing to put me through the business, beginning with Dispatch, in a year of training. "There is the question of money," he said. I replied, largely, that this was not of first importance to me: I was living at home. "How about £500?" he asked. Elated, I said, "Surely that is too much to pay a trainee?" The elation did not last. He explained that the money was to pass not from Chapman & Hall to me but from me to Chapman & Hall. I took up my duties at Burns & Oates without further delay.

Having, I hope, gained your sympathy on the financial plane, I must exploit it to go back even further—to my childhood. And what determines me to do this, apart from the general backward looking that belongs to this, my seventy-fifth year, was a phrase in a letter of my mother's. "Please," she had written to the poet Francis Thompson, "return the revise proofs sixteen pages at a time." First of all (said I to

Sir Francis Meynell, book designer, publisher and poet, founded the Nonesuch Press and designed all its books, has been typographic adviser to H.M. Stationery Office, and is the author of *The Nonesuch Century* and an autobiography, *My Lives* (Bodley Head and Random House, 1971). Lecture given March 24, 1966.

myself) I am the son of a mother who was not only a poet but who knew also that page proofs have to be dealt with in units of sixteen. Yes, and that was only a trifle of the family's knowledge. I have often seen my mother unflinchingly cut a treasurable phrase in one of her essays so as to make a fitting end to the line or paragraph, and correct a proof so that a word deleted here would be promptly balanced by an added word there, to save the overrunning of the corrected lines. Where did she learn this tenderness towards my craft? But from my father, of course. Of him more in a minute.

My childhood had a literary background and foreground, the great names and exciting personalities of the writers who were my parents' friends. There was George Meredith, whose limping descent of the staircase I can just recall, and whose yearly tip of a pound at Christmas I can *very* easily remember. There was the silver teapot which I never carried to be replenished without remembering my father's solemn sanctification of it: "Robert Browning has taken his tea from this." There was W. B. Yeats standing owl-like at the door, blinking to discover my mother through the smoke from the Cyprus cigarettes which I had lately been sent at top speed to buy, my father sometimes going twice through his pockets before he assembled the necessary tenpence halfpenny. (Tenpence halfpenny was also the price of a box of toy soldiers, and once I thought of buying soldiers instead of cigarettes and running away from home.) There was Francis Thompson, "The Poet," as we children always called him, fragile, mannered, and complaining of the weather.

My mother and father edited a literary monthly magazine, *Merry England*, as well as *The Weekly Register*—and as well as doing much miscellaneous journalism, rearing their large family, and caring for a multitude of young poets and friends. The whole editorial work of the monthly was done by my parents and amateur helpers on and about the library table. If I was allowed in the room on press-days, the bargain was that I was to sit under the table. So I came to know these and other illustrious helpers as much by their feet as by their faces.

When he was over fifty, my father added the last segment of the circle. Magazine proprietor, editor, writer, he now became book publisher, as managing director of Burns & Oates. He gave me my first job. He also gave me my first lesson in detail. *The Collected Works of Francis Thompson* was planned a few months after I had joined the firm, and I was allowed to have a hand in designing the edition. When it was printed, my father discovered that a number of the kerns of the letter "f" had been broken. Day after day piles of the imperfect volumes were massed in his flat, which was immediately above the office. We had a sort of fire-bucket drill. One of my sisters would find the page, my father would dab in the kern, I would do the blotting, and another sister would restack the books. Some scores of thousands of pen corrections were thus made. I don't think my father would have trusted any one of us to do the actual pen work. He leant back, he quizzed, he admired after every stroke.

It was at Burns & Oates in 1913 that I began my long association with Stanley Morison. My cousin Gerard Meynell, whose example and influence in good printing has somehow missed the historians—Gerard Meynell, with Edward Johnston, the great calligrapher, published the remarkable magazine *The Imprint*, a notable venture not, alas, destined to live for long. They wanted a clerk, and Stanley Morison, then in a bank, applied for the job. When *The Imprint* came to an end my father came to the rescue. Morison was engaged—thank goodness I can't remember at what minimal salary—to help me in the invention and design of Burns & Oates books. These were of course Roman Catholic, and that suited Morison well, for he was a convert to that church. We used the seventeenth-century Fell types for prayer books, for altar cards, for ritual books. We had fun, and handsome fun. Books then, just before the First World War, were hand set. The Monotype was yet to find its face—and typefaces.

In 1914 I bought an Albion press which I kept in my dining room, and persuaded the Delegates of the Oxford University Press to lend me some of their Fell types. The Romney Street Press was my new style and I issued a prospectus. If ever there was a gold-brick prospectus this was it!

> The Romney Street Press has been set up for the better and un-affected production of Books, Pamphlets and single sheets of poetry. The preliminary costs of equipment amount to £40 [in those days about $200] and Francis Meynell, the Director of the Press, invites subscriptions to cover this amount. Subscribers will have first call upon the publication of the Press at cost price.

The only two small books that I managed to produce were, with a good deal of difficulty, disposed of—yes, the whole fifty copies each— but there was no general subscription, and that past cost of equipment bore heavily on me.

Meantime decisive things had happened to me. I had met George Lansbury, the Socialist leader, apart from my father the greatest masculine influence on my life. In Lansbury I found a most ready support for my "propaganda" view of good printing and good craftsmanship of any kind. Lansbury secured the financial support which made it possible for me to start the Pelican Press. We set advertisements for commerce, which was in those days something of an innovation, and we printed political pamphlets in the Minority Socialist interest. These pamphlets are odd to look at now. The slogan of "fitness for purpose" had not yet informed us. A report of the great meetings which we held at Albert Hall to welcome the first Russian Revolution was designed in Cloister Old Style, with a mannered elegance which would have suited better an essay by Walter Pater.

To return to Stanley Morison: when after the war Lansbury's *Daily Herald* was started, and I joined its staff, it was Morison who took my place at the Pelican Press. Soon after that war I began making proposals from the Pelican Press to various publishers. Would they allow me to print for them this, that, and the other book in a "really nice" edition? I pointed out that if they were in fact wrecked upon the conventional desert island and wished to take with them the conventional choice of two books, Shakespeare and the Bible, they would not find a current edition of either fit for a *tasteful* shipwreck.

My arguments were fruitless—except of a plan for myself. Why shouldn't I do what I wanted the publishers to do? Why wait on them? So I began to hanker after the as yet unnamed, unmanned and un-financed Nonesuch Press. The next step was to bind David Garnett and Vera Mendel to the adventure. The first provided a cellar in his book-shop for our premises; the second supplied $1,000 for our capital. Among us we planned to give as much editorial as physical value to our books, and we adopted the phrase "books for those collectors who also use books for reading."

Whence the corporate name? I began by looking not for a name, but for a device; I found in a tapestry surviving from the Nonesuch Palace the elements which Stephen Gooden (a first-rate copper engraver) made into our first "mark." In adapting the device, we also took the name, and I silenced an early objection that it was too boastful by pointing out that Nonesuch means "nonpareil" and so had an esoteric meaning. For, as you know, "nonpareil" is the name of a very small and humble type size. "Nonesuch" was chosen in a spirit of mixed hope and humility.

So there we were in 1923, in our cellar under Birrell & Garnett's book-shop, book-enthusiasts, *amateurs* in the literal, though not, I hope, the derogatory sense of the word, tackling the donkey work of book production and the mule work of distribution. For nearly two years we continued in the half-light of our limited premises, producing illuminating works in limited editions, and varying the daily task with such occasional diversions as "invoice bees"—parties to which our friends were bidden in order to help us between drinks with the task of writing out invoices and statements.

It is scarcely worth recording the vicissitudes of those underground activities. Only when we tried to stem an ever-rising tide of Congreves—which I eagerly unloaded from the lorries—only then did we wonder whether, for purposes of self-preservation, the Press might not have to expand. (Indeed, one of our old walls *did* bulge alarmingly.) Happily, part of the edition of Congreve got temporarily lost. The lorries which were carrying the bound books from the printers broke down just before we did.

My stock-in-trade was the theory that mechanical means could be made to serve fine ends, that the machine in printing was a controllable tool. Therefore we set out to be mobilisers of other people's resources; to be designers, specifiers, rather than manufacturers; architects, rather than builders, of books. This gave me a freedom that the great private presses, bound to one or two types, could never have: the freedom of the fine new faces and revivals of old faces that Stanley Morison was leading the English Monotype Corporation to make.

Nonesuch led the way in popularising these faces, and Monotype was handsomely ready to gratify my whims. When I wanted linked italic letters for *as* and *is* and *us*, they humoured me. When I wanted smaller roman capitals for Fournier and long ascenders and descenders for Plantin, they produced them.

It isn't proper for me to say much about the flurry that Nonesuch made in the twenties. *The Times* gave us a leading article. Booksellers—and there *were* booksellers in those days—queued up for Nonesuch editions. An undergraduate would put down his name at four bookshops for a Nonesuch book, be served, if he were lucky, by two, and then sell his second copy at a premium which largely paid for his first.

We kept back no copies, though of course we knew that many book-sellers put some copies aside for the rich secondhand market. We had a wonderful assurance both from this oversubscription of the English

George Macy.

BELOW LEFT Title page from Heritage Press edition of *John Brown's Body*, 1948, designed by Meynell.

BELOW RIGHT Title page from The Limited Editions Club's *Old Goriot*, 1948, designed by Meynell; courtesy George Macy Companies, Max M. Stein.

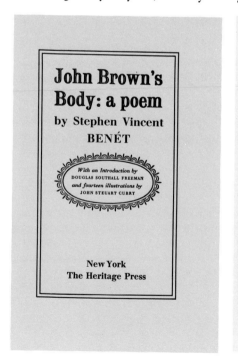

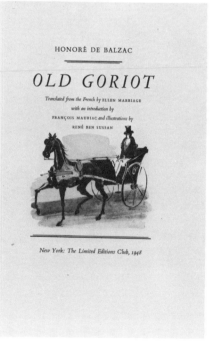

market and from our sales in your country. For on a spring day thirty-nine years ago, there came unannounced into my new office (a room in our early eighteenth-century house) a young American, hatless, coatless, swinging a gold-headed cane. He was direct and gay in his manner and in declaring the purpose of his visit. "What is my business with you?" he said, taking the words from my mouth. "Why, I come as the future distributor of Nonesuch books in the United States."

I'm not equal to resisting so purposeful an approach from someone whose whole attitude is so radiant and decisive, and so I said to Bennett Cerf—yes, it was he—"Right you are." And right indeed we were for many years. What a pleasure, and profit, that long association was! We had a contract drawn up, I believe, but certainly neither of us ever thought of referring to it.

In the middle of the thirties I felt that Nonesuch had completed its immediate programme. There seemed no longer any obvious gaps in the English classics which needed to be filled by books better edited and better printed than those already in existence. At least, that was the argument I used to explain to myself a certain exhaustion of my interest. Moreover the depression of the early thirties had taken its toll; it wasn't so easy to sell our kind of book in what an Indian friend of mine called "this mundial badtime." I needed money and I accepted a new challenge. I became a twice-weekly columnist for an English newspaper. Then I was induced into the film trade by United Artists—on the commercial, the distribution side; and then to an advertising agency.

Here I have to report on another American visitor. I had received from the United States fine-looking and enticing prospectuses from The Limited Editions Club, and even a suggestion that I might design a book for it. Then one day into my office walked George Macy. Nonesuch was neglected and flagging; he would take it over. I trusted him and his work; the deal was made, on a basis which relieved my anxiety about my total staff of two and about my debts of $800 or $1,000, and cost George little money but great effort besides. So began an interregnum in which George was the master of Nonesuch and I his part-time assistant. He was the publisher, the inventer; I was his designing (in the innocent sense of the word) aide.

It was he who decided to make the Nonesuch Dickens—to procure its superb editing, to buy the treasure of the original engravings, to include one with each set of volumes. That set the limit to the edition—the number of these steel plates and wood engravings was 877. Although, or perhaps because, Dickens was almost in my family, I was skeptical, I fear. My grandfather and Dickens had been close friends, and co-actors as well in the amateur dramatics that Dickens was fond of organising. It was Dickens who introduced my grandfather to the young lady who was to be my grandmother. And he, Dickens, wrote of her to my grandfather: "Good God what a madman I should seem if the incredible feeling I have conceived for that girl could be made plain to anyone!" Forgive this digression about what is precious in my purely family feeling.

I return to George's Nonesuch Dickens. I designed it, after persuasion, with loving care. Its twenty-three volumes took two full years to make—and then came the war. Even Dickens was submerged by that, as was the Nonesuch office which George had set up in London. But after the war the Dickens came into its own, and it is a lucky buyer who can get it today at five times its published price.

In the Macy-Meynell prewar period there was another book which I would place with the Dickens pretty well at the top of the Nonesuch achievement: *The Masque of Comus.*

After the war George produced a very few books in the United States with the Nonesuch imprint, while I was occupied, believe it or not, with setting up a vast research organisation for the British cement industry. And then, in 1951, George gave the Nonesuch name back to me—*gave* it back. I shall tell briefly what I did with it as a hobby, not as a living, from my desk in the midst of cement technicians.

First I had to find a friendly publisher who would do all the business of financing and distributing the books I wanted, with a new zest begotten by my technical and alien surroundings, to design. I found my perfect collaborator in Max Reinhardt, who had acquired the romantic business of John Lane—romantic for me because the original John Lane had first published the poems and essays of my mother, Alice Meynell. How lucky I have been in my associates—Random House, George Macy, Max Reinhardt.

What was my thesis now? It was what you might call a sociological one. The new world, after the shattering war, was for British people's homes a greatly narrowed one: not large houses, now, with a library and ample bookshelves, but many small flats—apartments to you. Well then, a new Bible, a new Shakespeare, a new Blake: could these be made in fine editions that would fit the new and narrowed scene and shelf?

The key to the problem must be paper. I searched the mills for so-called India paper that would be marvelously thin and opaque but would yet have just that minimal roughness of surface that would prevent pages sticking together—the vast disadvantage of standard India papers. My search was a failure. Then I had a brainwave. One of the most competent paper mills in England belonged to our Imperial Tobacco company, and made cigarette papers exclusively. To them I put my problem. Would they experiment? Yes, they would. And they finally produced precisely what I hankered for. The new Shakespeare occupied 234 cubic inches as against the 720 inches of the old. The new Bible was 199 cubic inches, the old edition 864; and the Blake, even more remarkably because its text was expanded, was only one-tenth the bulk of its forerunner.

There were new books as well, but always the aim has been elegance, not opulence. Now we are in the midst of a series of children's and "young people's" classics, the Nonesuch Cygnets.

I have perforce to mention my own book, *Poems and Pieces*, published four years ago; for if ever my ashes are deemed worthy of an epitaph, I should like it to read, "Printer and Poet."

In 1799 an amateur printer and historian described one of his acquaintances as "a gentleman of a typographic turn." The phrase came spontaneously into my mind when I came to think of what I should say here about George Macy.

George Macy was a gentleman, gentle of speech, of humour, of deportment, of thought; gentle too in thoughtfulness, which is something different. And also, like many a gentleman of the old school, he was an autocrat! And he was an amateur. It has always shocked me that "amateur," or as we English still say of an unpaid cricketer, a "gentleman," should have the word "professional" set as its opposite. For a professional may be a gentleman, and an amateur may be no gentleman.

But George Macy gives another turn to the terminology: he was a professional, he was a gentleman, and—with all the heart that he could spare from his family, he was a lover, an *amateur*, of books. And he was—how much indeed he was—"a gentleman of a typographic turn." Though of all the 300 fine books that he caused to be published, less than half a dozen carry his name and involve his sole responsibility as designer, I believe that his influence was felt by every typographer and by every illustrator in every book made for him. This influence was often plain autocracy, but when it served his purpose it could be mild.

Whence did his authority spring? Hans Mardersteig once wrote that "no one who has not composed a book with his own hands and prepared it for the press knows the extent to which the same page may, with the same means, be given a beautiful, an indifferent, or an ugly form." I will go so far as to say that George Macy's authority was in part developed from the fact that he himself, with his wife Helen, had, for their own pleasure, set and printed books at the case and on the handpress, and so achieved the knowledge, the discipline, and a freedom of permitted movement within that discipline.

When one received from him a commission to design a book, all the data were there in the commission: no questions need be asked as to text, editorship, illustration, place of printing, or time schedule. He might suggest a size, a paper, a general manner of binding; and though these were options, not instructions, they properly made at any rate a bias in one's mind, because of his experience and taste, the general experience and generous taste of a "gentleman of a typographic turn" who was also a professional in his judgment and technique. But receiving a commission was only the beginning; one studied the problems, made one's trial layouts, and submitted them to him.

The problems of book design are always problems of communication: the communication of the author to the reader, of the designer's intention, first to the publisher and then to the printer. Indeed, the smart thing today, I am told, is to regard *all* human problems as problems of communication. In the University of London the subject has been elevated to departmental status. It has not yet reached our older universities if the story be true of a distinguished medievalist at Oxford who was observed attending to his bicycle in the street. The front tyre was flat, but he was vigorously pumping up the back one. When the oddity of his ways was pointed out he said, with some surprise, "What, do they not communicate?"

Once, and only once, as I shall describe in a few minutes, George Macy told me that *I* was pumping up the wrong tyre. My own submissions were from England, and the books made there for The Limited Editions Club by a variety of designers would by themselves furnish half a library. But England was only one of G.M.'s larders. He drew the riches of his books from the United States—think of the Bruce Rogers Shakespeare—from France, Italy, Spain, Russia, Japan; in all, from twenty-five different countries on four continents. All these tributary

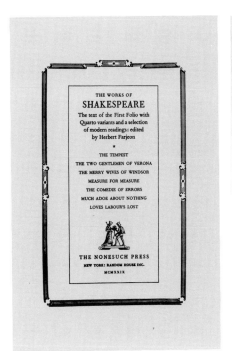

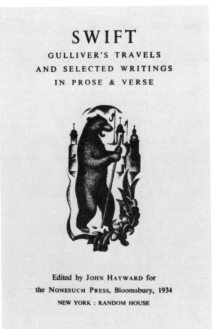

ABOVE LEFT   Page from the Nonesuch
Shakespeare (Nonesuch and Random
House, 1929).

ABOVE RIGHT   Title page of the Nonesuch Swift (Nonesuch and Random
House, 1934).

RIGHT   Title page from The Limited
Editions Club's *Casanova*, designed by
Meynell, 1940, from The Limited
Editions Club's *Quarto Miscellany*;
courtesy George Macy Companies, Max
M. Stein.

countries he visited constantly, besides commanding their printers by cable. You doubtless know the pleasing rhyme that runs, "Geography is about maps/Biography is about chaps." Believe me, it is hard to maintain that distinction in the case of George Macy. His biography could easily become a geography. He himself became a man of many countries but also a man of the world—by no means the same thing. (You will remember that G. K. Chesterton once made the proper distinction between Mother Earth and Fatherland.) No one, I say, *no one* has ever had the equal of Macy's knowledge not only of national styles but, in detail, of the chief and the best printing houses, paper makers, binders, illustrators, in well-nigh every book-producing land. No one but George Macy could have persuaded both Picasso and Matisse to illustrate books for him. Much more even than that, no one else could have induced them to carry through their undertakings! All this added to his confidence and command. He saw the foothills from a mountain.

And year by year, book by book, his vision and his authority grew. Ventures into the making of limited editions are usually short-lived. The Kelmscott Press lasted only seven years; the Doves Press, fifteen; the Vale Press of the painters Ricketts and Shannon, seven years. One reason for their short lives is a failing interest on the part of the promoter; if his favourite plans are fulfilled his attention wanders. Another reason may be a failing in the interest of a fickle public. George Macy was not merely persistent but consistent for twenty-seven years; he remained ardent and inventive, and he had the conviction and skill, through depressions and booms, hot wars and cold wars, in swiftly changing circumstances, always to find and furnish a responsive public. His wife, who worked at the case and at the handpress with him in their private hobby, was also his one and only intimate confidante and counsellor in the large affairs of The Limited Editions Club.

The thinker, the writer, the speaker about another man's performance is in a dilemma. It is the dilemma of a choice between impersonal generalities and judgments on the one hand and factual, personal experience on the other. The second has the unpleasant feature of involving the first person singular, the "I." On the other hand, the approach by generalities and judgments is only deceptively "non-I"; it depends on the credence that can be accorded to the "me," to the critic. So, I choose the frankly personal role—and I will make it a case history of one book, because that history will include many features that are illustrative of George Macy's general attitude towards bookmaking.

The book is *John Brown's Body*. The entrepreneur is George Macy. The designer is Francis Meynell. The scene is New York and London. Scene I of Act I is a letter to G.M. from F.M. dated 13th January, 1944. "I have just read Stephen Vincent Benét's *John Brown's Body*, and as I think it is one of the best books ever written I rush in dangerously and ask you to put it into your list of projects and, even more dangerously, to ask you to let me design it."

Five weeks later George Macy replies with the characteristically friendly call-to-order that my unbounded enthusiasm needed. For Macy was by nature a composed and balanced man who disliked my habit of excessive statement.

"I was delighted," he wrote, "with the note which expressed a burst of enthusiasm for Benét's poem. There are of course other tellings of the John Brown story. I will arrange to send you *God's Angry Man*, which seems a superior telling to me." However, he writes two years later, in January 1946, and here works his pertinacious memory fortified by his excellent file:

> You will remember that you wrote me recently [recently, mark you!] out of a burst of enthusiasm for *John Brown's Body*, to say that you would like to plan a new edition typographically. The time has come, it is here.
>
> John Steuart Curry has completed a set of illustrations. I am sending you, in a separate package, a set of photographic prints. They reduce the paintings to the size which John would like to have in the book. If you feel that more pictures are desirable, and have definite suggestions, let me know.
>
> I do hope you can address yourself quickly to the typographic plan. My suggestion is that you plan the title page and other special pages, a sample page for the opening of each chapter, a sample page for the text; and that you get these sample pages made up in London. The text for these special pages I am including with the set of prints.
>
> You might at the same time send me a sample of the kind of paper you would like to see used, and a sketch for the binding.

You will notice that after a lapse of two years George almost casually grants me my ambition and is in complete command of me and of all the details. But I—I seem to have been a little slow; for four months later, in May 1946, he writes:

"I am sending you a telegram to tell you that I am very anxious to have the typographic plan for *John Brown's Body*, since the illustrations are languishing for reproduction and the whole problem of the production of books these days is so great that I hate to see any part of a book in a languishing state."

In the summer George came to London, and I showed him the typographic plan, which he liked. It is always an anxious moment, this immature, tentative pencil realisation of one's intention, whether one is designing for himself or for another. I have always taken humble warning from what happened to the great historian Gibbon. It is recorded that it was Gibbon's custom to present by his own hand a copy of each volume of the *Decline and Fall* to the Duke of Gloucester. "One day," says a contemporary chronicler, "elated with pride at the delightful office, and imagining as he went, what handsome things the Duke would say to him—all he got from his Royal Highness was: 'What? Ah! Another damned big square book, eh!' "

No, George Macy was more kind and more recondite than this!

But I began to argue about the illustrations, and the argument went on with an obstinacy on my part which equalled his. My general objection had been this: that Benét's poem was its own illustration, its own illumination, its own projection. We discussed a compromise: the illustrations should be in a pocket in the binding, not in the pages of the book itself. The separation of the pictures from the text seemed for a time a happy solution to us both. A year later Macy was decisive:

"I have been puzzling and puzzling about the problem of the inclusion of the illustrations; puzzling so much, in fact, that I have sometimes felt that it would be better to strike the book off our publishing list. Unfortunately I can't do that. So, I have come to the conclusion that I must proceed with an edition of this book in which John Steuart Curry's illustrations are given the prominence which he expected them to have.

"Therefore, I now propose to proceed with this book in this country, to have an entirely new typographic scheme made here and to compose the text here with great speed."

The characteristic here is Macy's loyalty to the wishes of John Steuart Curry, who had lately died. For the same reason he discarded also the countersuggestion of mine that the illustrations, if they were to be within the book, should be reduced to "in-text" proportions instead of whole page and double-page plates.

"In an attempt to be fair," wrote G.M., "I have spent some time and money in making colour photographs of the pictures just to see what they looked like when reduced as sharply as you have marked them for reduction. They look like nothing at all. It would be a libel on the illustrator."

Cold-war telegrams and letters passed, in which George was more temperate than I. For I, having done a great deal of editorial and sub-editorial work on the text of *John Brown's Body*, told him that if he issued the book in a format not mine he must not use my editorial apparatus. And he was shocked at the mere notion that he could contemplate such a thing. We were reduced even to sending messages to each other via a third person. . . . An impasse!

Well, he came to London again, he greeted me with his fantastically, his annoyingly, persuasive charm, the contest was over, and he had of course won hands down. And this too was characteristic: that once the storm was over, there was an absolute and utter return on his part to confidence, to encouragement. He issued a handsome pamphlet which he called "what a typographer does to, for, with a book, as exemplified in the contents of a letter from Francis Meynell to George Macy." In that letter of mine there were, I find, some 1,500 words of description and instructions (and I don't think a word of this "communication" was misplaced or superfluous!).

In this account of the making of one book, which shows in sequence George Macy's accessibility to suggestions, balance of judgment, attention to details, persistence in developing a difficult project, loyalty to an obligation, and obstinacy—especially obstinacy—I will note only two more things. First, George went with his wife and son and daughter to the dramatic reading of *John Brown's Body* at the New Century Theatre in 1953. He sent me the playbill signed by all the family: "To our beloved Francis. We have looked on John Brown's Body and we think of you." So that I must add also warm tenderness to the qualities evoked by this single book. And the second thing to add is his humour. In his *Monthly Letter* he printed my first letter of proposal about *John Brown's Body*. Monstrously, unjustifiably, but quite delightfully, he inserted a few words, making me write: "Did you ever hear of it? Is it at all known in America?" Those words were wholly his, not mine! He invented them in order to raise a smile at the superior, condescending Englishman! And a smile it did raise, from at least this example of the superior, condescending Englishman. I hold in honour this "gentleman of a typographic turn."

Victor Hammer.

VICTOR HAMMER

by Carolyn Reading Hammer

VICTOR HAMMER told the story of a Florentine craftsman who was commissioned by a Signor Praetesi to make a square-topped table for his Signora. Some time later the Signor came to the craftsman's shop to fetch the table. A table with a round top was brought forth. "But," said Signor Praetesi, "I commissioned a square-topped table!" "Ah," said the craftsman, "but it turned out round."

When I was invited to write this paper, my main concern was with discipline: how to write objectively about Victor Hammer's work as a typographer. But, like Signor Praetesi's table, my paper, in the writing of it, turned out differently than I had planned. And so, my story begins.

That Sunday afternoon in mid-July, 1948, was a humidly typical Kentucky summer's day. But we natives ignored it as we had for nearly two hundred years, and assembled at five o'clock to greet Transylvania College's new professor of art and to see the first exhibition of his paintings in Lexington. The artist's presence produced for me a situation in which I am always at my most awkward: meeting artists. For I have very few words for art.

But soon after entering the exhibition room I forgot the artist for his work, and for a long first time I looked at his printed books. Later that afternoon I did meet Victor Hammer and the only thing I can remem-

Carolyn Reading Hammer was a professional librarian and a private printer when she began studying with Victor Hammer, became his wife and joined with him in his Stamperia del Santuccio in Lexington, Kentucky. Lecture given February 16, 1966. Victor Hammer, born in 1882, died in 1967.

ber saying to him was, "Did you *really* print those books?" and his amiable answer, "Yes, I really did."

In September I was enrolled at Transylvania College as a student in one of Victor Hammer's evening classes. Amelia Buckley and Joseph Graves, my co-printers, were with me. We had previously told Victor of our interest in printing and had shown him strong evidences of our need of his help: the products of the Bur Press and the Gravesend Press. He was kind without much comment, but did suggest that we come to his class in beginning drawing, which, though surprised and not encouraged by the suggestion, we did.

I had never attended an art class, much less faced up to a live model whose head I was to sketch. I must have begun with the eyes—drawing very big ones—for I recall that I soon found my sheet too small to accommodate a head in proportion to the eyes.

The model was seated before a white drop curtain which hung from the ceiling in the center of the studio, dividing it into two almost equal parts. As we worked, Victor moved about among us to observe our progress. To a student seated quite near me I heard him say, "The head is an egg. You know? Just draw an egg!" I looked at my two headless/ eggless eyes and decided that Victor Hammer would never see them. But just as my hand moved to rip the sheet from my pad, a voice from behind me said, "Are you interested in calligraphy?" I turned and there was Victor motioning me to go behind the curtain where I found Amelia Buckley and Joe Graves already happily seated. The three of us were at long last safely on the right side of that curtain—and Victor had known it.

From this time on, the class was divided. While the other students drew eggs and eventually whole bodies, we took broad-edge pens in hand and filled sheet after sheet with verticals, diagonals, horizontals, and circles. Once these strokes were controlled, we filled sheet after sheet with the roman capital letters formed from them. Launched with the steel nib, we learned to cut quill pens by cutting forty, one after the other, and proceeded with that tool to copy from old manuscripts their fine Latin hands, and illuminated our efforts after their illuminations. We also copied uncial and half-uncial hands, gothic minuscule hands, and the so-called insular hands. Victor taught us to control our hands, but gave us our heads. No doubt "writing and illuminating and lettering" can become heady affairs.

These evening classes prolonged themselves happily and had we been cloistered Irish medieval scribes, we could not have taken our efforts more seriously. No ink, no paper went untried; we wrote on parchment in raised gold letters and attempted elaborate illuminated capitals. How impractical a teacher we had! His only worry seemed to be Joe Graves's prodigality with gold leaf: one sheet to an initial letter. But especially did Victor take delight in the work of Joe Graves.

As we worked in Victor's scriptorium, we slowly began to find our own letter-forms, forms which we could adapt to the English language in which we would write. For Victor, this was the turning point in our learning from him: to see for ourselves the subtle rightness of a Latin line in one hand, the rebuke of an English line in the same hand. In devious ways—through the capital roman letter, the uncials, the frakturs, the "Caroline" minuscules, the court hands—we learned that one can judge a letter-form only as a *line* of written letters, or printed letters, composing words and sentences. Inevitably we were led to the knowledge that the language is a letter-form's restriction.

For two years we shared the one table in Victor Hammer's "Scriptorium"—a scriptorium very much a part of the studio, for that drop curtain had long since been taken down. Over us all, Victor presided with the greatest of patience and kindess and, for a while, with a hope—which none of us was able to fulfill.

Only for very short periods in his long life was this hope—the creation of a fruitful master-apprentice relation—fulfilled: once in Florence, when Fritz Kredel came to him for a year, and following Fritz, Edgar Kaufmann came—with him, too, Victor could share his work and thoughts. There, too, Victor had two gifted young men as apprentices: Fritz Arnold and Paul Koch, the son of Rudolf Koch. Once again, briefly, he had apprentices at his school at Grundlsee in Austria, and felt a justification for teaching.

In 1938, Wells College, and in particular Nicholas Nabokov and William Rusk, received him and gave him warm haven and warm friendship, but within the student body he found no lasting resonance. "In true belief," said Victor, "art is an *unteachable* subject."

His years in the East were certainly fruitful in friends: among the first he found here was Paul Standard, and Robert Middleton and Ulrich Middeldorf (though rather farther westward), Joseph Blumenthal and Norman Kent, the two Dard Hunters, August Heckscher (who was the first in this country to write about Victor's work), Graham Carey, Paul Bennett, Robert Leslie and James Laughlin and the

Kurt Wolffs, for whom he printed books; the gifted Harry Duncan at the Cummington Press, and Lewis Mumford, who has long been a comforting friend. For Herbert Steiner, whose "Mesa" and "Aurora" series were printed by the Hammers at Wells College, Victor had deep respect and gratitude. I name these persons for I, too, knew, or know them now, and in my turn am grateful for their interest and kindnesses to Victor.

In noting so many names throughout this paper, I intend to try to weave them into a tapestry—a tapestry in which Victor Hammer too is as a thread; these touching threads form a pattern and then move on to form another. In these Wells College days he could also meet and talk with John Howard Benson, who, as Victor said, "invited me to a feast and gave me a diploma;" Frederic Goudy, whom he several times visited; Elmer Adler ("a faithful friend bold enough to use my first uncial in his *Beowulf*"); D. B. Updike ("who oddly enough wanted my uncial types, but could not get them"); W. A. Dwiggins; Porter Garnett; Carl P. Rollins; Arthur Rushmore; Frederic Warde; Herbert Davis and the Clarence Kennedys at Smith College; Rudolph Ruzicka; Philip Hofer. Each of these people left a memory in Victor's life and though no "working" friendships nor alliances were formed, deep respect for their work—so different from his own—remained. And this is as it should be. Each had his own orbit. I have shared less than a fourth of Victor's eighty-three years. But through him, I can share vicariously his European years (another story) and these early years in the eastern United States as well.

The evening classes at Transylvania expanded into weekly afternoon sessions in Victor's home, as well as an added evening for the calligraphers and would-be calligraphers. The afternoon sessions were our wonder and delight—and our frustration; during these seminars we came to know another mind—a philosophic mind, if you will. Victor's translation, with Thornton Sinclair, of Konrad Fielder's *Posthumous Papers*, Victor's own *Four Dialogues*, his essays, *Concern for the Art of Civilized Man*, and the little notes on which he worked ("Pebbles" he called them) reveal the content of those hours. The evening for the calligraphers' gathering was less formal and might take any turn. Very often Victor read to us from whatever he had in hand when we arrived. (I never saw Victor "wait" for anyone or anything—if a burin, a brush, a pencil or the handle of a press was not in his hand, a book was—or always in his pocket ready to be brought out.) The books in hand, as I

remember from those evenings, were often poems of Goethe, Hoelderlin, Leopardi, the stories of Johann Peter Hebel, or Carlyle's translation
of the German romances—particularly those of Musaeus. When he was
reading Wright's *Islandia*, "a world that is traditional yet free," he
would share with us certain passages. Mark Twain's writings were
Victor's pleasure and he would have one of us read that delightful
passage recording the question and answer conversation between Jim
and Huck on language. I know now that it was not by chance that these
books were in hand, but rather by design. And once, we persuaded him
to play on his clavichord—one of the two he had made in Florence.

Victor believed only in learning, never in teaching: "Nothing can be
taught," he said, "but everything can be learned." He was the best of
teachers, he was the worst of teachers. Here in Lexington there were
seeds sown, but we were such frail plants. His years here, valid and rich
as we find them for ourselves, left him almost as alone as ever. Raymond
McLain, then Transylvania College's president (and Victor's student)
tried to obtain a grant so a workshop could be established for a three-
year period in order that Victor could have paid students and paid
apprentices to work with him. There were gifted applicants, but unfortunately no grants came forth. Perhaps it was a pity.

Other than his work, Victor's activities, then and now (1966), are
few. He has no sporting accomplishments, nor inclinations to observe
another's. There is no competitive spirit in him. Friends take him to our
Keeneland races, where he remains in the paddocks most of the time,
observing the horses. The only card game I ever saw him willingly play
was solitaire. In conversation he is most attentive, but he claims that our
general conversations and small talk here in Kentucky are incomprehen-
sible to him: too many dropped consonants and too-soft vowels. "I can't
possibly understand how you can understand one another," he says. He
delights in concerts and to recordings he does sit quietly listening; for
him "background" music has no appeal, and his social "rudenesses" (so
far as I have witnessed) have, for the most part, consisted of his em-
phatic request, "If we are not to listen to the music, just turn it off,
please." On one occasion, he forcibly removed a cocktail glass from the
hand of a guest who, as he sipped, was examining a rare edition of
Goethe's poems belonging to our host. Our host was quietly grateful,
but the guest was not so quietly placated. I would say that Victor is
usually gently reserved in conversation except when it takes a turn
towards art, and then he speaks, strongly defending "modern" art.

eva & zeno
polycarp
alexius
quintilian
winifred
kenneth &
imogen
benjamin

Page of American Uncial from *Chapters on Writing and Printing* (The Anvil Press, 1963; courtesy Carolyn R. Hammer).

This initial consists of two pieces. One is a brass piece, one-fourth inch in thickness, in which (in reverse) the letter E has been cut to a 1/16-inch depth; the other piece is the E, cut from another piece of brass and forced into the letter form cut from the first piece. The assembled pieces are rubbed on stone to a common smoothness, and then the ornamentation is punched into the first piece; the whole is rubbed smooth again and the E piece is removed. The first or letter form is now mounted on a block to make it type-high, and is inked. The separate E is inked by itself and inserted into the letter form with pinchers, and the united block is printed as one.

placed into the press and is inked with a roller supported by roller-bearers. The letter (fig. 2) is placed into a 'devised' holder and is inked with a brayer. Finally, with pincers, it is transferred from its inking block to its groove in the 'letter-form' block and the once a-gain united pieces are printed as one:

XCEPT THE LORD build the house, they labour in vain that build it: except the Lord keep the city, the watchman wak-eth but in vain. It is vain for you to rise up early, to sit up late, to eat the bread of

6   THE

A letter T is cut out in reverse from a 1/16-inch piece of brass; the outline of this letter is traced in reverse on a second piece of brass, also 1/16-inch thick, and is cut out of it. The T is then fitted into the result-ing groove and left there until the ornamentation is punched, and then removed. The orna-mented piece is blocked; this block and its fitting letter are separately inked, united in the press and printed as one.

HE TRUTH WAS found already long ago, It bound the noble spirits into one Hold to the ancient Truth Do not let go!

Das Wahre war schon laengst gefunden, Hat edle Geisterschaft ver-bunden; Das alte Wahre, fass es an!

From *Notes on the Two-Color Initials of Victor Hammer*, by Carolyn Reading Hammer (Stamperia del Santuccio, 1966; courtesy Carolyn R. Hammer).

But I have digressed again and must return to my story. Amelia Buckley and I abandoned our work at the Bur Press—our tastes had changed—and Amelia devoted what time she now had to calligraphy. Joe completed his manuscript copy of Rudolf Koch's little essay, "Wer ist Victor Hammer?" which Ulrich Middeldorf had translated into English, and Joe found a handpress which Bob Middleton and Victor helped him to get in working order.

What happened to me was this: determined to print, once my "Scriptorium" days were, I felt, nearing an end, I casually suggested to Victor (with the most uncasual of feelings as I did so) that I might not be a bad bet as an apprentice at the press, and that as a start, I might learn quite a bit if I were just allowed to look on as *he* worked at the press. There was not a pause of indecision on his part. "My dear young woman," he said, "one does not learn anything by what you call 'looking on.' This makes no sense." I doubt that I *really* forcibly urged his reconsideration, but a little later, when I was graciously and kindly being escorted to the door, I remember Victor saying, "I am so very sorry, but it just can't be the way you want it." I went down the walk to the gate and as I heard the large white doors close behind me, a sort of small madness came over me and I vowed to myself, "Victor Hammer or no, I will find myself a handpress and print!"

I wrote to various places and finally got a letter from a firm in Toledo, Ohio, saying that they had some odd parts of old handpresses which they were getting ready to scrap and that maybe I could piece together a whole press; so I went to Toledo. That storeroom in Toledo looked so forbidding, the pieces looked so immense, so mixed up and unconnected with one another, that I left in dark despair.

But this trip to Toledo was the turning point. Very soon afterward, Joe Graves offered me his small Reliance Press, for he and Victor had coerced the local photogravure company into parting with its large proof press for Joe, just so I could have the smaller one. Seeing my persistence, Victor took me as his apprentice and with the exception of the Hoelderlin, he let me share in the printing of all subsequent Stamperia del Santuccio books, and in their casing and binding.

At Wells College, Victor had written a paper which he entitled "A Unique Plan." In it, he presented the necessity for an artist to have a patron who knew what he wanted. This patron might be a group of people who wished to commission a certain artist to provide them with a piece of sculpture or a painting. Of course Victor's aim in writing this paper had other ramifications peculiarly his own. Joe Graves and I had read "A Unique Plan," and when Jacob Hammer came to Lexington to live we took advantage of him to fulfill our version of the "plan": We would commission Jacob to print books which Victor would design, for a jointly owned press whose associates would publish titles of their own choosing. Some ten other friends of Victor's got quite as interested in "the plan" as we were, and so it was that the Anvil Press came into existence. Victor served as its "Honorable Designer" (he has never had a vested interest in it as such). Jacob's pressmanship was excellent, as evidenced by the Pico della Mirandola *Dignity of Man,* the Hebel *Francisca,* the Tyndale *Gospels,* and the Shakespeare *Sonnets.* After Jacob left Lexington, the printing went on more slowly, but surely, with its distaff printers: Nancy Chambers, Anne Williams (together with her husband, Wayne), and myself. In press now is the *Phenomena* of Aratus, reproducing some forty of the Ratdolt woodcuts printed in two colors, and in the spring, quite appropriately, the Anvil Press will begin to print a portfolio of Harriet Holladay's wild-flower woodcuts— products of her work with Victor and Fritz Kredel. The layouts for all of the Anvil Press books, with small exceptions, continue to be Victor's.

The Stamperia del Santuccio has its plans apart: its next publication will be a new translation of nine poems of Li Po, then Victor's "Pebbles" and some "pebbles" as well to come from our beloved friend, Thomas Merton.

When, to our delight, Beatrice Warde was with us last summer, she definitely determined that, per capita, Lexington has more printers and binders than almost any other place. It is true that there are quite a few of us gathered around the handpress and the binding table as a result of Victor's being in our midst. Especially important to us is that Mrs. Lawrence Crump was at the binding table; Victor forced her to it, recognizing the skill in those hands of hers, urging her to work under Hope Weil when she could; and now she most willingly and capably fills our needs. There is no beehive of activity surrounding Victor, but rather a small and quiet stream of work of which he is the source.

Lexington is rich in local friends and not so remote that new friends have not come to our quiet corner there. Jack Stauffacher brought Hermann Zapf to us from Pittsburgh for a weekend (the facile perfection of Zapf's work is, Victor feels, unsurpassed). Here we first knew Norman Strouse when he came to give a lecture at the University of Kentucky Library, and once, in search of another historian, Blanche and

Alfred Knopf chanced upon us. The type designers at our local IBM plant, quite gratuitously, brought Stanley Morison, Adrian Frutiger and Max Caflaisch into Victor's studio. Liam Miller came to us from Dublin all on his own, Herbert Simpson from Evansville, Indiana, Sir Frank Francis from London. Every now and then we must travel to meet those we want to know: the Lewis Allens who live far away in California had to be met in Paris one fall, the Muir Dawsons and the Harman Cohens in New York, John Dreyfus in Cambridge.

Robert Middleton's tribute to Victor Hammer has been published by Champion Papers as its *Book 14*. This "book," and a chapter which I contributed to the Anvil Press publication, *Chapters on Writing and Printing*, document Victor Hammer's uncial typefaces and many of the books he printed in them. To name Victor Hammer is to name an uncial type, for he has cut no other. In tracing the chronology of the uncial letter, I shall begin with the words of its first critic, Saint Jerome (ca. 340–420) whose denunciation, in the *Codex Amiatinus*, is written in the very letter he denounces:

> Let those who want them have ancient books or books written in gold or silver on purple parchment or in what is commonly called uncial letters—written burdens [I call them] rather than books. (Translated from Migne's *Patrologia Latina*.)

When Dr. E. A. Lowe's book, *English Uncial*, was published, Victor was asked to review it for the *Papers* of the American Bibliographical Society. A part of the review reads:

> It interests us that Dr. Lowe again introduces the tantalizing question of the meaning of the word *uncial*. After quoting from Jerome in his preface to the book of Job . . . Lowe suggests that the books may have been in square or rustic capitals as well as in uncial. It is an intriguing question and "merely in size" leaves one unanswered, and leads to further suppositions. "Size" may infer height (the exaggerated "inch-high" of a letter; it may infer width of a letter (for the rounded form of the uncial does not permit our narrowing it, whereas the rustic capital may be narrowed and soar to any height); and it may infer length of line (for the uncial line in inches is wasteful of space). Or, Jerome may well have been referring to the weight of a book (in "ounces") and the corresponding size of a book written in such a waste-of-space letter! But enough of added suppositions; we can only think that had Jerome not lived in a cave, we may not have been puzzling over the word *uncial*, but another.

> Jerome was not a scribe; we can only imagine what facilities he had in his cave, but he seems to have been wishing for a paper-back to fit into his pocket, or for an Oxford edition printed on India paper.

Victor also wrote of E. A. Lowe, and I quote it now as I feel that the author and the reviewer are here reflected in the same mirror:

> Positively to be enjoyed is . . . [his] sincere love for, and attachment to, the historical forms of the letters—sentiments so characteristic of him. Yet he is able to assert his preferences and determine his judgment on the basis of the excellence of execution. One has heard him compare certain letter-forms and certain pages with the taste of delicious foods: with his eyes he "tasted" these black marks on a yellowed parchment. . . . [Some of his words have the fine flavor] of a love letter. . . . Love is there and one can hear this venerable gentleman . . . speak in terms of love and see him caress an ancient page. (From *Papers*, vol. 55, 1961, pp. 267–268.)

The Latin manuscript to which Victor kept returning—to taste with *his* eyes—was one which he first saw reproduced in the German translation of Edward Johnston's *Writing and Illuminating, and Lettering* and later saw in its original in the British Museum: a late sixth-century Gospel, Latin Vulgate (Harley MS. no. 1775). Its letter-form is more nearly the prototype to the Hammer uncial than any other.

The Hammer cursive-uncial Andromaque has not been cast in any but a trial cast and Victor has used it sparingly, for there is little of it and it is difficult to set in its present form. There was no prototype for the Andromaque face. Victor tells of its origin in his paper, "Digressions on the Roman Letter" (published as a chapter in *Chapters on Writing and Printing*, Anvil Press, 1963):

> A number of years ago I was commissioned to paint a triptych of a mother and child, a Madonna with the Infant. . . . Finally, only the back of the center panel remained to be completed. I had decided to write upon it, in gold letters, part of a text from John the Scot. I made several trials in uncial letters and even did the inscription in Roman capitals on the back of the panel itself. But it was not right; it just did not fit.
>
> One morning, however, without much thinking or hesitating, I lettered the inscription in a cursive made up of Latin and Greek characters in combination. . . . Though the inscription was in Latin, I was careful to take French, English and German into con-

sideration when I cut the ten-point type from it; I made smoke-
proofs of words and sentences from these languages. . . .

I was with Victor when we left the punches in Paris with Charles
Peignot, who the year before had seen a photograph of the inscription
and had reacted in a very unbusinesslike way: "Victor," he said, "if you
cut punches for these letters, bring them to me next year when you
return and I will make a trial cast for you." We remained in France a
number of weeks after having left those punches cut to the 10 point, and
when we returned once again to the foundry, Victor was met with
incredulity by Monsieur Mouchel, who had been assigned to prepare the
matrices and oversee the casting. "It is a miracle! Do you realize that
you have cut these punches to within one-hundredth of a millimeter by
your eye alone?" "Was it not necessary that I do so?" asked Victor.

Again I will quote Victor's "Digressions on the Roman Letter." This
section was written in the form of a dialogue between A (Victor) and
B.

> B questions A: "You told me once that E. A. Lowe does not con-
> sider your uncial a real uncial . . . ?"
>
> A responds: "No, dear old friend that he is, he did not. Even when I
> first met him in Florence, in the early 1920's, he argued about
> this. He deals with things of the past and does not want them
> disturbed. But I am neither a paleographer nor an historian. I
> felt the spark of life still lingering in that eternal creation—the
> Roman letter—and tried 'to fan its flame.' In the beginning my
> efforts seemed stillborn. The prejudices against my type only
> now begin to give way a bit; its 'flame' will never burn high but
> after more than a generation's time, this child proves to be still
> alive—at least to a few. I may be wrong, but I attribute this
> 'life' to the fact that these letters were cut, not designed, that no
> pantograph machine interfered at the moment of creation.
> Somehow, people feel this quality too in all things made by the
> human hand. . . ."

In November of 1965, Victor received a letter from David Johnson
McWilliams of La Casa del Libro in San Juan. McWilliams wrote that
he had arranged an exhibit on "The Initial Letter"—an exhibit devoted
to "the decorated letters to be seen at the opening of MSS, their chapters
or divisions, etc." A last section in the exhibit "was given over to the
initial letter in modern books"—those of William Morris, Grailey

Hewitt, Eric Gill, Anna Simons, Victor Hammer, and others. "For your books," he wrote, "the legend in Spanish and English read: 'When one thinks of the work of Victor Hammer, the Viennese typographer and printer now in America, what is most likely to come to mind is his fondness for uncial typefaces such as he has designed and used in the books on display. Rarely has . . . attention been given to the colored initials etched in metal which he creates to compliment his typefaces. . . . Hammer creates a ribbon-like figure, seemingly the least complex form that the required letter might take, and lays upon it a rectangular background all sprinkled over with a small white pattern or with a large pictorial allusion to the text. The result is similar to that achieved with enamel, as in cloisonné or champlevé.' "

This paragraph in Mr. McWilliams's letter led me to the thought of writing about printed initial letters and, in particular, the two-color initials of Victor Hammer. I approached the two-color initials historically, that is, I searched in the books which we had in the house in order to find out who else had written about such two-color initials, especially about the Schoeffer initials in the 1457 and 1459 editions of the *Mainz Psalter*. I began with Thomas Moxon, who yielded nothing to me; in Hánsard's *Typographia* I found uncertainty: he quotes Papillon and Savage as affirming that the *Psalter's* letters had been "printed in *colours* with *suites* of *blocks*." Prior to this quote, Mr. Hánsard had affirmed that each of the blocks was printed separately and that justification had been obtained by points fixed upon the tympan so as "to act upon the margins of the print: thus, every block of which the suite consists will require separate beating, pointing and pulling." So tiring and tedious did this seem to Mr. Hánsard that he offered his "stereotype" method in its place. (Hánsard, pp. 912–913.)

In his *Printing Types* (vol. 1, p. 280) Mr. Updike wrote:

> Mr. Rudolph Ruzicka, who had thoroughly investigated the ingenious processes employed in printing these coloured initials in the Fust and Schoeffer *Psalter*, tells me that they were not stamped, as generally supposed, but printed. He writes, "A solid metal block, type high, was made for the filigree work, with a shallow mortise cut in the shape of the initial. The initial itself, also of metal and exactly as thick as the mortise was deep, was inked separately and dropped into the mortise of the filigree block, already inked. The combined blocks were then printed in one impression and in exact register, separately from the type. Of course the initial was a little

narrower than the mortise, leaving a fine white line between the letter and its decoration."

Then I turned to Dr. Victor Schoelderer's *Johann Gutenberg*, published in 1963 by the British Museum, and found, beneath Plate IV, facing page 25 (the plate illustrates the famous initial "B") an explanation very much in agreement with Mr. Ruzicka's. Also in 1963, in *Printing and the Mind of Man*, which has as its frontispiece the same remarkable "B," there are two other generally agreeing accounts (pp. 12, 31–32).

If there were other cutters and printers of two-color initials between Schoeffer in the 1450s and Hammer in the 1950s, I could not locate them. In writing that the *Mainz Psalter* initials were a "magnificent but solitary trial," S. H. Steinberg in his *Five Hundred Years of Printing* (p. 54) has put an authoritative end to *my* search at least.

The Stamperia del Santuccio has printed a little book entitled *Notes on the Two-Color Initials of Victor Hammer;* these notes are very brief statements on the work involved in cutting and printing such initials. I can remember the day when we saw our first reproduction of a Schoeffer initial (actually it was the stereotyped "B" in Hánsard's *Typographia*). "Ah!" said Victor, "he cut his initials just as I do—that fine white line surrounding the initial letter tells the story." In the Schoeffer print and the Hammer cut one can see the goldsmith's art.

A copy of the catalog of the exhibition planned by Justus Bier of Victor's work (North Carolina Museum of Art, April, 1965) shows facing page 71 his woodcut, "The Front Wall of the Chapel at Kolbsheim. A Diagram of Measurements and Auxiliary Lines." The chapel at Kolbsheim is on the estate of Madame and Monsieur Alexandre de Grunelius; it is their private chapel, commissioned when Victor was living with them in the 1930s. I call it Victor's chapel because he planned it and worked alongside the masons as they shaped the blocks of red sandstone brought from old vineyard walls or from old quarries— the same quarries which had given stone for the Strasburg Cathedral some ten miles from Kolbsheim—and raised the ashlar walls forty centimeters thick. He had carved the seven figures over its door and the ornamentation inside; he had drawn the plans for its stone altar and the four candlesticks, woodturned and gilded, which stood on it; he had modeled the door of the Tabernacle to be cast in bronze in Paris. The ironwork on the heavy oak door and the door's fish-shaped handle were his work, and a hanging brass vessel for holy water was from his drawing. For over two years he worked to complete the chapel, waiting until the last to paint the Crucifixus. The second year was 1937, when he had to return to Vienna. Not until twenty years later was he able to return to Kolbsheim and paint the Crucifixus. It is there now, over the altar.

As an artist Victor belongs to no school, has created no school; as a typographer too, his thread has been of a different color. In a letter to Victor, Wallace Stevens humorously suggested a title for a paper which he knew Victor was writing: "Why not call it 'The Opinions of a Contrary Man'?" Victor answered him in the last of his *Four Dialogues* (p. 103):

> You labeled me the Contrary Man, but you did not say contrary to what. Truly, I am contrary to mediocrity, though I know we could not live on this planet without it; I am contrary to sloth, and contrary to waste, which will go on in spite of me, and I am contrary to blasphemy against the Spirit. I have proved to myself that I can change the world, but only within the reach of my hands.

Those hands have cut the 10-point letter on a slim shaft of steel; they have carved in sandstone the seven figures over the doorway to the chapel at Kolbsheim. How far have those hands reached? Not far perhaps. But for some of us, deeper than Victor knows.

As though for him, Hoelderlin wrote these lines:

> True, the gods go on living,
> But they are over our heads
> high in a different world.
> Endless there is their work,
> and little it seems they consider
> Whether we live, so much spare us
> the heavenly ones.
> For a frail vessel not always commands
> the force to contain them,
> Only at times can Man bear the abundance of Gods.
>
> *(Brot und Wein)*
> translated for V. H.
> by B. Q. Morgan

Jan Van Krimpen.

JAN VAN KRIMPEN

by John Dreyfus

JUST AFTER Holland was liberated in 1945, I met Jan Van Krimpen (1892–1958) for the first time. Some of his English friends knew I was in the vicinity of Haarlem, where he worked for the ancient printing house of Enschedé en Zonen. No news of him had reached England during the occupation of his country, and I was asked to find out if he was still alive and well. My commanding officer agreed to drive with me into Haarlem, where we found the house of Enschedé in the shadow of the great church in the centre of the town. From there we were guided out through the suburbs by Frans Enschedé until we reached Van Krimpen's house. Despite a winter diet augmented by tulip bulbs, the type designer was in good health, but on no later visit did I ever again see him looking so slim.

He took us up to his book-lined study. On the mantelpiece were three framed photographs. I immediately identified a good likeness of Stanley Morison and an excellent photograph of the English calligrapher Edward Johnston, but I could not recognize the third photograph, which Van Krimpen told me was of a distinguished Dutch poet, P. C. Boutens, who had also been his friend. This was an impressive trio of heroes, not one of them a narrow specialist. Boutens was a scholar as well as a poet. Johnston had been a philosopher as well as a writer and calligrapher. As to Morison, I knew at first hand his many-sided gifts as typographer, type designer, historian, critic, editor and friend.

John Dreyfus, printer, critic and consultant on design, numbers among his titles those of typographic adviser to the Cambridge University Press and the Monotype Corporation, and European consultant to The Limited Editions Club. Lecture given October 14, 1965.

The bookshelves made it abundantly clear that I was visiting a lover of literature and not merely a designer of books and types. In that last harsh winter of the occupation, he had conserved his strength and contrived to keep warm by spending a great deal of time in bed, where he read voraciously in English, French and Dutch. His favourite reading was poetry, and his knowledge of English and French was so profound that he was really able to appreciate the subtleties of such poets as Rimbaud and Donne. His library was also well stocked with technical and historical treatises on the art of typography and letter design.

My first visit to his house was quickly followed by a longer stay, for, as soon as hostilities in Europe were over, I was allowed to take short leave of up to seventy-two hours on the Continent. The Van Krimpens invited me to spend two days at their home, and I was delighted to return. I was able to bring with me generous rations of food and drink, which I soon learnt were of more than routine importance to Van Krimpen. Later we travelled together to Brussels, and before long he resumed his visits to London, where I often met him after my demobilization.

As I came to know him better, he introduced me to some of his Dutch friends. One of them was a young publisher in Utrecht who had taken note of the fact that Van Krimpen would celebrate his sixtieth birthday in the spring of 1952. He asked me to write an account of Van Krimpen's work, to be designed by Van Krimpen himself and printed at Enschedé. I agreed to write the text and to choose the illustrations, and in due course the book was published with a foreword by Stanley Morison, under the title *The Work of Jan Van Krimpen* (London: The Sylvan Press, 1952). Although that book contains a fuller record of his work than can be given within the space alloted in this volume, it still does not present a complete record of Van Krimpen's output, for in the six years between the publication of my book and his death, Van Krimpen produced some excellent work.

Van Krimpen's achievements can be better appreciated in the light of some knowledge of his background and development. He was born in 1892 in Gouda, the third son of a corn merchant. Both his parents died before he left school. At the age of sixteen he went to the Academy of Arts in The Hague, where he learnt anatomy, drawing, and all the usual art school subjects. But it was student life at The Hague which really developed his tastes and interests. At about the age of eighteen he became deeply absorbed in poetry, notably in the works of young contemporary Dutch poets, many of whom became his friends.

One of these poets was Albert Besnard, who, in an affectionate memoir of his early friendship with Van Krimpen, recalls the atmosphere at the meetings of these young literati. "It was really remarkable," he said. "We learnt to hate people we had never even met."

Van Krimpen steadily developed an interest in the physical appearance of books. He became absorbed not only by the craft of printing but also in the art of lettering. He studied Edward Johnston's handbook, *Writing and Illuminating, and Lettering*, which had been published when Van Krimpen was fourteen. Then he turned to other books on the subject. He had a good knowledge of English and became a subscriber to *The Imprint*, a new English magazine which first appeared in 1912, just when he left the Academy of Art. The principal aim of *The Imprint* was to raise the standard of commercial printing in England; among its contributors were Johnston and Morison. A small number of Dutchmen were keen to advance the same cause in their own country, and to this end a small monthly magazine was started in 1912 by the Dutch poet Jan Greshoff. Van Krimpen drew a fine title page and vignette for this magazine, called *De Witte Mier* (The White Ant), and became friendly with its editor. The circulation of *The White Ant* was not large, but it was influential in literary circles, and it was instrumental in establishing Van Krimpen's reputation.

Greshoff wrote of that period as a time in which both he and Van Krimpen were very orthodox in their views. They detested everything which resembled symbolism or ornament. As Greshoff put it, "We wanted to make a book beautiful irrespective of its text."

Van Krimpen's enthusiasm for printing was fired by a visit to the remarkable exhibition of the typographic arts put on at Leipzig in 1914. He then struck out as a free-lance designer and began to specialize in lettering covers and bindings for literary publications.

In 1917 he started to publish lyric poetry written by his friends in a series known as "Palladium Books," for which he designed a uniform format for the most divergent texts. For the third book in this series he chose Caslon as the text type, attracted by its unpretentiousness, a quality which he particularly admired in the best English books of that period. Although Caslon's types had been modelled upon Dutch types of the seventeenth century, they had nevertheless taken on a distinctly English character which also appealed to Van Krimpen.

He already held strong views on typographic design for serious reading; nothing was to obtrude typographically between the text and the reader. If the reader wondered why he had enjoyed the physical act of reading, Van Krimpen was satisfied. He had no desire to indulge in showy typography, and never manifested the slightest sympathy or interest in what he called typography for publicity and propaganda. (Writing for an American publication in 1956, he acidly remarked, "I might say I have no particularly high regard for it [publicity] either; and that publicity—typographical and of any other variety—is apt to work with me the *not* intended way round.")

It was his gift for lettering which first brought him into association with the printing house of Enschedé en Zonen. The Dutch Post Office commissioned Van Krimpen to draw the lettering for the special issue of stamps printed by Enschedé in 1923 to commemorate the twenty-fifth jubilee of Queen Wilhelmina's accession to the throne. The lettering formed an important part of the design, and it caught the attention of Dr. John Enschedé, who, in 1923, invited Van Krimpen to design a new typeface for his firm.

The results were first shown in 1925 at the International Exhibition of Modern Decorative and Industrial Arts in Paris, and the type was accordingly named Lutetia. It was so great a success that Enschedé engaged Van Krimpen to design further types for his firm. He was also given the task of designing printed specimens in order to publicize their unique range of historic and contemporary typefaces. He quickly acquired an international reputation and designed a wide variety of printed matter for Enschedé, with whom he remained associated until his death.

Van Krimpen's status within the firm was moulded by his own force of character. Although he never became a director of the firm, he was given a great deal of liberty to work at home and to travel abroad. He became friendly with artists, poets, papermakers, printers, publishers and clients in many lands, especially in France, Belgium, Luxembourg, Italy and England, countries in which he travelled extensively. Some of his finest work was done for the Nonesuch Press and The Limited Editions Club, but his enthusiasm went beyond the limits of artistic and literary productions. He developed a great interest in liturgical printing, which extended his travels to monasteries and religious printing houses in Europe and North Africa. He also showed great skill in designing encyclopaedias, commemorative volumes and catalogues of specialized collections. His reputation as a letterer, type designer and calligrapher brought him many commissions. Apart from the numerous typefaces which he designed for the house of Enschedé, he took on special commissions from Bible printers and from the Monotype Corporation; and at the time of his death he was at work on a new type for the Lumitype (or Photon) machine.

His success with lapidary inscriptions culminated with the design of a huge monument in Amsterdam, the Dam Monument, on which are recorded the names of the victims of the occupation years.

He drew several series of stamps, lettered numerous elegant book jackets and wrote a number of articles, monographs and lectures. He was not left without honour, either at home or abroad. In his own country the city of Amsterdam gave him its first award in typography in 1945. In England he received the gold medal of the Society of Industrial Artists in 1956. He was the first Dutchman to be elected an honorary member of the Double Crown Club in London, and the pleasure which he derived from his attendance at its dinners led him to found a similar dining club in Holland, the Nonparel Gezelschap, of which he was the first president and prime mover. He joined the Association Typographique Internationale after its inaugural meeting in 1957 and played an active part in its affairs as a member of the board of directors.

After his retirement from Enschedé en Zonen in 1957, he continued to make frequent visits to the printing house, and he remained active in its affairs. He died, as he had hoped to die, suddenly, painlessly and while still at work. He had just arrived one day at the entrance to Enschedé, and was about to step out of the car when he slumped back, collapsed in his seat and died. He was close to a fine stone which had been cut to his own design to commemorate the two hundred and fiftieth anniversary of the firm to which he had brought so much honour.

From this brief record of his achievements and from the illustrations and type specimens which accompany this article, it can be seen that Van Krimpen completed an impressive range of graphic and typographic work during his lifetime. Nevertheless, he did not end his days in a contented frame of mind. As his compatriot Professor Willem Ovink observed, "Van Krimpen died at the peak of his ability, his fame and his influence, embittered and disappointed even as a craftsman, because he had not succeeded in gaining acceptance for all his ideas and because he saw them falling into disrepute, as he thought, through misunderstanding."

That he was misunderstood was partly due to defects in his own character, and partly due to the harm done by inept would-be imitators

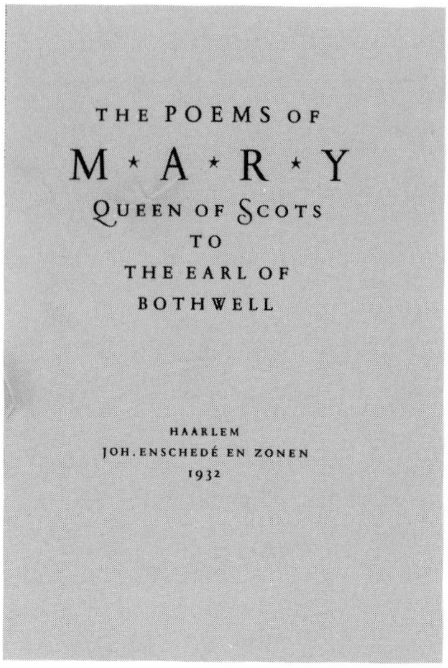

THE POEMS OF
M ★ A ★ R ★ Y
QUEEN OF SCOTS
TO
THE EARL OF
BOTHWELL

HAARLEM
JOH. ENSCHEDÉ EN ZONEN
1932

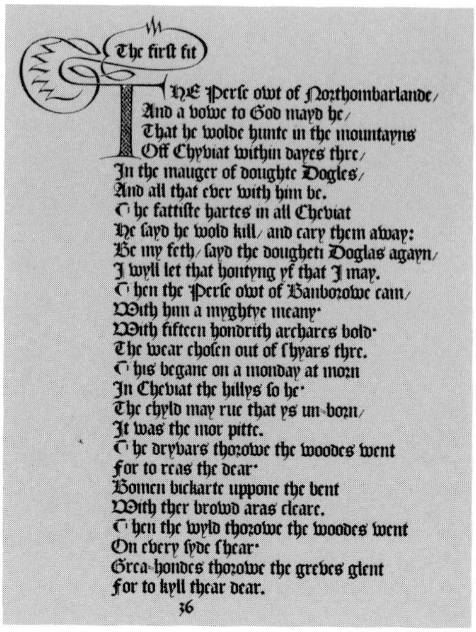

ABOVE LEFT   Van Krimpen's Romanée type used on the title page of an Enschedé book (the letters of "Mary" are in blue).

ABOVE RIGHT   Van Krimpen's Dutch Black-Letter No. 5, with calligraphic initial in red.

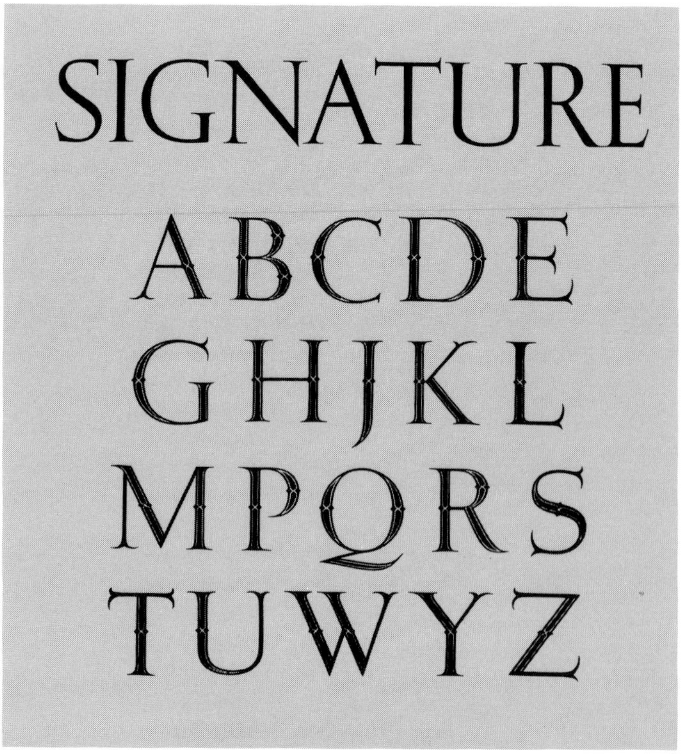

HART EN LAND

Mijn hart wou nergens tieren
En nergens vond het vreé
Dan tusschen uw rivieren
Nabij uw groote zee,
Mijns harten eigen groene land
Dat voor mij dood en leven bant.

De wind zong door de boomen
Tot in mijn stille huis
De stemmen uwer stroomen,
Uw volle zeegeruisch:
Daar brak mijn hart in zangen uit,
Daar werd de stem van 't bloed geluid.

Wel hebt gij mij gegeven
Al wat ik andren bood.
Ik zong van dood en leven,
Van liefdes rijken nood:
Des harten teederste ademhaal,
Hij werd verstaanbaar in uw taal.

Al dieper zoeter wonder
Fluistert uw stem mij voor . . .
Laat mij niet sterven zonder
Uw levenwekkend koor!
De wind die in uw loover huwt,
Is 't afscheid dat mijn hart niet schuwt.

P. C. BOUTENS

C'EST de 1880 qu'en Hollande on fait partir la grande rénovation artistique. Elle fut surtout sensible à cette date dans le domaine de la littérature, mais un mouvement parallèle dans les arts industriels s'était déjà dessiné en Angleterre sous l'inspiration de William Morris, et ne tarda guère à se répandre en Europe.

Il convient toutefois de signaler un courant précurseur: le rationa-lisme, dont Viollet-le-Duc fut l'initiateur en France et Cuypers l'in-troducteur en Hollande. En architecture ce rationalisme, utilisant les formes gothiques traditionnelles, fut confusément interprété. On prêta en effet plus d'attention à l'expression formelle du go-thique qu'au solide principe de construction rationnelle sur lequel il s'appuyait. Cuypers notamment remit en vogue la voûte et cher-cha en outre à obtenir de nouveau dans les divers métiers une pure exécution du détail.

C'était là une tâche fort difficile, exigeant de nombreuses années de préparation, ne permettant d'ailleurs pas d'espérer la possibilité de porter la pratique professionnelle au degré de perfection qu'elle atteignit au moyen-âge. Cuypers ne la poussa pas plus avant parce que, s'il faisait lui-même les dessins, il n'exécutait pas de ses propres mains. Elle fut reprise par des artistes œuvrant dans diverses bran-ches des arts industriels et qui s'inspirèrent des idées de William Morris et de Semper. Les sculpteurs taillèrent eux-mêmes leurs statues dans le bois ou la pierre, les céramistes moulèrent et tour-nèrent leurs vases, procédèrent à leur émaillage et à leur cuisson, les fresquistes et les peintres verriers exécutèrent leurs travaux, les artisans du batik, les graveurs, les imprimeurs, les tisserands et les relieurs étudièrent leur métier, se familiarisèrent avec les maté-riaux et la technique et consacrèrent toute leur activité à l'exercice

8

of his own style. Although Van Krimpen could be a delightful host and companion and was extremely generous with his time with young and old alike, there were occasions when he became suspicious, vain and obstinate. He refused to discuss certain matters, and his writings generally lacked the clarity of his own graphic work. His influence, therefore, depended more upon his practise than his precepts.

As practised by Van Krimpen, both type design and typography were made to appear deceptively simple. Some of his admirers were consequently deceived into believing that they too could produce fine work with the minimum of effort merely by copying his mannerisms—such as his use of widely spaced capitals in displayed lines. As a result of such facile copying, the masterly simplicity of Van Krimpen's own style deteriorated with his imitators into aridity, unrelieved by his own gift for decorative touches by calligraphic embellishment or by a stylish use of colours and materials.

The true basis of Van Krimpen's mastery of type design and typography lay in a combination of four qualities which are rarely found to so marked a degree in one man. These qualities were, first, a disciplined, reflective and literary mind; second, a trained taste for line, mass and colour; third, an observant and accurate eye; and last of all, a hand which was unerringly obedient to his intentions. Lacking these qualities in equal measure, his imitators could not match his achievements. They could, nevertheless, benefit from a close reading of some of Van Krimpen's writings on typography. Unfortunately, he sometimes expressed himself in an excessively fractured style, so I will focus attention on only two of his remarks, the first of which is both brief and clear.

"Everything that counts in typography is a subtlety," he wrote. To emphasize this point he liked to quote the following sentence from an essay by Frederic Warde. "As long as we work with the arbitrary signs of the alphabet, we shall be dependent on the past and—like the Greek vase makers—we shall derive our finest effects from the subtle personal variations on a traditional style and shape."

Van Krimpen's next remarks are unfamiliar to English readers, as they appeared in his introduction to a Dutch translation of Stanley Morison's *First Principles of Typography*. "Those who see typography as a possible art should not lose sight of two things: first, what makes a *profession* can very well be taught or learnt, but the essence of *art* can never be taught; second, typography—like so many professions—can be useful, appropriate and even good when it is far removed from art."

Here, then, was a man who, despite his own considerable powers as an artist, preferred to discipline himself to the service of a craft—and here I again quote his own words— "the only purpose of which is, and therefore the only purpose of which should be, to serve." Van Krimpen thus added his own authority to those who steadfastly believe that the prime duty of typography is to communicate the thought or image intended by the author with the utmost clarity and grace and with the least degree of self-assertiveness or obtrusiveness.

During his lifetime, Van Krimpen used his own types with greater distinction than any other designer who worked with the same types. Founts of Lutetia were promptly acquired in the U.S.A. by D. B. Updike for use at his Merrymount Press in Boston, but it would seem that Van Krimpen's types are still only at the outset of their popularity in the U.S.A. His Spectrum types have recently been used with distinction by Jack Stauffacher in publications issued by the Hunt Botanical Library (in conjunction with a bespoke new display face designed by Hermann Zapf), and a set of Spectrum has recently been acquired by Saul Marks for the Plantin Press. Cancelleresca Bastarda has been used with grace and wit by Leonard Baskin at his Gehenna Press. No doubt the use of these types by designers of the calibre of Baskin, Marks and Stauffacher will lead to their more widespread use in the U.S.A.

Typographers throughout the world will long have reason to be grateful to Van Krimpen, not only for providing them with a fine heritage of original type designs, but also for showing them how these types could best be used. It is a rewarding experience to examine the books and pamphlets designed by Van Krimpen and printed under his own rigorous supervision.

Few typographers in this century have measured up to the definition of the word "typography" given in the eighteenth century by that great practitioner, Pierre Simon Fournier. According to Fournier, the craft consists of three parts, "each distinct and indispensable, namely punch-cutting, founding and printing." He explained that the practise of the three different branches produced artists of three different kinds—punchcutters, founders and printers. "But," said Fournier, "only he who combines a knowledge of all three branches is fit to be styled a typographer."

Van Krimpen's knowledge and achievements certainly merit him the name "typographer." But he was something more than that—he was also a distinguished graphic designer, and a man of letters in the literary sense of that phrase. He enriched the field of typography by the breadth of his culture and the range of his talents.

Giovanni Mardersteig.

GIOVANNI MARDERSTEIG

by John Dreyfus

THE NAME of Giovanni Mardersteig is linked by many bibliophiles with the Officina Bodoni, his hand press in Verona. Yet it would be quite wrong to assume that he has retreated from the twentieth-century world to print by hand with Bodoni's types. His hand press does indeed produce some three hundred sheets each day, and these are still immaculately printed under his direction by a staff of four. Nevertheless only a small part of his time is now devoted to the operation of the hand press, nor is it any longer customary for him to use Bodoni's types. In the past forty years he has designed several fine text types and display faces for his own use, and his most recent type enriched the typographical resources of printers throughout the world when it was made available for mechanical composition.

In addition to the hand press, he now directs a compact and modern printing house equipped with carefully chosen machinery for composing and printing. From this plant, the Stamperia Valdònega, he exacts a standard of work which bears comparison with the standard of excellence established at his Officina Bodoni.

Printing, whether it be by hand or by machine, does not monopolize his entire working life. Since his youth he has been passionately interested in literature, and he has consistently followed his own predilections in publishing texts which interest him or in reproducing work by artists whom he admires. He is a fastidious scholar whose books and monographs display an impressive range of knowledge, coupled with a remarkably acute perception of things seen as well as read. He is widely

Lecture given October 5, 1966.

travelled—and incessantly visited. Only those visitors who cannot speak to him in Italian, German, French or English need to rely on his classical Greek or Latin. He is a scholar and an artist.

If an artistic temperament is inherited, Mardersteig's might be traced back to both his grandfathers—one a professional painter, the other a sculptor. From his father he received a training which was deliberately calculated to develop his manual and intellectual gifts. Mardersteig's father was a successful lawyer in Weimar where Giovanni grew up with three brothers and a sister. All the boys were taught to use their hands by spending their Saturday afternoons or Sundays on manual work, with carpenters, printers or other skilled workmen. His father was personally interested in every kind of manual skill and encouraged his sons to acquire it; but he did not neglect their intellectual development. A constant stream of distinguished visitors who came to his home helped to open up the minds of his children to the delights of the mind. Among these visitors was Count Harry Kessler, patron of the arts, man of letters, diplomat, publisher, and also the proprietor of a private press.

When Mardersteig was a boy, Ludwig Thelemann ran a bookshop in Weimar where Giovanni was free to browse for as long as he wished. Books of every kind were to be found there, and the assistants were so well informed that they were all able to satisfy his youthful curiosity with great exactness. A lifelong passion for books was formed in those hours of browsing, and his mind was rapidly stocked with a great deal of knowledge which later stood him in good stead.

In choosing a subject to study at the university, he expressed a preference for the history of art, but his father insisted that he should read law, so that he would have some professional qualification and some means of earning his livelihood. He began to study at the University of Bonn, but soon moved to Vienna: at this safe distance from his father he was able to devote a good deal of his time to the history of art. He later completed his studies in Kiel and Jena.

Mardersteig suffered from tubercular trouble and was not fit for military service. He spent the early years of the war gaining experience in legal administration in Germany, but his health obliged him to go to Switzerland in 1916. There his health gradually improved and he worked for a while as a teacher in a school at Zuoz. But he was unable to speak continuously for any length of time and soon had to abandon teaching. In 1917 a large exhibition of German painting of the nineteenth and twentieth centuries was held in Zurich, where, acting on a suggestion from Count Kessler, he arranged a section devoted to expressionism. It was the first time that this new movement of German art had been shown abroad.

Faced with the problem of making his career, he decided to approach Kurt Wolff, a gifted publisher with an established reputation. Wolff already had an impressive list of literary works, but Mardersteig presented him with a memorandum in which he set out detailed proposals for extending the list to cover the field of art. He suggested several new series, and gave titles for books which should be included, as well as the names of people who were competent to write them. He also proposed launching a new review of art, later called *Genius*. After a lengthy discussion, Kurt Wolff invited him to come to Leipzig and to carry out his plans there.

The first of six biannual volumes of *Genius* appeared in 1919. It was hard to bring any appearance of unity into these large volumes which contained so many separately printed woodcuts, lithographs, coloured plates and text pages. This experience impressed upon him the need for one man to assume the tasks of printing, binding and publishing.

Working with Wolff was not his first experience of publishing. Thelemann's bookshop in Weimar had been taken over by a bookseller named Kiepenheuer, with whom Mardersteig became very friendly before he left school. When Kiepenheuer's first book was published, he began to have regular discussions with his young friend, who despite his youth was already well informed about publishing and book design.

In the first years after the war, the poor quality of printing led Mardersteig to consider setting up a press of his own. He was dissatisfied with the books produced by others under his direction, and he saw how badly they compared with the attractive work produced by English and German private presses.

Count Kessler had demonstrated that the high standards of the English Private Press Movement could be successfully transplanted: no other book made a greater typographic impact on Mardersteig than the edition of Goethe's novels which Kessler published in his Grossherzog Wilhelm Ernst series of German classics. The Goethe was published in 1905 with a fine title page lettered by Eric Gill. Mardersteig was also familiar with the work of Willy Wiegand at the Bremer Presse, but his work did not wholly accord with Mardersteig's convictions; for as a young man of intelligence and taste, he had his own ideas about what he wished to print and how he wanted to do it. He had gained some useful experience by working for a time with Tieffenbach at the Officina Serpentis, but here too he was not wholly in sympathy with the style of the house, or its methods. He was impatient to set up his own press.

He could not afford to start with a new type, so he had to find a type which was already in existence, but not in common use. For years he had admired the types of Giambattista Bodoni (1740–1813) from whose printing house in Parma a magnificent series of books had issued, culminating in the posthumously published volumes of his *Manuale Tipografico*. One of these books had caught Mardersteig's eye during his first visit to Italy in 1912. As time went on, he acquired many more of Bodoni's books, and came to know his work in considerable detail.

His interest in Bodoni was shared by a friend in Rome, a young man who suffered from lung trouble caused by a wartime gas attack. Because of their health, the two men decided to set up a printing press jointly in Switzerland. Influential acquaintances of his friend's father, a sculptor in Rome, obtained permission from the authorities for type to be cast for their use from Bodoni's original matrices, which were still preserved in Parma. In 1922 Mardersteig set up the press in Montagnola near Lugano, but unfortunately his friend did not respond well enough to treatment and was never able to join him at the Officina Bodoni.

From Bodoni's enormous range of types, Mardersteig selected only a small number of founts. Those used at Montagnola were a 12, a 16 and a 20 point text type in roman and italic. In addition a 20 point decorated italic and a large 32 point fount were used, with a variety of titlings.

With these types, he produced a handsome set of books, which were nevertheless unlike Bodoni's own books. From the outset of its activity, the Officina Bodoni produced books of distinction and of impeccable quality—there was no preliminary faltering or fumbling.

In the early days of the Officina Bodoni, Mardersteig composed the type and printed it with his own hands. Later he engaged a compositor and employed a girl to help by damping the paper, hanging, pressing and folding the printed sheets, and then sewing the finished books. He himself had some experience of bookbinding, but soon he had the good fortune to be joined by an experienced Greek binder named Demeter, a fine craftsman who had previously been with Cobden-Sanderson at the Doves Press, and also with Gruel in Paris. Demeter executed some magnificent binding designs at Montagnola. He was able to help Mardersteig by telling him how work had been done at the Doves Press, and also revealing the source from which it obtained vellum. Printing on

EPILOGUE

SPOKEN BY PROSPERO

Now my charms are all o'erthrown,
And what strength I have's mine own,
Which is most faint: now, 'tis true,
I must be here confined by you,
Or sent to Naples. Let me not,
Since I have my dukedom got,
And pardoned the deceiver, dwell
In this bare island, by your spell.
But release me from my bands,
With the help of your good hands:
Gentle breath of yours my sails
Must fill, or else my project fails,
Which was to please: Now I want
Spirits to enforce... art to enchant—
And my ending is despair,
Unless I be reliev'd by prayer,
Which pierces so, that it assaults
Mercy itself, and frees all faults....
    As you from crimes would pardoned be,
    Let your indulgence set me free.

A page from a brochure by Mardersteig, *On G. B. Bodoni's Type Faces*, printed at the Officina Bodoni, Verona, in 1968 as a keepsake for a lecture by Mardersteig at the Morgan Library Gallery, New York.

vellum is an art in which the Officina Bodoni has excelled. No surface is more difficult to print upon than vellum, but no other surface yields a more satisfactory result if it is successfully printed.

The Jansenist severity of Bodoni's original style was tempered by decoration on Mardersteig's bindings, as well as by deliberate use of Bodoni's more decorative types. None the less it soon became clear that there were limits to the variety which could be introduced into the typography of the press if the range of types was to be confined to the original Bodoni trio. A further disadvantage was that these types were all, with the exception of the italic, unsuited for use with modern book illustrations, and it had been Mardersteig's intention from the start to produce fine illustrated books as well as fine editions of carefully chosen and scrupulously edited texts. The first extension of the range of types was the result of a visit to Montagnola by Stanley Morison.

A few years after the press had been established, Morison came at Christmas time and stayed for a week. During a series of lively discussions he spoke of an American friend, Frederic Warde, who had designed an Arrighi type based on a letter-form found in a sixteenth-century writing book by Lodovico Vincentino. Mardersteig was familiar with the original, and when Warde later explained to him in Montagnola that he would like his book to be printed there on the hand press, the proposal was readily accepted. Warde returned to Montagnola as soon as the type had been cut in Paris, and then composed the text with his own hands. Three hundred copies were printed, with an introduction by Morison. Both Mardersteig and Warde enjoyed their collaboration so much that they promptly set to work on another book, an edition of the *Crito* for which Warde made a few modifications to his type. Both books were published in 1926.

The year 1926 was marked by two other events which were to have a lasting effect upon the development of the Officina Bodoni. In that year Mardersteig was first introduced to a French punchcutter, Charles Malin, who was then at work on the punches for Eric Gill's Perpetua type. Malin later cut punches for all the types designed by Mardersteig for hand composition, and the two men became close friends. But the first result of their collaboration did not appear until 1929, because another event in the year 1926 entirely changed the activity and location of the Officina Bodoni.

A National Institute was set up in Italy in 1926 to produce a complete edition of the works of Gabriele D'Annunzio. To find out which printer deserved the honour of carrying out this task, a competition was arranged in which about a dozen printers were invited to take part. Mardersteig's name was included by an Italian publisher and printer, Arnoldo Mondadori. The specimens set in 12 point Bodoni and submitted by Mardersteig were judged to be the best; but when he was invited to print the series of more than forty volumes, it was discreetly suggested to him that he might set up his printing press on Italian soil.

The idea of removing to Italy had already been in his mind for several months. He had even gone as far as to print a prospectus for a new Accademia Tipografica which he had intended to set up in Florence with Frederic Warde. Now he decided instead to settle in Verona, conveniently close to D'Annunzio's home on Lake Garda, a centre in which he was able to find new quarters and additional staff in 1927. Existing staff were transferred from Montagnola, but as the entire edition had to be composed by hand, extra compositors were engaged, and in due course a second press and a bindery were set up. To provide him with the quarters he required, Mondadori covered in a large court-yard inside his own printing plant. Mardersteig enjoyed complete auton-omy over this press within a press, and at the same time was given great assistance with his domestic problems. After five years the bulk of the work was completed, although the last volumes of the index did not come out until 1936, by which time 200 copies had been printed on the hand press, and an additional 2,000 by machine.

Work on the D'Annunzio editions did not bring all other printing or designing activities to a halt. Facsimiles of two more writing books were printed, and in 1929 there appeared a *catalogue raisonné* of the books published by the Officina Bodoni in its first six years, with an introduc-tion by the printer. More types were added to the typographical resources of the press, first Janson from the Stempel Foundry and later Monotype Poliphilus and Blado. An entirely new fount cut by Malin became available in 1929. The type was inspired by the magnificent roman used by Aldus Manutius for his edition of Bembo's dialogue *De Aetna* (Venice, 1495) and was named Griffo in tribute to the punch-cutter of that name who had made the prototype. Another of Griffo's designs was used as a basis for the accompanying italic.

While recovering from a bout of meningitis in 1931, Mardersteig designed a second roman type which he named Zeno after the patron saint of Verona.

Completion of the D'Annunzio edition was both a relief and at the

THE
ALPHABET
IS A MIRROR
OF THE MIND
OF MEN

IN PRINCIPIO ERAT VERBUM,
et Verbum erat apud Deum, et Deus
erat Verbum. Hoc erat in principio
apud Deum. Omnia per ipsum facta
sunt, et sine ipso factum est nihil,
quod factum est; in ipso vita erat,
et vita erat lux hominum; et lux in
tenebris lucet, et tenebrae eam non
comprehenderunt. ✠ Et Verbum caro
factum est et habitavit in nobis; et
vidimus gloriam eius, gloriam quasi
Unigeniti a Patre, plenum gratiae
et veritatis.

Zeno, a roman type by Mardersteig, first intended for use in a missal;
punches cut by Malin from 1935 to 1936.

PRIOR TO PRINTING THE PAPER is slightly damped, which even if it is hard or strongly sized renders it lissome and causes it to accept every kind of ink more readily. Compared to printing "dry" only a fraction of the amount of ink is used on the hand press. The image of the type is clearly impressed in flawless black upon the paper as though the character were engraved. The type image must not be grey, for such a state of affairs would point either to bad inking, bad preparation or to bad printing. There are typefaces, however, which when printed in perfect black look and should look grey on the page, but this is due to the cutting of the type, to a certain pallor of the typeface. It is particularly difficult to obtain the correct and most perfect effect from type when printed upon vellum, the noblest of all printing surfaces. As it is extremely sensitive animal substance, it expands or contracts at the slightest variation of humidity and its vitality is a well-known thorn in the flesh off all bookbinders.

same time a slightly unsettling experience. Other considerable tasks were still in hand within the department at Mondadori, such as the Albatross editions which Mardersteig designed and produced for John Holroyd-Reece. Soon after the D'Annunzio editions were completed, Holroyd-Reece asked Mardersteig whether he felt inclined to work for a short time in Glasgow at the Collins Cleartype Press. The suggestion came just at the right moment. Some way had to be found of filling the vacuum created by the completion of the D'Annunzio, and Mardersteig decided that a completely new experience in fresh surroundings would do him good. He went to discuss the matter in Glasgow and then agreed to work there for six months. He stayed a whole year.

One of his first questions in Glasgow was, "Where is your clear type?" It was explained to him that no such type existed, although all their types were in fact clear. This did not satisfy Mardersteig, who suggested that if they called themselves a Cleartype Press, they ought to have a type which would distinguish them from other printers. A type of Scottish origin seemed to be indicated, and his choice finally fell upon a type used in Glasgow by Foulis in the eighteenth century. He redrew this type and handed over his drawings to the Monotype Corporation, which made the type for the exclusive use of Collins. Mardersteig was nevertheless allowed to use it himself for an edition of Walter Savage Landor's *Imaginary Conversations* which he designed and printed for The Limited Editions Club (and which George Macy considered to be one of the ten finest books he had ever issued). Collins later allowed this type to be sold to other printers without any restriction.

In addition to making this contribution to Collins's typography, Mardersteig was able to improve the standard of their presswork. Once when one of the Collins pressmen declared that it was impossible to produce better work with his old machine, Mardersteig gently suggested that he go off to the canteen for a few minutes; by the time he returned, Mardersteig had rolled up his sleeves, and had so adjusted the makeready that he was able to show the pressman that the required quality *could* be obtained, despite the age of the machine on which he was working.

After his return to Verona, Mardersteig was invited by Mondadori to become his typographical adviser and art director, but he declined. He had enjoyed his experiences in Glasgow, but he now wanted to devote himself to creating some more new types, and he also wanted to resume work with his hand press. He was not yet ready to work with mechanical presses for his own ends. Moreover he wanted to devote more of his time to his own researches in various libraries until he had sufficiently regained his strength to work again with the hand press.

In 1937 the Officina Bodoni was removed from Mondadori's to its present quarters in Mardersteig's private residence on the outskirts of Verona. Within a month of his first arrival in that city in 1927, he had conducted a methodical survey of suitable houses on the hills which overlook Verona. His choice soon fell on a magnificently sited house off the Via Marsala, which runs northwards out of the city. The owner's son occupied part of the house for several years, but eventually the entire house became available and the opportunity was taken in June 1937 to transfer the hand press to its present location.

The period from 1936 to 1939 was marked by the production of more books with illustrations by contemporary artists, and also by the introduction of a wider range of types. During these years he used his Zeno and Griffo types for the first time, and also acquired Monotype Garamond, Baskerville, Bembo Centaur and Imprint.

Work did not halt during the Second World War, but the war's effects were nevertheless deeply felt. With a suitable sense of occasion, the Officina Bodoni issued a new edition of *Candide ou l'Optimisme* in the autumn of 1944.

In the immediate post-war years, Mardersteig took stock of the incredible changes which were taking place in the world. He could not escape the conclusion that a hand press must now be regarded as an anachronism. This led him to decide to put his knowledge of printing to better use by starting up a second department, in which machinery would be used for typesetting and printing. He even intended to abandon the hand press and concentrate entirely on his new department.

Encouragement to go ahead with his scheme came from a group of industrialists who approached him in 1948 with a request that he should print a number of finely printed editions to heighten respect for Italian culture in foreign countries. He was asked to draw up a plan to show how this might be achieved. A few months later this group withdrew from the scheme, so he was unexpectedly left to carry out a plan which was not entirely his own. Fortunately he had sufficient capital at his disposal to build up a small printing establishment further along the Via Marsala; it was opened in 1949 and was named the Stamperia Valdònega, after the valley along which the road runs.

The new plant attracted new customers, notably the managing director of the Banca Commerciale, Dr. Raffaele Matteoli, who was keenly interested in Italian literature and in philological problems. With Dr. Matteoli's encouragement, work began on a compendious series of Italian classics, of which more than sixty volumes have so far been published, and several already reprinted, at the Stamperia Valdònega.

Although it had been Mardersteig's intention to abandon the hand press, the Officina Bodoni continued in operation. There were still some patrons in Italy, in the United States and in the British Isles who would accept nothing less than the product of the hand press. He therefore decided to keep up the Officina Bodoni as an active printing house in addition to his new printing plant up the road. It was not a hard decision, for he still wanted to produce more illustrated books, and he again felt an urge to make some new types for hand composition.

Before Malin died in 1956, he completed the engraving of a set of punches for a titling face, named Pacioli after the writer of a sixteenth century treatise on letter design which contained the patterns used by Mardersteig as the basis of his drawings. Malin also cut an original text type from drawings made by Mardersteig; as this type was first used in 1954 for Boccaccio's *Trattatello in Laude di Dante*, it was given the name of Dante. It has since been cut by The Monotype Corporation and is now extensively used by printers throughout Europe. At the time of his death, Malin was still working on Dante Titling.

Of all the post-war products of the Officina Bodoni, the four volumes by Tammaro de Marinis which describe the library of the Kings of Aragon are certainly the most massive, and they may also be regarded as one of the finest typographical achievements of the press. With an output ranging from works of such remarkable scholarship to finely printed modern verse or modern book illustration, Mardersteig's work was the subject of a series of major exhibitions in various European cities.

One of the books shown in the later exhibitions is of particular interest—an edition of Felice Feliciano's *Alphabetum Romanum* printed at the Officina Bodoni in 1960. This book is remarkable because it was the outcome of prolonged research by Mardersteig, who personally prepared the facsimile reproduction, edited the text from the original manuscript, wrote a lengthy introduction which incorporated the fruits of his research, planned the typography of the book, then had it composed in types of his own design and printed on his own handpress. It should be added that in fact—and typically—three editions of the book were printed—in English, German and Italian.

Mardersteig clearly understands both the advantages of printing on a hand press and the potentialities of machines. In his *catalogue raisonné* in 1929 he wrote ". . . only he who has actually printed a book on a hand press and has thus trained his eye in the slow course of preparation, choosing the right tone of ink and printing, is able to appreciate that a handpress is just like the pencil of a draughtsman, whose subtlety no machine can ever attain. At the same time it is obvious that there are of course bad craftsmen, and machines under the direction of masterly mechanics." The mechanics at the Stamperia Valdònega have the advantage of being subject to the controlling eye of a man who has formed his own standards with a hand press, and who will not lower them. The staff at the Officina Bodoni work for a master printer who can still perform for himself any of the operations he requires of them. By applying the knowledge he gained at the Officina Bodoni to the benefit of his mechanically equipped establishment at the Stamperia Valdònega, Mardersteig has vindicated his faith in the hand press.

Lucian Bernhard.

LUCIAN BERNHARD

by Karl Bernhard

WHEN DOC LESLIE of the Composing Room, genial director of Gallery 303, asked me to give a short talk on the life and times of my father, Lucian Bernhard, I readily consented. Who, after all, was better qualified by long association and calm temperament to do the job? But soon I realized a slight predicament, and begged the good doctor to let me talk about Gutenberg or Goudy or Babe Ruth—none of these could talk back. I sympathize with biographers of living personalities apt to correct you in mid-sentence, to blush when you overpraise, or in my case, to withdraw my allowance for several weeks! But Bob Leslie was not easily put off, and I proceeded to prepare these notes.

To an even greater degree than most people in the graphic arts worthy of biography, Lucian Bernhard is a person of many facets— type designer, poster artist, devoted Tango dancer, architect, father of five, grandfather of eleven and great-grandfather of two; also, package designer, admirer and interpreter of feminine beauty, state and costume designer, reformer of our idiotic spelling system, and, according to latest research, the only U.S. citizen who owns neither a radio, a television set, an automobile, nor an electric carving knife! To live long and happily while so afflicted, the man must have a well-developed sense of humor. And he does.

A few years ago, Gallery 303 sponsored an exhibition under the title "55 Years of Bernhard," and it was remarked at that time that a similar exhibit of work spanning that many years could be made by only very

Karl Bernhard, son of Lucian Bernhard, is a typographer, graphic designer, editor and writer who conducts the Lucian Bernhard Studio in New York. Lecture given November 30, 1966.

few men in the graphic arts. How time flies! Here, we are able to report on well over sixty years of professional activity that started soon after the turn of the century in horse-and-wagon Berlin and carries us to the smog-ridden, traffic-congested New York of 1966.

Like any life that has spanned so many decades, so many people, so much history, and two continents, Lucian Bernhard's story is full of facts, anecdotes, and legends—some of the latter made up by the artist himself to keep reporters and biographers on their toes. Birthplace, family, youth and early career are pleasantly clouded, and a person's idea of how and why Lucian got where he is depends on whether he heard him introduced at an Art Directors' meeting in Cleveland in 1926 or at the Chicago Advertising Club in 1936, or studied under him at Pratt Institute in 1946, or read about him in Doc Leslie's *PM* magazine.

This, our honored subject thinks, is as it should be. Whether he *really* ran away with the circus because he was distantly in love with the bareback rider, whether he *really* had to leave home because his mother didn't approve of his having painted all her somber oak furniture in bright "modern" colors while she was away from home for a few days, seventy-some years ago—these matters are of little help or relevance in judging the man and his work.

To give the younger readers an idea of how unpromising it is to ask certain questions, the following is the story told by Lucian in answer to a lady's question as to how he happened to become a poster designer. As we all know, he explained, a person's talents are determined on the day of birth, when an angel descends from above to kiss the baby on a decisive part of the anatomy. A kiss on the forehead dooms the child to life as an intellectual; a kiss on the fingers makes a great pianist or brain surgeon. Mom had just burped little Lucian and put him face-down in the crib, when the angel came down and kissed him gently on his posterior. His fate as a poster designer was thus sealed.

In any case, it is a fact that Lucian Bernhard was born at a time and place most favorable to the development of his natural talents. It was a time when the burgeoning of the creative arts in Europe opened unlimited horizons for individual effort, and the rapid growth of consumer industries called for more and more work in the applied arts. Above all, it was an ideal climate for individualism, when businesses of considerable wealth and influence were run by men of strong convictions, long before the advent of group-think, brain-storming, committee decisions and diluted personal authority. Also, and this too had real influence on the individuality of style, of a distinctive personal "hand," before the invention of rubber cement, Bourges sheets, photostats and efficient typographic service and variety, all of which we take for granted today.

The Germany of sixty years ago was the seedbed for innovations in the graphic arts that subsequently spread through the continent and the world. Into that scene came school dropout Bernhard, impatient with the colorlessness of the poster columns and the interiors of homes, his eager eyes wide open and his pockets empty. Arriving in Berlin in the first years of this century, he began to look for opportunities to exercise his undefined talents. And, to his good fortune, the printing and business world was looking for him and the other bright young artists who were populating the coffee houses of the city, discussing art and the meaning of life, and watching girls go by.

It was in those days, traditionally romanticized as "carefree," that the profession of "commercial art" was born. The development can be traced in the graphic arts magazines that were launched sixty years ago. Bernhard was one of a group of four men responsible for the first of these, *Das Plakat* (The Poster). Two of the other three, both in their middle eighties, Rudy Bleston and Hans Sachs, are also living in New York today. So, when you see the latest copies of *Gebrauchsgraphic* or *Graphis*, keep in mind that they are the direct descendants of the trail-blazing *Plakat*.

In this fertile setting the talents of many of those first commercial artists found expression in all areas of design. Posters were for many the jumping-off point that led into books, store fronts, types, fashion, furniture, packaging, wallpapers, textiles, interiors—all of which came to be taken for granted as subjects of any good designer's attention. Specialization was far away.

When, a dozen years later, self-taught Bernhard was appointed professor of poster art at the Royal Art Institute in the German capital, he entered a classroom for the first time since having left school in Zürich at age fifteen. His appointment to a professorship established especially for him was an official recognition of his contribution to the revitalizing of the poster, the undisputed advertising medium of the time. It was a medium which, except for some theater posters, had deteriorated to a wordy, overdecorated style, or lack of style. Initially eliminated from a poster competition, because it obviously did not conform to the "trend" (how familiar!), but saved by a perceptive jury member who had arrived at the judging late, the Priester match poster became recognized as the first "modern" poster and launched Lucian on that part of his career.

Posters in Europe's cities functioned in a favorable setting. In slow-moving traffic their design and colors could afford to be subtle, actually beautiful. L.B.'s sense of color could be employed at its very best, and for fifteen heady years his work was sought after by the leading firms of the continent. Extensive work in interior design of residences and public places, design for stage and cabaret, work with leading book publishers, brought the young designer into contact with the most vital section of a lively society.

But Germany had lost the war (we'll never know for sure to what extent Lucian's unenthusiastic service in the Kaiser's army contributed to that!) and things were not as "carefree" as they had been. So, when in 1922 the lithographer Roy Latham invited Europe's leading poster designer to New York in the hope of injecting some continental style into the American poster scene, Bernhard accepted enthusiastically. Latham did not realize, nor could his guest, that he was fighting a losing battle: the automobile was about to displace the pedestrian; sidewalks were about to be narrowed to make room for more cars; the neon sign and other blatant techniques were about to pollute the city's visual landscape. And ever newer advertising media were on the horizon.

In love at first sight with what was soon to become his adopted country, speaking broken English, L.B. proceeded nevertheless to spread the message of the poster as a medium demanding a design style of its own, before advertising people and the then newly invented art directors from coast to coast. There was always much interest and applause. Occasionally, there were even a few courageous agency people who commissioned designs for their big clients. These commissions rarely went beyond the sketch stage: American advertisers of the twenties still wanted not posters but genuine oil paintings, suitable for impressive display on the walls of the president's office.

This was something of a disappointment to a man who had been conducting a poster studio employing thirty artists in Berlin just a short time ago. But, always the pragmatist, Lucian reasoned that the city that leads the world in the number of pretty girls per block can't be all bad. So he decided to settle in New York, and proceeded to busy himself with the design of millionaires' homes, books for Random House, Elmer Adler's Pynson Printers, and Knopf, furniture for Grand Rapids, silks for Seventh Avenue, and typefaces for the American Type Foundry.

BRAZIL AND THE
It shows to civilized

THE EARLY PRINTER
They instructed some local

BRAZIL AND OTHER
It shows civilization at a

BRAZIL HAS A
It shows phases

BERNHARD
MODERN
roman & italic

BERNHARD
Modern BOLD
& BOLD ITALIC

AUTOMOBILE S
Owner Drives Excellent B
Rebuilt Cars Giving Satis

ENJOYS PERFORMA
Delightful Musicale by Splendid M
Beautiful Souvenir Programs Dis

ABOVE LEFT Some typefaces
designed by Lucian Bernhard,
shown in American Type Founders
specimens, with a sampling of the
faces in the Bernhard Gothic series,
which includes the Light, Medium
Italic, Medium Condensed, and
Extra Heavy versions shown here.

BELOW LEFT Specimen lines
of Bernhard Fashion,
also cast by ATF.

ABOVE Titles of three additional
Bernhard type designs, Modern,
Modern Bold, and Tango.

Being an essentially modest man, he saw to it that each typeface carried his name, thus making it easy for type buffs to spot his work in any type catalog.

Finally, in 1926, an understanding and courageous client came from Baltimore and commissioned a series of Bernhard posters, which helped make Rem cough syrup a household word, and which were followed for the next twenty years by commissions for innumerable posters and car cards throughout the country. In these American designs the subtle hues typical of Bernhard's European work gave way to stark primary colors more in keeping with the needs of the garish, bustling city street, the crowded subway rush, the speeding traffic on the highways. The red, white and blue became the mark of the Bernhard poster. The advertising business of that day being, even more than now, a business of word people rather than picture people, the poster's contents became words, and the colorful, eye-catching Bernhard lettering poster resulted.

But again, the scene was changing. Businesses were run increasingly by impersonal management. Ad decisions were made by committee; art directors took the place of designers, and looked for specialists to execute their ideas. Lucian, accustomed to diversity, had no taste for the limitations of specialization in any one narrow area. But, if he was to be forced to specialize, he was going to choose a speciality worth specializing in. And so, starting in the early thirties and in essence going back to a major interest of his coffee house days, he spent more and more of his time in the pursuit and glorification in painting and sculpture of New York's outstanding product, the pretty girl.

This is not to say that he abandoned active participation in the graphic design world. Aided at various times by his brilliant but modest son Karl, his debonair son Manfred, and Alex the taciturn, Lucian continued producing posters, trademarks, packages and other commercial work until about ten years ago. It was then that someone at a type-lovers' luncheon asked him about his ideas on the future of type design, and he casually replied that yes, indeed, he was already working on it. Would he be willing to prepare a talk on the subject for a meeting six months hence? Yes, of course, he answered, always ready to promise anything *that* far away. But the six months passed, and he had hardly started on his favorite project, an alphabet essential for the reform of English spelling, when the appointed date came around and something had to be presented, no matter how tentative. The reception of his Fonotype was nevertheless enthusiastic. Inquiries came from various quarters, and what had started out as not much more than a challenge to a type designer's imagination grew into a major project which was to occupy Lucian for the next eight years.

The easy, humorous style of the presentation of Fonotype, as it first appeared in *Printing* magazine, belies the work and suffering that went into its preparation, and which accounts for Lucian's firm resolve to keep his mouth shut at type-lovers' luncheons!

As of this writing our hero, nearing the middle of his ninth decade, is occupied primarily with his paintings, still of his favorite subject matter, and with correspondence with interested people all over the English-speaking world, in the further "missionary work" of making Fonotype a tool in overcoming the handicaps to our children's education represented by our mysterious orthography.

This short outline of a long and fruitful life of one whose work has contributed to the heritage of the graphic arts may or may not explain the major statement of Lucian Bernhard's philosophy stated at increasingly frequent occasions: "Life is too complicated and a waste of one's time."

Tɛr is no sûch ting as an exákt fuulpruuf rekórding of spiich-sounds on pɛ́per

A sample block of Bernhard's simplified phonetic spelling alphabet, known as Fonotype, from a showing in *Printing Magazine*. Copyright by Mr. Bernhard.

Fred Anthoensen.

FRED ANTHOENSEN

by Walter Muir Whitehill

I MET FRED ANTHOENSEN (born 1888) for the first time thirty years ago, when he came to my office at the Peabody Museum of Salem to discuss the printing of a museum publication. I knew nothing of him or his work, for I had only returned to New England the previous spring after spending the better part of nine years in Spain, and was out of touch with recent developments in fine printing. He was then in his early fifties—a short, stocky, trim, gray-haired man, dressed in dark sobriety that suggested an established doctor or lawyer rather than artist. I found him to be a quiet, shy man, totally without the false *bonhomie* and mendacious blandishments of the salesman. All that he said was brief and to the point. It was clear from the beginning of this first meeting that he instinctively understood what the Peabody Museum wanted, and intended to use the full extent of his craftsmanship to give us *that*, rather than something quite different, however good that something different might be.

It was fortunate for me that I met Fred Anthoensen when I did, for I was in the awkward situation of knowing the difference between good and bad printing when I saw it, without having the slightest technical knowledge of how this difference was achieved. In this first meeting we briefly looked through the typescript (of a mid-nineteenth-century journal of travel in South America) that the museum wished to publish,

Walter Muir Whitehill has been since 1946 director and librarian of the Boston Athenaeum, and is a faculty member of Harvard's Peabody Museum of Archaeology and Ethnology. He is a former president of the Club of Odd Volumes, Boston. Lecture given February 23, 1966.

chatted a bit about books and the world in general, and that was that. Fred returned to Portland, and shortly submitted some sample pages, which delighted me. When proofs came, they were clean and handsome, free of printer's errors. In due course there appeared what became one of the Fifty Books of the Year 1937, achieved at a fair and mutually satisfactory price, without haggling of any kind. So began a friendship, based on trust and sympathetic understanding between craftsman and customer, that has enriched my life and made my work easier over the past thirty years.

As a Harvard freshman in the academic year 1922–1923, I wandered into the Widener Room in the library and encountered George Parker Winship, who had a singular genius for infecting undergraduates with a love of books and fine printing. I often returned, and as a junior enrolled in Winship's highly individualistic course entitled Fine Arts 5e, History of the Printed Book. It met on Tuesday and Thursday afternoons at three o'clock in the Widener Room, and was conducted with extreme informality. Winship would bring up from the Treasure Room armfuls of incunabula, Aldines, French illustrated books of the eighteenth century, products of the Kelmscott, Doves, and Ashendene Presses, and simply talk about them in the most offhand manner. Through George Winship I came to know the work of Daniel Berkeley Updike and Bruce Rogers, and eventually made the acquaintance of the printers themselves. To me Updike's work was particularly sympathetic, and the Merrymount Press the ideal of twentieth century American achievement in bookmaking.

Thus, when I found myself at the Peabody Museum of Salem in need of having a book printed, I would instinctively have turned to the Merrymount Press, and was not wholly enchanted when my boss, Lawrence W. Jenkins, seemed inclined to turn to a printer in Portland, Maine, of whom I knew next to nothing. As matters turned out, nothing could have been more fortunate than this somewhat accidental encounter, for Fred Anthoensen's tastes in bookmaking and mine were very similar. He and I were both striving for perfection in our different areas. The museum had things that needed publishing, which he instinctively knew how to clothe in appropriate dress. As the work that we gave the press was unaccompanied by hampering restrictions, it afforded him a useful opportunity to exercise his talents in design to the fullest extent.

Few men are still active in the same printing office that they entered some sixty-eight years ago. Fred Anthoensen is a native of Denmark, born on 14 April, 1882, at Tonder in Sleswig, but at the age of two he was brought by his parents to Portland, Maine, where he has lived ever since. In 1898, after completing his grammar school education, he was apprenticed in the composing room of the Southworth Printing Company. This firm opened in 1875 when the Reverend Francis Southworth bought a small press and a few fonts of type to produce a religious newspaper and tracts for distribution among the seamen who then abounded in Portland. Originally his four sons manned this press, and after a time outside work was taken in and a printing business established. "This was," as Fred Anthoensen recalls, "the era in printing history when the use of twisted rules in imitation of lithographic effects was much in vogue, and taste in printing called for a different type for each display line." The outside work of the company was not stimulating, for it consisted largely of Sunday-school lessons and law books, but it provided the means of learning the craft. In 1901 Fred Anthoensen became a full-fledged compositor, and in 1917 was made managing director of The Southworth Press. In 1921 he gained his first out-of-state client, and in 1923 his first book to design and print, a narrative of shipwreck in the Fijis, edited for the Marine Research Society of Salem by Lawrence W. Jenkins. By the time I came to know him, Fred Anthoensen was not only managing director but part-owner of the establishment, which hyphenated its name to The Southworth-Anthoensen Press. Eventually he bought out the family interest and became the sole owner of The Anthoensen Press.

This is a very American nineteenth-century performance which, if edifying tracts were still in vogue, would have furnished the Reverend Francis Southworth with a good subject—the son of immigrant parents who, without established friends, rose by consistent hard work and self-education to the top of a craft that he entered as an apprentice, and became a cultivated gentleman into the bargain. The key to all this is that, although Fred Anthoensen's formal schooling stopped at sixteen, his education has never ended. In a recent letter to me, he remarked, "In learning to be a printer I discovered there was both good and bad printing, and I soon decided which I wanted to do. I also knew it would take study to perfect myself." In notes on the press that he wrote in 1943, he observed that when he became a compositor, "Mr. D. B. Updike and Bruce Rogers were working in Boston and Cambridge, well on the road to distinguished careers. It was through the specimens of their work shown in *The Printing Art*, that handsome and scholarly printing journal without a peer, before or since, under the editorship of Henry Lewis Johnson, that I became interested in fine printing. I have always felt that this journal never received due credit for its share in the revival of American fine printing. At that time it was the best source of study for the apprentice who had but few dollars to spare for books. It was to this journal, too, that I owe so much in determining and shaping my own career."

He owed even more to his habit of reading widely in good literature of every kind. As a young man he bought volume after volume of Everyman's Library, and gradually read his way through the series. Thus to meet Edward Gibbon, Herodotus, Plato, Richard Hakluyt, and Jane Austen—to name only a tiny fraction of the riches there available—provided a broader education than many institutions manage to convey. The English eighteenth century especially attracted him, both in prose and typography, and gradually he began to assemble favorite authors in contemporary editions. His studies of literature and book design went hand in hand, and thus gave him the basis for the uncannily intuitive sense of appropriateness in design that marked his mature work. When I received proofs of the October 1942 meeting notice of the Club of Odd Volumes, at which Professor F. N. Robinson was to speak on the "Poetry of Dafydd ap Gwilym, a Welsh contemporary of Chaucer," I found with them a note that I had better ask the speaker whether the decoration—a pair of medieval lovers kissing in a tight clinch—was appropriate to the subject. I telephoned Fritz Robinson to say that Fred Anthoensen wanted to know whether a medieval necking party was a suitable symbol, and received the answer: "Absolutely. That is all Dafydd ap Gwilym ever wrote about." Over and over again I have had cause to be delighted by the subtlety with which Fred Anthoensen has caught the spirit of what he is putting into type, no matter how abstruse the subject may be.

His process of self-education was a solitary one, for he worked long hours and he knew few people who shared his interests, for he seldom left Portland. A few years before World War I, he revisited Denmark and took pleasure in the fanciful rococo palace façades of Copenhagen, as well as in the admirable Danish food and drink. In 1924 he made a second trip abroad, visiting Kelmscott House, the Caslon Letter Foundry, the British Museum, and other sources of typographical inspiration. Although in the twenties and thirties, when he was developing the kind of business that he had always wished the press to do, he made occasional trips to Boston and New York in search of orders, such excursions eventually became unnecessary. Instead customers came to 105 Middle Street, Portland, and climbed the steepest and most vertiginous stairway in New England to the third floor of an unexciting loft building in order to see him. Only occasionally could he be persuaded to vary a routine which was happily filled by his printing office, his library at home, and his garden with its yew and lilac hedges. Although he has long been a member of the Club of Odd Volumes in Boston and done most of its printing for the past quarter of a century, his appearances in the convivial surroundings of 77 Mount Vernon Street have been all too infrequent.

Early in this century Fred Anthoensen decided what kind of printing he wanted to do. He then spent twenty-five years of unremitting work to reach the point where he could do it. From 1923, when he began to design and print books that were to his taste, he was continually seeking types and ornaments that would enable him to carry out his ideal. Following his visit to the Caslon Letter Foundry in 1923 he acquired a supply of the Caslon fonts, complete with accents, ligatures and swash characters. In 1931 he printed for the Mergenthaler Linotype Company a *Specimen* of George W. Jones's new cutting of the Baskerville face. Through friendship with Paul A. Bennett and C. H. Griffith of that company, he followed with especial interest the recutting for the Linotype of such essential book faces as Caslon Old Face, Janson, Baskerville and Scotch to conform to the original fonts, and the creation for the Linotype of new faces by W. A. Dwiggins and Rudolph Ruzicka. Although he made extensive use of the constantly improving resources of the Linotype, he nevertheless consistently sought castings from original matrices for hand composition whenever possible. In 1931 the Press acquired the Binney and Ronaldson "Roman No. 1;" in 1932, some of John Bell's types from Stephenson Blake and Company of Sheffield, England; in 1933, Joseph Fry's double small-pica italic of 1766, and a stock of Anton Janson's types, cast from the original matrices by the Stempel foundry at Frankfurt-am-Main. From Stephenson Blake and Company he also obtained a remarkable range of eighteenth-century type flowers and ornaments, which gave Fred Anthoensen the material for the evolution of the engaging decorations that have enlivened so many of his books.

The evolution of this stock of original types and ornaments, and of the use that Fred Anthoensen made of them, is simply and delightfully set forth in a 170-page volume entitled *Types and Bookmaking* that the Press issued in 1943, on the twentieth anniversary of the first book completed that represented the type of work that he wished to do. For this he wrote a sixty-eight page essay, commenting on the search for types; the late Ruth A. Chaplin—long a faithful assistant—prepared a bibliographic catalog of the 265 books printed in these two decades, and specimens were given of the types and ornaments. Here is the autobiography of twenty years of the work of the Press, similar in concept to the volume that Mr. Updike and Julian P. Smith prepared in 1933 on the fortieth anniversary of the Merrymount Press. I have always hoped for

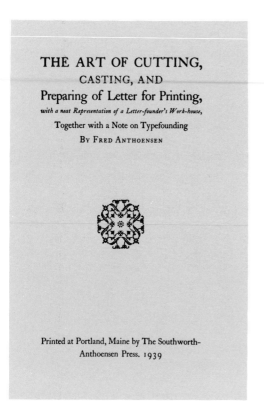

THE ART OF CUTTING,
CASTING, AND
Preparing of Letter for Printing,
with a neat Representation of a Letter-founder's Work-house,
Together with a Note on Typefounding
By Fred Anthoensen

Printed at Portland, Maine by The Southworth-
Anthoensen Press. 1939

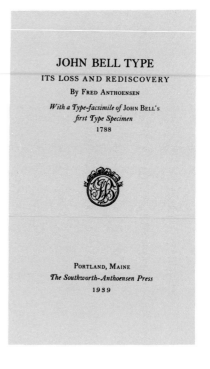

JOHN BELL TYPE
ITS LOSS AND REDISCOVERY
By Fred Anthoensen

With a Type-facsimile of John Bell's
first Type Specimen
1788

Portland, Maine
The Southworth-Anthoensen Press
1939

FACING PAGE, LEFT   Title pages from books and booklets of Fred Anthoensen's press include his own *The Art of Cutting, Casting, and Preparing of Letter for Printing*, 1939.

FACING PAGE, RIGHT   Anthoensen's *John Bell Type: Its Loss and Rediscovery*, 1939.

BELOW LEFT   Edward F. Stevens' *Thomas Bird Mosher*, 1941.

BELOW RIGHT   Edmund S. Morgan's *Paul Revere's Three Accounts of His Famous Ride*, letterpress portions by the Anthoensen Press (Massachusetts Historical Society, 1961).

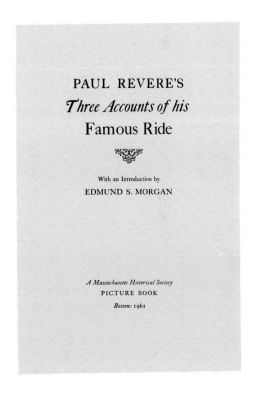

a sequel. I know that Ruth Chaplin had it in mind until her death, and I strongly suspect that bibliographic entries from number 266 and beyond were somewhere in her desk. I hope that Fred Anthoensen may have jotted down some further notes, or, if he has not, that he will do so now that he is leaving more and more of the daily routine of the Press to his able ally, Warren F. Skillings. Twenty-three years have passed since *Types and Bookmaking* appeared.

Several factors have combined to make The Anthoensen Press a uniquely useful institution. There has been first of all Fred Anthoensen's meticulous striving for perfection, which has gone beyond design and presswork to the training of singularly able compositors and proof-readers, who relieve the customer of anxiety and drudgery. The second is the remarkable intuition of this printer-designer that leads him to propose the appropriate treatment of any kind of material that may be submitted to the Press. Copy sent with only the most general instruc-tions, or with no instructions at all beyond the minimum required, is translated into type that seems inevitable in its appropriateness. The third is the ability of the Press, through the presence in the same build-ing of John W. Marchi's bindery, not only to produce a complete book under one roof but to distribute it, if required. The fourth, and by no means the least, is its willingness to attempt to achieve a sound piece of work at a price that the customer can afford to pay. Thus an important part of its work has come to be done for learned institutions and for individuals who wish to have something printed for noncommercial distribution.

There has scarcely been a week in the last thirty years when I have not had at least one job of some kind in process at The Anthoensen Press, yet in this time I have visited Portland very seldom, had extraordi-narily little correspondence with Fred Anthoensen, never had a dis-appointment in the result, or a disagreement about price. The notion that one has to be near one's printer is erroneous if the printer is good enough. When I have had books to do, Fred would give me an estimate for budgetary purposes and a sample page, or general indication of his plan. When the bill came, it was almost always less than the estimate, unless I had made unanticipated additions to text or illustrations. It has never been necessary to dot i's and cross t's in giving instructions, or even to spell out financial considerations with the detail that is cus-tomary in general business. Such a relationship has greatly simplified my work over thirty years, as it has that of many other bibliographers, librarians, and learned institutions.

Miss Margaret Bingham Stilwell, in the preface to *Incunabula in American Libraries, a Second Census of Fifteenth-Century Books owned in the United States, Mexico, and Canada*, printed by the Press in 1940, observed of this listing of more than 35,000 incunabula: "The fact that copy for the main text of the *Census* was set up and read within seven months from the time it went to press has been due, in no small part, to the efficiency of the Southworth-Anthoensen Press and its compositor, Mr. Warren F. Skillings, who with a minimum of error set the main text single-handed." In the same year, Fred Anthoensen worked out for me the format of *The American Neptune, A Quarterly Journal of Maritime History*, set for the most part in 12-point Linotype Baskerville, with certain sections in smaller sizes in double columns. After twenty-five years this format has accommodated the most diverse types of material, always readily and handsomely. Statistical tables and architectural drawings fit into its pages as readily as articles for general reading. By such performance the Press became an indispensable ally of the Bibliographical Society of America, the Peabody Museum of Salem, the John Carter Brown Library, and many other institutions. After the closing of the Merrymount Press in 1949, many of its long-standing customers, like the Massachusetts Historical Society, the Colonial Society of Massachusetts, and the Boston Athenaeum, moved their work without question or hesitation to Portland.

The variety and skill of Fred Anthoensen's design is most readily seen in small compass in the work he has done for the Club of Odd Volumes over the past quarter century. The notices of monthly meetings, usually printed on short notice, are as varied as they are numerous.

In 1947 Bowdoin College, by the conferring of an honorary degree, made Fred Anthoensen officially what he has already been for many years in fact—a Master of Arts. Colby College conferred the same degree upon him in 1951. It is singularly appropriate when a man is honored by his neighbors rather than by distant admirers. It is fitting that two Maine colleges, both of which have benefited by the typography of the Press, should have enrolled Fred Anthoensen on their lists of graduates.

But honorary degrees pale beside a little volume entitled *In Tribute to Fred Anthoensen Master Printer*, containing bibliographic essays by Paul Standard, Carl J. Weber, Charles R. Capen, Rudolph Ruzicka, E. Harold Hugo, Edward F. Stevens, Lawrence C. Wroth, Paul A. Bennett, Edward Page Mitchell, and myself. It bears the uninformative imprint "1952 Portland, Maine," but the remarkable thing is that it was printed under Fred's very nose, in his own shop—where his eyes were then accustomed to inspecting the inking of every form put on a press—through the amiable conspiracy of his own employees. The organizer and generalissimo of this benevolent plot was Ruth Chaplin, who proved herself as able in a cloak and dagger act as in the customary routine of a printing office. In the preface, where her fellow conspirators were named, I wrote: "One of the soundest principles of administration is what is called in the United States Navy the 'initiative of the subordinate,' which involves the premise that all members of an organization are competent in their several duties unless and until they themselves prove otherwise. Those who know The Anthoensen Press cannot fail to admire the manner in which everyone knows his or her job and deals with it—a situation far too uncommon in 1951." Parenthetically, even more uncommon in 1966. Continuing, I said: "It is not surprising that friends of Fred Anthoensen should wish to honor him by the publication of this series of essays. Neither is it surprising that his staff should have devised the means of printing the present volume without his knowledge or guiding hand."

This little volume inspired a chain reaction of benevolent conspiracies. Two years later Julian P. Boyd, Lyman H. Butterfield and I produced a little tribute to Harold Hugo that, although printed at the Princeton University Press, was illustrated by collotypes produced under Harold's nose at Meriden. Then in 1958 Lyman Butterfield joined forces with Fred Anthoensen and Harold Hugo to print a handsome account of my varied writings and confused activities, the material for which was extracted from my office and house, again without arousing suspicion. In 1959 Wendell and Jane Garrett and I, with the assistance of the Harvard University Press, paid Lyman Butterfield back by printing his letters home during a research trip to Holland in the manner and style of *The Diary of John Adams*. Only four nights ago, when Wendell Garrett was leaving the Associate Editorship of The Adams Papers to come to New York to assume a similar post with *Antiques* magazine, Lyman Butterfield presented him with another surreptitious volume, strongly resembling The Adams Papers, containing various extracts from the writings of several generations of Adamses concerning New York City. Thus the tribute to Fred Anthoensen established a pattern by which printers and historians have been honoring and mystifying their friends ever since.

The naval principle of the "initiative of the subordinate," which I came to know during wartime service with the late Fleet Admiral Ernest J. King, has more applications to printing than the one which I indicated above. It amounts in essence to believing that a naval commander should tell his subordinates *what* to do, and *when* to do it, but never, under any circumstances, *how*. It is the business of a competent subordinate to know *how* to carry out his duties; if he doesn't, he isn't worth having, and the sooner one gets rid of him the better.

It is equally the business of a master printer to know *how* to do his work, without being told, or without the intervention of an outside designer. If he doesn't, he is not a master printer. The client should confine himself to *what* and *when*, and have confidence that a real craftsman knows the *how*. I suppose, in retrospect, that an unconscious recognition of this principle—long before either of us had ever heard of it in naval language—explains the singularly happy relation of mutual confidence that Fred Anthoensen and I have enjoyed for thirty years.

In closing, I permit myself a final naval analogy in regard to the work of Fred Anthoensen. In the last chapter of my biography of Admiral King, I quoted a striking passage from John Buchan in which he analyzed the qualities invariably found in "great captains." There are three powers, Buchan wrote, "which raise their possessor to the small inner hierarchy of leadership." The first, in brief, is "visualizing power or synoptic power" or better still "the power of seeing a battle-front as a whole." The second is "the power of reading the heart of the enemy." These require some explanation in reference to bookmaking, but I translate the first as the ability to see a manuscript in all its implications of historic style, present-day use, and practical cost before devising a plan for its printing. The second is more quickly translated as "the power of reading the heart of the client;" of knowing instinctively what he wants and offering him that rather than something else. Buchan's third quality needs no translation. It applies as well to a master printer as to a great captain in arms. It is "the power to simplify, the capacity to make a simple syllogism, which, once it is made, seems easy and inescapable, but which, before it is made, is in the power only of genius. No great step in history, whether in war or in statesmanship"—and I might add in printing—"seems to us otherwise than the inevitable in the retrospect. The ordinary man flatters himself that he could have done it too, it seems so easy."

Robert (above) and Edwin Grabhorn. Photos by Marjory Farquhar

THE GRABHORNS

by Roland Baughman

DANIEL BERKELEY UPDIKE, the great Boston printer, once said in an address that was billed as his message to his follow craftsmen, "Printing is a trade and not an art, but it has frontiers on the arts." Now it would be very difficult indeed to select any printer from any period or place who would have fewer points of similarity with Updike than the brothers Grabhorn have, but I believe nevertheless that, deep in their hearts, they would agreed with his statement—though I also believe that they would laugh at anyone who would say so. Edwin and Robert Grabhorn have most assuredly practiced the trade of printing as an art, and the books which they have produced over what is now almost half a century have their source in an artistic inspiration which, if it is not in fact unique, is at any rate very rare among American printers. Grabhorn books have a personality, a hall-mark, an aura; like Kelmscott books, they can be imitated but they cannot be equalled at the hands of imitators.

But before this discussion becomes too deeply mired in the philosophy of "fine printing" and its relationship with "art," perhaps I should say a little of the history and background of these two typographical geniuses who work in the glow of the Golden Gate. Edwin Grabhorn is the elder of the two; he was born in 1890 (or thereabouts—the authorities can't agree and the Library of Congress won't venture a guess; and who would have the temerity to ask Ed directly?). [However, upon Edwin's death, December 16, 1968, his age was reported by the Associated Press to have been 89.—*Editor.*] Robert Grabhorn is some ten

Roland Baughman, who died in 1967, was head of the Special Collections Department of the Columbia University Libraries. Lecture given December 2, 1965.

years younger; rumor has it that he was born in 1900. Both are natives of Indianapolis.

Ed Grabhorn learned the printer's craft in the shop of an uncle. He was barely out of his teens when he answered the siren call of the West in 1909, obtaining a job with a music publisher in Seattle, Washington. That first western sojourn of his was brief and disillusioning, lasting only two or three years, but it included a turn at being his own boss—it had so happened that the man who had hired him as a compositor decamped, leaving him in sole possesion of a debt-encumbered business. The most enduring consequence of that experience was that Ed Grabhorn would never again be happy taking orders from someone else—not even from clients!

In any event, late in 1912 Ed Grabhorn was back in Indianapolis, where he spent the next three or four years working wherever his printing talents could command a wage. By 1915 he had had his fill of that, and he established his own "Studio Press," having acquired a stock of Goudy's Forum and Kennerley types. Somewhere along the line he had married, and the early Studio Press imprints include the name of his first wife, Florence. In a year or two his brother Robert, then in his later teens, became associated with the venture.

The products of the Studio Press were rather arty and self-conscious, in keeping with the tradition that had begun with William Morris, and which during the first two decades of the twentieth century made so deep an impression on the younger generation of American printers. However, it should be emphasized right here that the Grabhorns always deprecated and soon fought off the tendency to imitate even the greatest of printers. Frederic Melcher once asked Ed Grabhorn if he owned the Kelmscott Chaucer or the Ashendene Dante. Ed replied that he *had* owned both of those typographical monuments, but that he would rather not have such books around too long because he might unconsciously get to imitating them. Melcher also recalled, in another connection entirely, that Ed had given away his copy of the Ashendene Dante as a kind of *quid pro quo* for the gift of a copy of the first edition of Mark Twain's *1601!*

Arty or not, the productions of the Studio Press were gaining for Ed Grabhorn a reputation which has remained his ever since. W. R. Voris, who eventually bought the Studio Press—lock, stock, and unbound sheets—has written that as a young man he had heard tales of "a queer old fellow" somewhere in Indianapolis who "would rather do a fine bit of work than make a dollar, a man who could do wonders with limited supplies of type and accessories." When, much later, Ed Grabhorn heard about these tales, he told Voris that "the old fellow would be carrying on for a long time and would yet show them how to print real books." That vow was made when "the old fellow" was barely 30, just before he moved to San Francisco in 1920.

But when Ed and his brother Robert threw open the doors of the "Grabhorn Press" in San Francisco, that city, remarks David Magee, the noted Grabhorn expert and bibliographer, was "already richly endowed with printers"—John Henry Nash (the "Aldus of San Francisco"), Taylor and Taylor, the brothers Johnson of the Windsor Press, to mention only a few. John Johnck, founder of the well-known firm of Johnck & Seeger, arrived in San Francisco from Iowa about the same time that the Grabhorns arrived from Indiana. There were not many jobs for newcomers, and the first months were pretty hand-to-mouth for the Grabhorns. The wolf was kept at bay by advertising work, notably for the Standard Oil Company, the American Trust Company, and the Bank of California. Most printers would have been happy enough with accounts like those, but, again according to David Magee, the Grabhorns wanted to be *book* printers, not advertising typographers.

Since no publishers stepped forward to have them do their printing, the Grabhorns issued a book or two over their own imprint. Looked back on today, in the context of later Grabhorn books, those early self-advertising efforts are not very impressive—but they caused someone on the publications committee of the Book Club of California to sit up and take notice. At any rate, in 1921 appeared the first of what has proved to be a long and distinguished series of Grabhorn books issued by the Book Club. It was Emma Frances Dawson's *A Gracious Visitation.*

Such printing was making powerful friends for the Grabhorns, friends who for more than four decades have sponsored the publication of books that do not have to meet too strict a budget—friends who could almost be placed in the category of patrons. One such, and perhaps the most openhanded of all, was Albert M. Bender, for whom the Press printed seven items during the critical first four years of its existence in San Francisco. Mr. Bender died in 1941, and in the twenty years he knew the Grabhorns he was responsible, partially or entirely, for at least twenty-five of their publications.

By 1924 the Grabhorn Press was able to concentrate more definitely on book printing and somewhat less on advertising work (though to this day a substantial part of their effort is devoted to that lucrative side-line; truly definitive Grabhorn collections, I have recently learned, must include bottle labels of a certain highly regarded California wine!). And now began one of the great periods of the Press, marking its emergence to take its place among the most influential and widely known in America.

The 1920s marked the zenith of the "press book" craze, the "fine printing" madness, the era of the "limited de luxe edition." It was a period made to order for the Grabhorns, who began to issue books that were strictly limited as to edition copies, highly decorated with hand work, and (by today's standards) very modestly priced. It was a time when printers and publishers everywhere could expect to sell nearly any sad old text, provided it was dressed up with all the elegance the illustrator and designer could bestow, and issued in a "limited" number of copies. I'll say this for the Grabhorns—their texts were never old and tired. When they issued *Leaves of Grass* in 1930 (under the imprint of Bennett Cerf's Random House), it was the first time that American classic had ever been printed in monumental form. The same can be said of the *Red Badge of Courage,* 1931 (also a Random House book). And many other Grabhorn books of this period—though not exactly qualifying as monumental—incorporated texts of lasting importance which had never received the "fine printer's" accolade before—*Salomé, Hymns to Aphrodite,* and *The Golden Touch* in 1927, *The Scarlet Letter* in 1928, and *Robinson Crusoe,* which was done in 1930 for George Macy's young venture, The Limited Editions Club.

As we look back on it all now, we cannot really fault the limited editions craze that swept the country during the 1920s. I like the way Ed Grabhorn put it in 1933 in his essay, "The Fine Art of Printing." "I am glad it all happened," he wrote. "I would go through any form of hysteria again if we could produce another *Leaves of Grass.*" The simple truth is that in that magic decade there came into being the important tenets that have stood up under the impact of a major depression, the restrictions and ersatz standards of a world war, and the spiraling inflation of the post-war period. In the 1920s the American Institute of Graphic Arts began its Fifty Books of the Year shows, their purpose being to hold up for all to see the American productions that, in the opinions of the various juries, best met the challenges of the times. In that decade, too, George Macy's Limited Editions Club got its start, and ever since, in bad times and good, it has sponsored proud publications that exemplify the best in design, illustration, and bookmaking techniques. I submit that we desperately *need* these fruits of nostalgia, so that, when hard metal at last completely disappears from book production, when type and decent paper become the private province of the hobbyist, when the glacier of computerized printing overruns us all, we will be able to remember the beauty and quality that once existed.

But let's get back to the Grabhorns. During the early 1920s, according to Gregg Anderson in his recollections of his years spent as a compositor and factotum at the Press, the Grabhorns were strongly influenced by Morris, Cobden-Sanderson, St. John Hornby, and even Bruce Rogers. But that phase soon passed—and in my own opinion it was not only because Ed Grabhorn outgrew it, although of course nothing would have availed if that had not been the case. I think that there was another factor that was equally important—the coming of Valenti Angelo to the Press in 1926. Thereafter Grabhorn books were never the same, never imitative of someone else's work, and never again was the Press to be without the services and vitalizing force of a ranking creative artist. Valenti remained barely a half-dozen years, but while he was with the brothers Grabhorn he had an important hand in some of the most beautiful books they have ever produced. And when he left finally to seek the greater satisfaction of being his own boss in the New York area, he was followed by an imposing succession of artists who could and did work in what had become widely known as the Grabhorn genre. To try to list all of these artists would be tedious, and to select from them would be invidious. It would be equally wrong, though, not to mention at least two who have served for substantial periods, and who have strongly influenced the personality of Grabhorn books— Mallette Dean and, more recently, Ed's daughter, Mary Grabhorn.

It is easily seen that the half-century career of the Grabhorns can be divided into five major phases—the "incunabula" years in Indianapolis, the imitative period (perhaps "allusive" is a happier word) in the early 1920s, the "fine printing" era of the late 1920 and very early 1930s, the years of the great depression, and the post-war period. Gregg Anderson goes a step farther in his analysis, correlating the phases with Ed Grabhorn's successive enthusiasms as a book collector. The imitative period, for example, came when Ed was primarily interested in acquiring the better works of the most famous modern printers. "Gradually," wrote Anderson in the summer issue of *Print*, 1942, "his collecting drifted from the field of printing to the buying of first editions of

had for the prodigious deal of Time and Labour which it took me up to make a Plank or Board: But my Time or Labour was little worth, and so it was as well employ'd one way as another.

However, I made me a Table and a Chair, as I observ'd above, in the first Place, and this I did out of the short Pieces of Boards that I brought on my Raft from the Ship: But when I had wrought out some Boards, as above, I made large Shelves of the Breadth of a Foot and Half one over another, all along one Side of my Cave, to lay all my Tools, Nails, and Iron-work, and in a Word, to separate every thing at large in their Places, that I must come easily at them; I knock'd Pieces into the Wall of the Rock to hang my Guns and all things that would hang up.

So that had my Cave been to be seen, it look'd like a general Magazine of all Necessary things, and I had every thing so ready at my Hand, that it was a great Pleasure to me to see all my Goods

88

[BOOK II] STARTING FROM PAUMANOK

1. Starting from fish-shape Paumanok where I was born,
Well-begotten, and rais'd by a perfect mother,
After roaming many lands, lover of populous pavements,
Dweller in Mannahatta my city, or on southern savannas,
Or a soldier camp'd or carrying my knapsack and gun, or a miner in California,
Or rude in my home in Dakota's woods, my diet meat, my drink
from the spring,
Or withdrawn to muse and meditate in some deep recess,
Far from the clank of crowds intervals passing rapt and happy,
Aware of the fresh free giver the flowing Missouri, aware of mighty Niagara,
Aware of the buffalo herds grazing the plains, the hirsute
and strong-breasted bull,
Of earth, rocks, Fifth-month flowers experienced, stars, rain, snow, my amaze,
Having studied the mocking-bird's tones and the flight of the mountain-hawk,
And heard at dawn the unrivall'd one, the hermit thrush
from the swamp-cedars,
Solitary, singing in the West, I strike up for a New World.
13

ABOVE LEFT Page from The Limited Editions Club's *Robinson Crusoe*, 1930, printed by the Grabhorn Press.

ABOVE RIGHT Page from Random House's *Leaves of Grass*, 1930, printed by the Grabhorn Press with drawings by Valenti Angelo.

RIGHT Page from the *Cabeça de Vaca*, 1929.

36   Relation of Alvar Nuñez

The departure of four Christians. [1528-19] vember and December. They have wears of cane and take fish only in this season; afterwards they live on the roots. At the end of February, they go into other parts to seek food; for then the root is beginning to grow and is not good.

Those people love their offspring the most of any in the world, and treat them with the greatest mildness. When it occurs that a son dies, the parents and kindred weep as does every body; the wailing continuing for him a whole year. They begin before dawn every day, the parents first and after them the whole town. They do the same at noon and at sunset.* After a year of mourning has passed, the rites of the dead are performed; then they wash and purify themselves from the stain of smoke. They lament all the deceased in this manner, except the aged, for whom they show no regret, as they say that their season has passed, they having no enjoyment, and that living they would occupy the earth and take aliment from the young. Their custom is to bury the dead, unless it be those among them who have been physicians. These they burn. While the fire kindles they are all dancing and making high festivity, until the bones become powder. After the lapse of a year the funeral honors are celebrated, every one taking part in them, when that dust is presented in water for the relatives to drink.

Every man has an acknowledged wife. The physicians are allowed more freedom: they may have two or three wives, among whom exist the greatest friendship and harmony. From the time a daughter marries, all that he who takes her to wive kills in hunting or catches in fishing, the woman brings to the house of her father, without daring to eat or take any part of it, and thence victuals are taken to the husband. From that time neither her father nor mother enter his house, nor can he enter theirs, nor the houses of their children; and if by chance they are in the direction of meeting, they turn aside, and pass the distance of a crossbow shot from each other, carrying the head low the while, the eyes cast on the ground, for

BELOW   Robert Grabhorn device, used on San Francisco Public Library program commemorating acquisition of the Robert Grabhorn Collection on the History of Printing and the Development of the Book (1965).

BELOW LEFT   Title page from California map book printed for the Book Club of California, 1964.

BELOW RIGHT   Lines from *A Bibliography of the Grabhorn Press, 1914–1940*, by Elinor R. Heller and David Magee, showing the Grabhorn Press private type, Franciscan.

Title page from *Landscape Prints of Old Japan*, printed for the Book Club of California, 1960.

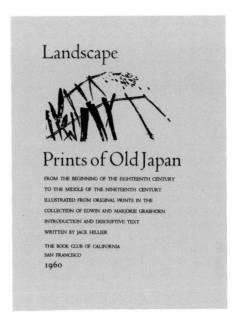

Landscape

Prints of Old Japan

FROM THE BEGINNING OF THE EIGHTEENTH CENTURY
TO THE MIDDLE OF THE NINETEENTH CENTURY
ILLUSTRATED FROM ORIGINAL PRINTS IN THE
COLLECTION OF EDWIN AND MARJORIE GRABHORN
INTRODUCTION AND DESCRIPTIVE TEXT
WRITTEN BY JACK HILLIER

THE BOOK CLUB OF CALIFORNIA
SAN FRANCISCO

1960

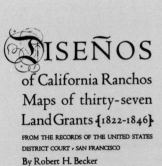

ꝹISEÑOS

of California Ranchos
Maps of thirty-seven
Land Grants {1822-1846}

FROM THE RECORDS OF THE UNITED STATES
DISTRICT COURT · SAN FRANCISCO

By Robert H. Becker

SAN FRANCISCO
The Book Club of California
1964

· 1922 ·

39. KWAN-YIN | BY STELLA BENSON
8½ x 6. One blank leaf; pp. (i-vi); pp. (1-10); one blank leaf: consisting of title p. (i), verso blank, text pp. (1-10), colophon on last page of text.
❡ Title printed in red; text in red and black. Type Garamond, handset; paper machine made. Bound in orange and gold Chinese paper boards with black satin back; black label lettered in gold on front cover. One hundred copies privately printed for Albert M. Bender in April, 1922.

40. DICKENS | IN CAMP | BY BRET HARTE | WITH A FORE-WORD BY | FREDERICK S. MYRTLE | [decoration] | SAN FRANCISCO | JOHN HOWELL | 1922
9 x 6¼. One blank leaf; pp. (i-vi); pp. 1-16; colophon; one blank leaf: consisting of title p. (i), verso blank, foreword pp. 1-11, p. 12 blank, text pp. 13-16.
❡ Title page printed in black and blue; caption title in blue; two initials in red. Title page decoration and two identical headpieces by Joseph Sinel. Type monotype Caslon, handset, and Original Old Style italic, handset; paper machine made. Bound in gray boards with linen back; white label printed in red on back. Three hundred and fifty copies printed for John Howell, publisher, in 1922. Price $7.50.
❡ The colophon reads three hundred and fifty copies. Actually only two hundred were printed and sold. The title page and headings are all hand-lettered.

41. A | LETTER | FROM B. FRANKLIN | TO | A YOUNG MAN
[caption title]
7 x 4½. Dp. (1-8): consisting of text pp. (1-7), colophon p. (8).
❡ One decorative initial; decorative headpiece. Type Original Old Style italic, handset; paper Van Gelder. Bound in orange boards with parchment back; black label lettered and decorated in gold on front cover. One hundred & ninety-four copies printed for complimentary distribution in 1922.
❡ Neither name nor any device of the Press appears. From the original letter on file at the Library of Congress, Washington, D.C.

[23]

English and American literature, and, before very long, to Californiana." Each of these interests has been reflected in the finer Grabhorn Press productions. At a later time, Ed took up the collecting of Japanese prints (David Magee credits him with owning "one of the finest collections of Japanese prints in the world"), and this interest, too, has resulted in a series of magnificent Grabhorn books.

But the story will be easier to tell if a chronological sequence is maintained. With the coming of the depression the limited editions bubble burst, leaving many printers who had flourished during the boom with little to do but gaze sadly at their idle presses. Although the west coast received the full impact of the depression somewhat later than was the case elsewhere in the country, San Francisco was eventually to suffer as much as any other city, and the Grabhorns would have fared no better than their fellows had Ed not come up with a brilliant idea. For several years the Press had issued occasional items that reflected his interest in works documenting the early history of California. Important among these were *The Harbor of St. Francis* (1926), *Relation of Alvar Nuñez Cabeça de Vaca* (1929), and *The Santa Fé Trail* (1931). These had all sold well, though typographically most of them (the *Cabeça de Vaca* is definitely an exception) were overshadowed by such masterpieces as the *Aesop*, the *Mandeville*, and the *Book of Ruth*. Accordingly, plans were laid to issue a series of reprints called "Rare Americana," featuring texts that in the original editions would have been far beyond the purses of ordinary collectors even in good times, and which no one had ever thought worthy of republishing. Between the years 1932 and 1937, the worst years of the depression, the Grabhorns issued *and sold out* twenty titles in three successive series of "Rare Americana."

The books were very modestly priced, even for those times, but despite that fact some of them stand among the most distinguished items the Grabhorn Press ever issued—*Wah-To-Yah & the Taos Trail* (1936), for example, and *The Spanish Occupation of California* (1934), with its unforgettable title page. And right here, I think, lay the real secret of their success, for it was almost as though the lower the budget for a given book, the more painstaking and lavish the effort to provide luxury for pennies. No volume among the ten items in the first series of "Rare Americana" could have had an expected gross return of more than $1,500, although the series included such permanent favorites as *Narrative of Nicholas "Cheyenne" Dawson* (1933) and John Bradford's *Notes on Kentucky* (1932). Under those circumstances the profits, if any, must have been figured in mills. But the books sold out as soon as they were issued; in not a single instance did the Grabhorns have to worry very long about an unsold inventory. Remember that those were dire times, and that the Grabhorns were competing not so much with other publishers as with the grocer and the man who collected the rent. The whole deal depended on three main considerations: first, low overhead (Ed and Bob did most of the work themselves, including, I rather think, the binding—even so the illustrator had to be paid); second, low inventory (the editions were held strictly to 500 or 550 copies); and finally, quick turnover (the first series varied in price from $1.50 to $3.00, the second was stabilized at $5.00 with 10 percent discount for prepayment, and the third again varied from $4.00 to $7.50). Almost at once, of course, the books doubled and tripled in the rare-book marts, but I have never heard it breathed that the Grabhorns ever expressed the slightest resentment of the fact that others reaped where they had sown. They just wanted to make certain that they would be permitted to go on sowing.

And, most happily for all aficionados of fine printing, it so turned out. The "Rare Americana" tided the Press over the worst years of the depression. The last of the three series, *Phoenixiana*, was issued in 1937, by which time business had picked up considerably. In fact, the project had begun to drag somewhat, and if I know the Grabhorns, they were probably getting tired of it; as other work increased, it became an increasing chore to finish out the promised series.

Nevertheless, the Grabhorn interest in early Americana—and particularly in early Californiana—was not dulled. Up to the time of the wartime restrictions of the early 1940s important California items continued to be produced, among them Wiltsee's *Gold Rush Steamers* (1938), Sutter's *New Helvetia Diary* (1939), and Meyer's *Naval Sketches of the War in California* (1939), featuring paintings owned by Franklin D. Roosevelt, who wrote the introduction for the book. This was the period, too, for three works aimed at a strictly local clientele, but which were snapped up by "Grabhorn collectors" over the whole nation—a W. P. A. book, *Festivals in San Francisco* (1939), Austin's *Around the World in San Francisco* (1940), and William Saroyan's *Hilltop Russians in San Francisco* (1941), all with plaintive and nostalgic illustrations by Pauline Vinson, and all published by James Ladd Delkin.

By this time the fame of the Grabhorn Press and its lasting place in the hearts of collectors were assured. Elinor R. Heller and David Magee bestowed the ultimate accolade by compiling a *Bibliography of the Grabhorn Press, 1915–1940*, which was printed by the Grabhorns, and which listed 338 major publications, plus innumerable ephemeral pieces. (A second volume was published later, bringing the record up through 1956 and the total of listed publications to 583.) I recall so well the reluctance with which my fellow librarians and I greeted the opportunity to pay $35 for that first bibliography—which nevertheless we bought. (We could sell it today, authorities permitting, for from five to ten times the original cost, and I think it most unlikely that any of us hesitated to pay the $75 needed to get the second volume.) The point to be made, however, is that after only twenty years in San Francisco, the Grabhorns were famous around the world for their colorful publications. Forty-odd of their books had been selected for the various Fifty Books of the Year shows, and one of them (*The Letter of Amerigo Vespucci*, 1926) had won the coveted A. I. G. A. gold medal. (The Grabhorns were awarded the medal again in, if memory serves, 1942, this time not for any specific volume, but in recognition of their total accomplishment and influence.)

During the war years, the Press's publishing activities were somewhat restricted, as might be expected. Perhaps the less said of those years the better, although the Grabhorns, who probably had an adequate stock of pre-war paper stashed away, did produce a number of outstanding volumes. Carl Wheat's *Maps of the California Gold Region* appeared in 1942, having unquestionably been in the works before Pearl Harbor, and early in 1944 Ivan Goll's *Landless John* was issued. Both were of folio size, both made the Fifty Books of the Year, and both were modestly priced (the Wheat sold for $18, the Goll for $12).

For my sins I give a course of lectures on the history of books and printing in Columbia's library school. As you may guess, the Grabhorns come in for discussion under the general heading of "Modern Fine Printing." Almost invariably the question arises, "How can they make any money?" To that I am forced to reply that I haven't the foggiest notion—and since only the IRS people know for sure, I can curb my curiosity. I rather suspect that the books the Grabhorns publish over their own imprint (the Shakespeare plays, for example, and the magnificent *Alamos* which has just come out) are figured on little more than a break-even basis, a kind of self-advertising, self-pleasing proposition in which a certain amount of red ink can be permitted in the interest, on the one hand, of attracting client work, and on the other, of satisfying the ancient Grabhorn compulsion to "show them how to print real books." It must be remembered that for the past twenty years Grabhorn publications for direct sale have been minimal in comparison with work done on order. It must also be remembered that the editions are extremely limited—the Grabhorns, as I said earlier, are not the least interested in giving self-room to a large inventory, nor, according to David Magee, in the drudgery of marketing, billing, shipping, etc. The Shakespeare plays are almost the only Press publications these days. They have been coming out at the rate of about one each year since 1951; they are beautiful books into which untold man-hours, artistry, inspiration, and loving care have been poured. And yet the price has been held to $30 and the editions to 185 copies. This means that the total gross expectancy from any one of them would be $5,500—and off the top of that must come whatever discount is allowed to dealers, usually, I understand, in the neighborhood of 25 percent. If the Grabhorns make a dollar on a deal like that I would be surprised.

This has been a very sketchy acount, and before I bring it to a close perhaps I should take the time for a generality or two. The Grabhorn Press consists [1965] of a very few key people—Ed, Robert, Robert's wife Jane, Ed's daughter Mary, and, until 1963, the pressman, Sherwood Grover, who had been with the Grabhorns so long that he was virtually a member of the family. It would be a good guess that ideas germinate freely among that group, so that there may be no way of being certain just *who* happened to be the one to think up a particular design or technique. But in general Ed is the designer, the idea man, Bob is the compositor and makeup expert, Jane oversees the bindery (while running her own show, the Colt Press), and Mary is a general factotum *cum* artist extraordinary. Each one, doubtless, would be quite capable of doing anyone else's job if the necessity should arise.

In 1948 Jane Grabhorn made what I consider a priceless summation of the way things happen at the Press. "[Ed]" she wrote [in, of all places, an open letter to her infant niece], "is what you might call an experimenter and an optimist—the inventor type. [Bob] is a perfectionist and a pessimist—the professorial type, in a sophisticated sort of way. Probably the reason Bob is a pessimist is because Ed is an optimist.

"I share their amazement," she continues, "every time a book is finished. There appears to be no organization, no planning, no system.

Not only does the right hand not know what the left is doing, but the left hand has no idea what the hell it's doing either. In fact, when the Grabhorns are 'at work,' the general effect is of both hands being tied behind the back and two men walking around blindfolded. Then suddenly, there's the book. Finished. I snarl, sneer, worry—but somewhere along the line someone must have been working. Because there's the book. Their team work is so successful that it is undetectable. Their combined talents are so perfectly synchronized that all appearance of effort as ordinary mortals know it, is completely effaced.

"I've seen many people come and go from this shop in the past fifteen years," she goes on, "and I don't believe that a single one of them, including myself, has left a single imprint, a trace, a mark, or a memory. I don't believe that one of us has exerted the slightest influence. These men are completely self-sufficient, and although entirely dependent one upon another almost for their existence, they are totally without need of anyone or anything else. This is a hell of a thing for a wife to contemplate. . . ."

And finally, a word or two about the Grabhorn product. The Grabhorns are experimenters and, because experimenting is always a chancy business, some of their projects turn out less well than might be desired. Gregg Anderson once commented (a little over-harshly, I have always thought) that "in almost any book where the text runs to more than 200 pages the Grabhorns are at a loss." He cited Wiltsee's *Gold Rush Steamers* (1938), which comprises 385 pages, as a case in point: the use of overly bulky paper and heavy binding boards made the volume nearly four inches thick! But, having made that mistake once, the Grabhorns have never repeated it. They apparently love thick, resilient paper which takes a deep impression, so their texts are usually short. When they are long, which of course sometimes happens, the paper is selected with the facts of life in mind.

The Grabhorns are masters of title page design, but they are not "title page printers." The exhilaration which one experiences on first seeing a Grabhorn title page is held at a high pitch as one leafs through the rest of the book. It is as though the designers had sought not merely to attract the eye by a brilliant beginning, but to set the theme for the decor of the entire volume. And to be successful in that is indeed a rare and precious thing.

Author's acknowledgment. No modern printers have been more copi-
ously written about than the Grabhorns. Their achievements and envied
way of life have inspired a voluminous *legenda aurea* (much of which,
we may be sure, the Grabhorns themselves regard as apocrypha). In any
event, there remains little that is wholly new to be set down, beyond
personal judgments. Especially as regards factual data, the foregoing
salute has necessarily echoed the following excellent sources:

American Institute of Graphic Arts, *Catalogue of an Exhibition* [of
Grabhorn printings], New York, 1942.

Gregg Anderson, *Recollections of the Grabhorn Press*, Meriden,
Connecticut, 1935.

Gregg Anderson, "The Grabhorn Press," *Print*, vol. 3, no. 2, Summer, 1942.

Jane Grabhorn, "Dear Victoria," *Book Club of California Quarterly
News-Letter*, vol. 14, no. 1, Winter, 1948.

David Magee, "Two Gentlemen from Indiana," in his *Catalogue of
Some Five Hundred Examples of the Printing of Edwin and Robert
Grabhorn*, San Francisco [1960].

W. R. Voris, *Notes on Some Early Grabhorn Items*, Tucson, Arizona [1939].

Prefatory matter by various persons and notes in the two definitive
bibliographies of the Press, 1940 and 1957.

Editor's note: Early in 1966, Robert Grabhorn retired from the Grabhorn Press, and in the fall, he and a young fine printer of San Francisco,
Andrew Hoyem, formed a partnership, Grabhorn-Hoyem, "for the
printing and publishing of books and the designing of printing that
merits individual attention but requires issuances in substantial quan-
tities." Edwin Grabhorn, until his death on December 16, 1968, gave his
primary attention to the publishing of a multivolume catalog of his
extraordinary collection of Japanese prints.

Jan Tschichold.

JAN TSCHICHOLD

by Paul Standard

IN THE PERSON and the practice of Jan Tschichold we have a fresh example of the difficulty of making plain common sense prevail, even in so old a craft as typography. The difficulty is by now largely past, for Tschichold is today acclaimed and honored for an achievement truly international. His thirty years' work in every field of typography has been done notably in three countries—Germany, Switzerland and England; and his crystal-clear principles accord with the finest graphic practices in Occident and Orient alike. Indeed, his close study of the older Chinese graphics may well have taught him to reconcile the graphic principles of east and west.

Born in Leipzig in 1902, Jan Tschichold was from boyhood exposed to letter forms, to their conversion into printing types and to their disposal in printed matter. His father was a designer and painter of letters, and Jan early made himself useful in the studio. He dreamed of becoming a teacher of drawing, but his study of the lettering manuals of Edward Johnston and of Rudolf von Larisch brought him instead a hope of becoming a calligrapher and letterer.

He studied at the Leipzig Akademie under Hermann Delitsch. The young Tschichold was soon entrusted, from his nineteenth to his twenty-second year, with Delitsch's evening classes, and proceeded to become a graduate student at the Akademie under Walter Tiemann and Hugo Steiner-Prag. In those early years he worked steadily in the Insel Verlag's design department, which has latterly summoned him back as a

Paul Standard is a leading calligrapher, teacher, lecturer, writer and translator in the fields of typography, lettering, and print-making and their history. Lecture given December 7, 1966.

consultant. His taste and capacity for type composition were meanwhile being cultivated in the famous printing-house of Poeschel & Trepte, which had long been printing many important Insel editions. A Bauhaus exhibition in 1924 quickened his responses to design and brought him in 1926 to the notice of Paul Renner (designer of Futura type), who engaged Tschichold to teach typography and calligraphy at the Munich Meisterschule für Deutschlands Buchdrucker.

Like Renner, Tschichold had been troubled by the decay of typography, which even after the First World War remained stubborn and rootless in its ineptitude despite the good example of Britain's printing revival since the turn of the century. To lift the craft clear of its corrupt foundations—or non-foundations—the young Tschichold published a pamphlet, *Elementare Typographie* (Leipzig, 1925), and followed this with *Die Neue Typographie* (Berlin, 1928). Together, these bold tracts opened every sleeping eye to the enormities so long accepted by the very nation whose Johann Gutenberg was still a revered name everywhere. Much of what those tracts contain remains true; but some of their conclusions and demands were grossly overdrawn and misconceived. The severest critic of these untruths today is their author himself. In defense he quotes a Chinese proverb, "In haste there is error," adding, "So many things in that primer are erroneous because my experience was too small."

Tschichold still recalls his deep satisfaction when at seventeen he saw by chance some English magazine pages set in Caslon type. By contrast, the busy and fussy German types and arrangements could only frustrate and exasperate him; and if he struck some wild resentful blows, his object was rather to restore some sanity than to set any rivers afire. His radical proposal was to scrap all the clutter and mediocrity of the then fashionable German types and to replace them with a single simple sans-serif face, perhaps because its very spareness served to banish the nightmare and confusion that surrounded him. While admitting this to have been a serious error, Tschichold yet pleads: "Very often error is creative. My errors were more fertile than I ever imagined. . . . It was a juvenile opinion to consider the sans-serif as the most suitable or even the most contemporary type face. A type face has first to be legible, or rather readable; and a sans-serif is certainly not the most legible type face when set in quantity, let alone readable." The other novelty his book recommended was asymmetrical arrangement to replace symmetrical. This, like the sans-serif dominance, was eagerly adopted by the younger graphic artists, and all went swimmingly until what Tschichold calls "the profane year of 1933," when Hitler took charge of Germany. Tschichold was promptly accused of creating "un-German" typography and "Kulturbolschewismus" in art; he and his wife were taken into "protective custody." Tschichold preferred to take refuge in Basle, Switzerland, where he has lived since 1933.

In 1935 he wrote another book, *Typographische Gestaltung*, which he still calls "a much more prudent and still useful book." Things had changed. "In time," he says, "typographical matters took on a very different aspect. To my astonishment, I detected most shocking parallels between the teachings of *Die Neue Typographie* and National Socialism and Fascism. Obvious similarities consist in the ruthless restriction of type faces, a parallel to Goebbels' infamous 'Gleichschaltung' (political alignment) and the more or less military arrangements of lines. Because I did not wish to be guilty of spreading the very ideas which had compelled me to leave Germany, I thought over again what a typographer should do. Which type faces are good, and what arrangement is the most practicable? By guiding the compositors of a large Basle printing office I learned a lot about practicability. Good typography has to be perfectly legible and, as such, the result of intelligent planning. The classical type faces such as Garamond, Jenson, Baskerville and Bell are undoubtedly the most legible. Sans-serif is good for certain cases of emphasis, but is now used to the point of abuse. The occasions for using sans-serifs are as rare as those for wearing obtrusive decorations." As to asymmetry, Tschichold still considers it a secret known to a group of initiates, and not easy to acquire, since its faults leap at once to the reading eye. Symmetry is, of course, less vibrant, but also less risky, even for the inexperienced. In sum, symmetry and asymmetry both are useful, but asymmetry demands a longer and harder discipline.

Since 1933 Tschichold's book typography and general typographic practice have been steadily along classical lines, tempered by a freedom that never exceeds the modesty of an ancillary craft. "The aim of typography," he says, "must not be expression, least of all self-expression, but pefect communication achieved by skill. Taking over working principles from earlier times or from other typographers is not wrong but sensible. Typography is a servant and nothing more. The servant typography ought to be the most perfect servant." Another commentator has lately put the matter more sharply by saying, "Self-expression is self-indulgence."

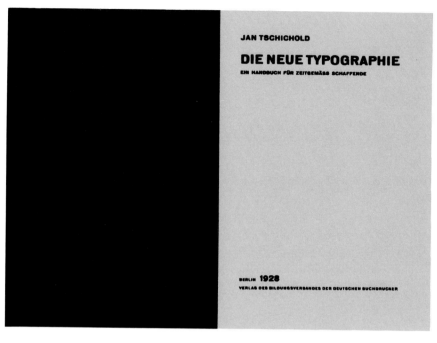

ABOVE   Title spread from Tschichold's *Die Neue Typographie*, 1928.
BELOW   Title spread, designed by Tschichold, of his *Asymmetric Typography*,
Reinhold, 1967, a translation by Ruari McLean of *Typographische Gestaltung*,
1935; courtesy Van Nostrand Reinhold Co.

As we have seen, *Die Neue Typographie* is a work of unequal merit. Yet (or should I say therefore?) it was rapturously embraced by the undisciplined as a gospel for all time. They saw this little book as the banner of a liberating pioneer. But as Tschichold's re-thinking of the fundamentals of typography brought forth a series of corrective tracts, his disciples became increasingly unhappy. Just as they felt they had solved all typographic problems for all time, here was the recreant Tschichold telling them to study closely the books of the typographic ancients and from them to learn anew the truly enduring principles of book design, so long forgotten or misunderstood. One disciple, the Swiss architect Max Bill, writing in the *Typographische Monatsblätter* blurts out the blunt accusation that Tschichold is a renegade from his own teaching, and he cites relevant passages to show the plain contradictions between the gospel of 1928 and the Tschichold practice since 1933.

Making his reply, in the same periodical, Tschichold sympathizes with the disillusion felt by his disciples; but, he asks in effect, would they be happier if he suppressed his youthful error and went on pretending he had writen a faultless book? Is it wrong to confess mistakes that must surely mislead the trusting? He goes further, and produces some fresh contradictions as yet undiscovered by his accuser, and he invokes the contrite sinner's privilege of seeking in all humility the remission of his typographic sins. He then in turn accuses his bigoted disciples of making a religion of asymmetry, recalling that they had once chided the classic typographer for making a religion of symmetry. The truth is, Tschichold concludes, that both symmetry and asymmetry are useful principles, dependable tools for the use of the practiced designer. The alleged "renegade" having thus given his altered views with such patient tact and good humor, the attacks ceased—ceased at least in printed form.

With his departure in 1933 from the Munich Meisterschule and his residence in Basle, Tschichold began his important career as teacher—a teacher in a classroom without walls, indeed without national frontiers. His widened audience was reached by his published articles and essays on particular aspects of his craft, by books designed for publishers, and by books of his own authorship, along with much commercial and promotional printing done to his specifications. His own published writings now exceed fifty titles, including translations, into five languages—all achieved in the thirty-odd years since he left the Munich Meisterschule. Indeed, it took this school only twenty years to realize

what it had lost; and in 1954 came its invitation to Tschichold to assume
the school's directorship—an invitation he in the end declined.

His students round the world have come to look forward to his in-
structional volumes, their texts and footnotes packed with discriminating comment. Most also contain extensive bibliographies of the subject
treated, and often of the author's other works as well. These latter, by
their very number, must be kept up to date in printed form lest order,
sequence and availability become confused. Each volume, a quiet ex-
emplar of working methods, has brought him assignments from many
western lands. The very latest, just published by Birkhaüser Verlag in
Basle as *Ausgewählte Aufsätze über Fragen der Gestalt des Buches und
der Typographie*, is now being prepared for publication here in 1967 as
something like *Selected Essays on Questions of Book and Typographic
Design*. And an earlier book's new version in English by Ruari McLean,
titled *Asymmetric Typography*, has been published by Cooper & Beatty
in Toronto and by Reinhold in New York, 1967. A few paragraphs
back I gave the German title of this book: *Typographische Gestaltung*.

In 1946 the late Oliver Simon of the Curwen Press of London flew to
Basle on Sir Allen Lane's behalf to engage Tschichold as re-designer of
the entire family of Penguin Books—a task that in three years brought
forth more than 600 titles, each newly made to suit the changing needs
of the world's greatest paperback publisher. Tschichold's precise draft
of instructions to govern the Penguin house style still reads like a dis-
tillation of wisdom patiently acquired by a versatile practitioner. The
call from Penguin had come just after his completion of the bright series
of Birkhäuser Klassiker in Basle, these including a twelve-volume
Goethe, a ten-volume Shakespeare and five other authors, each quarter-
cloth volume virtually given away at three Swiss francs; and all these
sequences were more than enough to promise well for Penguin, too. In
fact, Tschichold's work imparted to Penguin titles a new dignity, a
family look overlaid with a British reserve hitherto lacking. The Penguin Shakespeares sing out as gently as a consort of viols and recorders,
the *Sonnets & Poems* alone (in Bembo italic) being at its two-shilling
price not only the cheapest but high up among the loveliest editions
anywhere in print today. Jacket and title show a version of the Droe-
shout portrait newly wood-engraved by Reynolds Stone—a touch of
neo-Elizabethan atmosphere rarely matched in far costlier editions. A
full comparison of the Penguin single-play volumes with the three-play

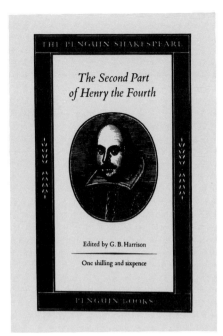

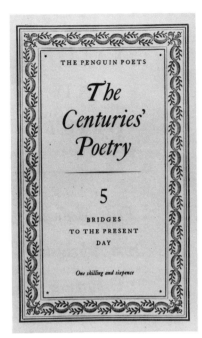

LEFT Cover of a title in The Penguin Shakespeare. Portrait from wood engraving by Reynolds Stone; lettering inside the panel in red (as reproduced in Tschichold's *Designing Books*, Wittenborn, Schultz, Inc.).

RIGHT Cover for The Penguin Poets; ivory paper, light green border (from *Designing Books*).

Illustrations in text, from *Treasury of Alphabets and Lettering*, Reinhold, 1966, showing how considerations of spacing and proportion determine the difference between good and graceless design. Courtesy Van Nostrand Reinhold Co.

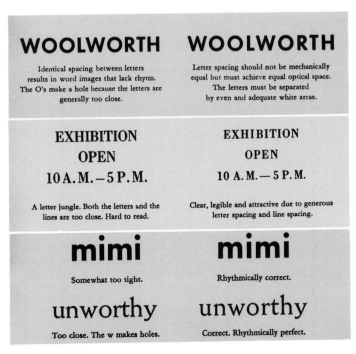

Birkhäuser volumes could become a profitable classroom discussion conducted by a perceptive typography teacher. Other books done for Penguin include works by Virginia Woolf, Homer, Apuleius, Turgenev, Voltaire, *British Wildflowers* with color plates, the Penguin Poets series, the two "Alice" volumes with Tenniel's illustrations, the small-quarto Penguin Prints series (beginning with Picasso), *Popular Art in the U.S.* (derived from *Index of American Design*), and the massive hardbound *Pelican History of Art* in royal octavo volumes.

The art books just cited seem the natural successors to Tschichold's earlier Holbein Verlag series of oblong quartos on the historic Chinese woodcut, a personal passion of his. The originals date back to 1620, when for recurrent ceremonial occasions such as a wedding or a royal progress, sets of them were often reprinted—here, too, the Chinese created the happy idea of presenting such prints to guests at a wedding, each print pulled from its historic block. Within the 1940s came simultaneous German, French and English editions of three major selections. The first two were titled *Early Chinese Color-Prints* and *The Wood-Cutter Hu Cheng-yen*, both being installments from *The Ten Bamboo Hall*, the most famous collection of its kind; the third, chosen from the next oldest such collection, bears the title *Color-Prints from the Mustard-Seed Garden*. But because this art flourishes today in China, a fourth volume was called for, this one a folio titled *Contemporary Chinese Color-Prints*, ten of its sixteen specimens being painted and then cut as woodblocks by Chi Pai-shih, who died at ninety-four only a few years ago. Finally there is a splendid octavo of Chinese *Poetry Paper by the Master of the Ten Bamboo Hall*. Each of these, in Chinese double-fold, is produced with the technical, editorial and bibliographical care of a true admirer who, perforce reproducing from *prints*, not from the original *blocks*, has taken a fanatical care to make all worthy of their originals. In particular, the small volume of poetry paper just has to be seen; there is no describing its tiny river scene, its waters "rippled" by delicate blind impressions that keep a tiny vessel afloat. Here is a world in miniature, so effortlessly shown as to require no ink for the buoyant water—another instance of the Chinese gift for art without technology.

Typophiles and calligraphiles are indebted to Tschichold for his studies of letter forms. All are models of expository prose: quick in marshalling the needed historical facts, orderly in criticism, discriminating in their corrective hints, encouraging in their practicality, and above all exemplary in their brevity. For they all possess what engineers call "terminal facilities"—that is, they stop when the topic is finished. Among these are his *Geschichte der Schrift in Bildern* (Holben Verlag, Basle; the English edition is titled *Illustrated History of Lettering and Writing*, 1947), with its ten pages of introductory text, four of descriptive summary, plus eighty plates acutely and critically captioned. This was one of the laurelled books of its year.

He has also prepared, for laymen seeking cultivation or for plain men of business seeking criteria for their own printing needs, two amusingly instructive books—but available for the moment, alas! only in German. They are titled *Was Jedermann vom Buchdruck Wissen Sollte* (or, *What Everyman Should Know about Letter-press*, 1949); and *Erfreuliche Drucksachen durch gute Typographie* (or, *Delightful Printed Matter through Good Typography*, 1951). In each, the reader is shown specimens of printed work, good and bad, with quick ways of turning the bad into good. The reader comes to recognize in printing a common-sense extension of his experience which will enable him to evaluate much besides printing.

It is now twenty-two years since the appearance of *Schatzkammer der Schreibkunst* (or, *A Treasury of Calligraphy*) published by Birkhäuser in Basle, 1945. This oblong quarto has a dozen pages of text and one hundred pages of plates, all specimens shown in true size. To carry the story of writing forward into the era of printing, there is the *Meisterbuch der Schrift*, which Reinhold has just published here in English. This small folio was first published by Otto Maier in Ravensburg, 1952. Its sixty pages of text with opposite illustrations, and especially its 175 annotated plates make this a volume profusely illustrated, as such books must be. And speaking of what such books must be, let me add that they *must be reviewed*—reviewed in the British and American daily and periodical press even if their small quantum of text is in an alien tongue; for unless the language be, say, Czech or Finnish, the preponderant illustrations will suffice. Now this book was duly reviewed in the London *Times Literary Supplement*, the notice running to fully 2,500 words. But the New York *Times*? It has yet to hear of this book, and of many another such; and I cannot help deploring this neglect by a newspaper unmatched for means and prosperity. What the *Times* of London has done habitually, the New York *Times* too can afford to do—especially as it once maintained an executive post entitled "Typographic Adviser." Had the New York *Times* done as its London namesake has so long persisted in doing, we too should by now have

developed here a comparably instructed laity in this important field of
the printed word. Our *Times* has long maintained its own Museum of
the Printed Word; it seems only natural to ask for a frequent Com-
mentary Upon the Printed Word.

But New York remains a fortunate city, fortunate especially in its
booksellers, of whom at least two can claim to be bookseller-publishers.
I mean, of course, Museum Books as nurturer-in-chief of the works of
Hermann Zapf; and George Wittenborn, who published in 1951 a full-
color Tschichold folio titled *Designing Books*. This volume's twenty
pages of text are straightaway instruction in the author's way of planning a book—principles which every aspiring designer can use to fashion
a style of his own. It will be remembered that Wittenborn issued in 1967
the latest Tschichold volume of essays on typography and book design.

In recent years Tschichold has been typographer and art director for
the Hoffmann-LaRoche pharmaceutical firm in Basle. When in 1960
Basle University celebrated the fifth century of its founding, the company presented to the University Library a copy of the second (1555)
edition of Vesalius's *De Humani Corporis Fabrica* in a contemporary
binding. This second edition is preferred to the first (of 1543) for its
improved text and finer typography. Both were printed in Basle by the
firm of Johannes Oporinus.

In order to share the quincentenary with its friends round the world,
Hoffmann-LaRoche issued a sixteen-page folio pamplet containing ten
loose single plates and three double plates reproduced in reduction from
the work itself. It was printed in separate editions for each of eight
languages, aggregating 62,000 copies. The pamphlet carries two articles,
one by Adolf Seebass on the book's importance to medicine, the other
by Jan Tschichold on its significance in the typography of learned
works. He speaks amusingly of a puzzle caused by the early engraver,
who cut positive instead of negative images on his blocks, thus "creating" lefthanders, contradictory shadows and inverted landscapes. On a
special double plate, Tschichold shows a dozen plates in miniature, each
laterally flipped to restore the original images and rejoin the landscape's
contours behind them, thus restoring nature's landscape of the
Euganean Hills near Padua, as identified recently by our own Harvey
Cushing of Harvard.

Hoffmann-LaRoche publishes *Roche*, a magazine for pure and applied chemistry, to which Tschichold contributes occasionally. In a
recent article about a visit to the Gutenberg Museum in Mainz he speaks

of the Gutenberg Bible and shows pages from Leonhart Fuchs' *Neu Kreüterbuch*, the pioneer volume of botany with illustrations, and from the pioneer anatomy book of Vesalius, both first printed in Basle in the year 1543.

As part of his unending concern with techniques and materials of printing, Tschichold produced in 1953, for a Basle paper firm named Kupferschmid, a comparative study to show the response of eight different papers to each of eighteen faces from the Monotype, Stempel, Bauer and Haas foundries, in the three major classes of printing: letter-press, offset and gravure. In this thirty-six-page quarto, double-column, half-width pages alternate with full pages to facilitate comparison of results of the permutations induced in a type by different papers and processes. It is a reference book of utmost value to the designer, for whom Tschichold had contrived to blend instruction with physical and professional delight.

Tschichold's strong talent as a scribe has often produced lettering commissions for publishers and for booksellers. But he always likes to show a departed artist's letters in their best possible state. When he was producing Alfred Fairbank's *Book of Scripts* for Penguin in 1949 he took special pains with the cover-panels of roman capitals from Juan de Yciar's Spanish manual of 1547. Because even the early editions were printed from blocks unduly battered, Tschichold used his pen and brush to restore the letters to their pristine finish. It is with him an act of simple *pietas*, and he has done it many times for many a departed writing master.

He has thus far created two type faces. The first, for the Schelter & Giesecke foundry (Leipzig) in 1935, is a slim, graceful end-stopped italic originally written with an edged pen and bearing the name of Saskia, famous as the wife of Rembrandt. In its range from 6 to 60 point it is even today a subtle and sinewy letter-family that is severely charm-ing or charmingly severe. It is still usable, with no nonsense about it. In 1965 he began the design of the Sabon roman and italic, running from 6 to 36 point thus far. An austere form of Garamond, this type is the first to be conceived for simultaneous triple issue as foundry type by Stempel and for machine composition by Monotype and by Linotype. This means a triple headache for the designer, since he has to devise subtle compensations for the three different sets of body-widths if the face is to be consistent in all three forms. But this is the kind of problem he likes.

And well he may, for Sabon's recent birth as a type for hand setting at the Stempel foundry already stamps it as a decided success. Gotthard de Beauclair has just completed a limited edition, at the Trajanus Press in Frankfurt am Main, of Joseph Bédier's established text of *Der Roman von Tristan und Isolde* in Rudolf G. Binding's German version, with 14 hand-colored woodcuts by Fritz Kredel. This tall octavo volume is nothing less than a triple masterpiece jointly achieved by Tschichold as type designer, by Beauclair as typographer and by Kredel as illustrator. The latter's blocks have here attained a new state of floating grace to suit the demands of this touching early romance. The Sabon gives the text a timeless look, ingenious in its fitting, balance and texture—altogether a happy augury for this Sabon-trismegistus among current type designs.

For all Tschichold's friends, the year-end must long remain a season of surprises—surprises of printed matter dealing with origins, survivals or revivals. For example, there is the large early Chinese portrait of Ts'ai Lun, credited with the invention of papermaking; there is an illustrated essay on the techniques of the early Chinese and Japanese color woodblock; some early Chinesse stone-rubbings; a picture in lace-maker's technique of the nineteenth century. This last, being part of his private collection, is now, with its seven companions, the means of illustrating a book of German baroque and rococo love poems, *Schönste, Liebe Mich,* published to his design by Lambert Schneider of Heidelberg.

But the latest of these *occasionalia,* his greeting for 1966, is from a unique document he discovered: a print of the earliest known poster for an established tradesman, originally cut in metal or wood about 1560— that is, 155 years earlier than any like poster hitherto known in Europe. It was issued by the Parisian milliner and hosier Pierre Baudeau from his shop in the Rue St. Denis. In that period silk stockings, which had hitherto been worn only at court, were gradually becoming generally fashionable.

Some day, one supposes, Tschichold's collection of color-printed fruitwrappers of the Mediterranean region will become first an illustrated monograph, and later a modest book on a fascinating subject. It will also be a surprise. Only the traveller in Italy or the Mediterranean who has seen (and therefore saved) such wrappers can have any notion of an art form undreamed of by the fruit-ranchers in Florida or California.

I began by saying that recognition, honor and acclaim have by now come to Tschichold. I consider it an honor for my country to have been the first in such recognition, when in 1954 the American Institute of Graphic Arts here awarded him its gold medal—the first such award to a Continental European. He is an honorary member of the Double Crown Club of London, and of the Société Typographique de France. When in 1965 the city of Leipzig celebrated its 800th birthday it awarded him its Gutenberg Prize, the highest European award for typography. And in June 1965 the Royal Society of Arts in London conferred on him the distinction of Honorary Royal Designer for Industry (Hon. R.D.I.), "for outstanding contributions as a typographer and book designer," making him the first Swiss artist to receive this award.

When in May 1966 he addressed the International Week of Typography at the Gutenberg Museum in Mainz, he confined himself to what he called the three needs of bookmaking: (1) indention for each paragraph save the first—and this he deems equally essential in a letter to a friend; (2) avoidance of formats large or ungainly in size, and of square formats generally; and (3) avoidance of white or glossy-white papers where at all possible. These all seem modest enough requirements. Even if we add his permissive symmetric and asymmetric typography it is hard to understand why such simple rules to preserve traditional printing practices should have been criticized as doctrinaire and even dictatorial. Perhaps his critics feel reproached by the common sense of his teachings, and so have come to regret their own gullibility in having plumped, in their own practice, for so much typography-à-la-mode. They can neither forgive him his quick renouncing of his youthful errors, nor come to a like renunciation of their own. He continues to demand of the typographer only a single obligation: so to organize a book as to make its reading easy and pleasant. "Grace in typography," he is convinced, "comes of itself when the compositor brings a certain love to his work. Whoever does not love his work cannot hope that it will please others." Is this a dictator, uttering some doctrinaire gospel? No; it sounds rather like the man whose work I have long admired for its rational care and for its clean, uncluttered design. Recalling that reading is the one remaining pleasure that must be enjoyed in silence, I can salute Jan Tschichold as a designer alert for every method or material that promises to deepen that pleasure. As such, he remains for me a conserver of those practices of the "art preservative" that have survived mere experiment.

Hugh Williamson.

QUALITY IN BOOK PRODUCTION

by Hugh Williamson

I'M PARTICULARLY PROUD to be taking a part in this series, because it is dedicated to the memory of Paul Bennett. Fifteen years ago, Paul spent time and effort on helping me with information and advice about printing types and their use in America. He gave this help not only liberally, but with encouragement and real enthusiasm. Today, whenever I encounter somebody younger and less experienced, who is in need of help, I remember Paul Bennett and *his* way with these things.

Paul was not the only citizen of the United States who gave me help. I also recall, with gratitude, the kindness of William Addison Dwiggins, and I would like to remind you of something he wrote. It appears in his *Extracts from an Investigation into the Physical Properties of Books as They Are at Present Published, Undertaken by the Society of Calligraphers*—1919:

"Mr. B, will you please tell the committee why you printed this book on cardboard?"

"To make it the right thickness. It had to be one inch thick."

"Why that thick, particularly?"

"Because otherwise it wouldn't sell. If a book isn't one inch thick it won't sell."

Hugh Williamson is a printing production executive (Alden Press, Oxford, England), writer and lecturer on printing. He is the author of the definitive *Methods of Book Design* (Oxford University Press). Lecture given September 20, 1967.

"Do you mean to say that people who buy books, select them with the help of a foot rule?"

"They have to have some standard of selection."

"So that it is your practice to stretch out the text, if it is too short, by printing it on egg box stock?"

"Not my practice, particularly. All publishers do it. We're obliged to use this and other means to bring the book up to a proper thickness. You must remember, that our prices aren't based on the contents of a book but on its size."

"You mention other methods. Would you mind telling us what other methods you use?"

"We can expand the letterpress—judiciously. We limit the matter to . . . seven words on a page, say, and so get a greater number of pages. We can use large type, and can lead—considerably."

"But doesn't that practice hurt the appearance of the page? Make a poor-looking page?"

"I'm afraid I don't get your meaning."

"I mean to say, isn't the page ugly and illegible, when you expand the matter to that extent?"

"You don't consider the look of a page in making a book. That's a thing that doesn't enter into the production of a book. If I understand you correctly, do you mean to say that it matters how a book looks?"

"That was the thought in my mind."

"That's a new idea in book publishing."

[The Dwiggins "Investigation" was first published under copyright, 1919, by L. B. Siegfried; it was reprinted in Paul A. Bennett's *Mss. by WAD*, Typophiles, 1947, and in Mr. Bennett's collection, *Books and Printing* (World, 1951; paper, 1963).]

I remind you of Mr. B's testimony of nearly fifty years ago, because it was not then, and is not now, the view of an imaginary enemy of good work. It's perfectly possible for a capable man to hold sensible and consistent opinions which oppose quality in book production. And oppose it successfully; and win the day.

Another witness in the Investigation is recorded as having told the Committee that "a book could have a good title-page as cheaply as a bad one."

I expect you remember the tale about the great Duke of Wellington. This fearsome old man, wearing the full-dress regimentals of a Field

Marshal—cloak, sword, plumes, medals, stars, chains and ribbons every inch—was walking across Green Park, from some freak-out at Buckingham Palace to his house at Hyde Park Corner. And he was stopped by a man who raised his hat and said, "Mr. Smith, I believe?" The Duke turned upon him the face which in its time had terrified an army, and said, in the voice which had launched the Guards at Waterloo, "Sir, if you believe that, you will believe anything!"

If anybody believes that quality is as cheap as rubbish, he must have little experience of book production, and even less of costing. A man who can design a good title page will probably cost more to employ than a man who can't. A printer who invests in a good range of typefaces, and uses them with meticulous accuracy, costs more than a printer who doesn't. Paper which deserves good type, well arranged and well printed, costs more than egg box stock.

I'm told the *Bowker Annual* shows that in 1965 the production of adult trade books by "general" American publishers—those covered in an industry survey—cost on average 39.5 cents per dollar of sales. In these firms, the profits before Federal income taxes average 10.6 cents per dollar of sales.

Now let's suppose that one of these publishers engages you or me to jack up the quality of his book production from mediocre to good. Perhaps he's been blackballed for membership in the AIGA or something. The company has no qualified staff, so you take on a first-class free-lance designer. You get in touch with the kind of printer who until then would have reckoned it uneconomic even to inquire after this particular publisher's ulcer. You gather together the publisher's entire inventory of paper—little of it being fit to feed pigs with—you deliver it to a warehouse somewhere in the sticks, and you arrange for a disastrous fire. You improve the materials and methods of your bookbinding so radically that the books get a better-than-ever chance of holding together after being read the first time. Your designing friend spreads his talent from the spine round the front board and the back, and over the staining of the edges to the headband. And these little adjustments are likely to increase the cost of your production by 5 percent or more.

I don't think these adjustments would necessarily bring about any increase in sales which you could prove to be a result of this physical change in your books; and even if they did, the editorial and sales people would certainly claim the credit. I don't think the firm would increase its prices by 5 percent; from 1964 to 1965, the publishers surveyed increased the average price of their adult trade books by only 3½ percent.

So your work on behalf of your company has increased costs by 5 percent, while sales and published prices have not increased proportionately. So your production cost rises from 39.5 to 41.5 cents per dollar of sales. So the profit before taxes goes down by 2 cents. And *that* is almost 20 percent of the profit.

A production man is said to look after a sackful of his employers' money. If a publisher sells a $1,000,000 worth of books a year, his production man is likely to be spending $400,000 a year. Profit-chopping, by 20 percent or any other percent you can see, is what he is paid *not* to do.

Fortunately for those of us who have *surreptitiously* carried out this operation in the past, this 5 percent increase may not be very conspicuous in the company's accounts; anyway, not in a form which can be dumped on the production man's doorstep. The burden is one which is dumped on the production man's *conscience*.

It goes without saying, that if the board of directors decides to nail the company's flag to the mast of good quality book production, as Alfred Knopf did long ago, that is another matter entirely. But my own experience has been that such changes tend to be brought about by a production man. And he would sooner sell his grandmother to the salt mines than ask his directors to spend more money on production. Almost all I remember of my Latin lessons is that you begin with *Nonne, Num* or *Ne* when you ask a question expecting the answer *No!*

Of course, there are fields of publishing in which quality does support sales. In the difficult years immediately after World War II, for example, the London publishers Thames and Hudson achieved a triumph in the marketing of art books with color illustrations. This triumph was based on standards of color reproduction which now are familiar enough, but which then only the formidable Doctor Neurath could have imposed upon his reluctant engravers and printers. Some of the states in the U.S.A. insist, in great detail, on minimum standards of layout and material in the textbooks they buy; so a badly produced book might have no sale at all. But I don't think we can maintain, because of this, that good quality sells more books over the whole field.

Some years ago, I was able to make some changes in the production of books by Graham Greene, Anthony Powell and J. B. Priestley, among others. People were good enough to take the view that these changes were for the better, even radically for the better. These authors published a book a year, more or less, and the sales performance of their edition showed a clear pattern. I didn't observe—and it wasn't for lack of looking—any change in this pattern which I could reasonably claim resulted from the different way in which their books were being made.

It's certainly possible to put up a better economic justification for good production than this one I've given. For instance, it was my *company's* decision to employ a production man who was notably interested in quality. Having taken him on, the company was entitled to expect only his best work. The increase in setting cost which I loaded on to Graham Greene's books was chicken feed in the context of his enormous editions. But economic ground is not the foothold on which I would choose to fight for quality in book production. I think it's slippery ground; it's a vulnerable position.

After a week in the U.S.A., I'm pretty sure that practitioners here have no cause to believe the battle is won. I'm quite certain the battle is far from won, whether here, or in Britain, or anywhere else. I'm quite certain the bad times are likely to come again. Perhaps events are going to remind us of the salty evidence of Mr. G before the Society of Calligraphers:

"What's the use of talking about standards in connection with things like *these?* These aren't books, they aren't fit to wad a gun with. I wouldn't have them in the house. . . . There aren't more than half a dozen presses in the country that know how to print. Most printing looks as if it had been done with apple butter on a hay press. . . ."

I don't mean we are apt to return to the situation of fifty years ago, when Dwiggins wrote these words. I do mean that we may find ourselves advancing into a situation of a kind different from that, and different from today's situation. The state of affairs I visualize is one we would all dislike, just as much as Mr. G disliked his. I don't think we have any reason for satisfaction with the present, or for optimism about the future. Let me give you an example.

Science is growing and advancing at a rate which is really astounding. Each new form of science requires not only existing forms of expression but also new forms of expression not previously seen in print. Everybody knows that we in Britain are lousy at languages; but a proportion—and a rapidly growing proportion—of our people are today using a second language in their work—the language of mathematics. This part of our people publishes and reads a far higher volume of printing than the general run of our citizens. The setting of type of calculus and similar mathematics is just about the most abstruse task a printer can be called upon to undertake—apart from arguing with the unions. A printer who takes it on needs to graduate through whole strata of difficulty of other kinds, such as complicated tabular composition. He needs to have behind him machinery suppliers who develop and maintain stores of thousands of matrices for special purposes. Meeting these requirements is going to be one of the most vital duties of the book printing industry in the next ten years—not vital to the printing industry, perhaps, but certainly vital to scientific progress.

I've been trying to think of the word, like Anglophile and Francophile, that stands for admiration of things American. I'm sure there is one, but it's curious that it doesn't come to mind. Anyway, whatever the word is, I *am* one. I think the writings of Theodore Lowe De Vinne and of Daniel Berkeley Updike, for example, are the best things of their kind that have ever been done.

I've also absorbed the impression—and it may be a false or *blind* impression—that the printing industry in the States is not developing in directions that will support the advance of the various sciences. There's a great deal going on here which has left Britian some way back. Your process photography for example; your camera work in offset printing; your paper; above all, perhaps, the extent of the professional book designer's influence on book production. All these are enviable advances. In general terms, American technology is in advance of ours. So it's particularly surprising to get this feeling, that if things go on as they are doing, British printers may perform a better service to the growth of scientific publication than American printers. Perhaps I'm quite wrong about this. But if I'm right, it can hardly be a satisfactory situation for scientists and publishers in the States.

Now I want to talk about book production as an activity, regardless of national boundaries. I may not succeed, but that's what I want to do.

First of all, we're all agreed that a really well-made book doesn't turn out that way by chance. Among other things, it takes skill. Now, some skill isn't enough; and one person's skill is nowhere near enough. You need a lot of skill, and you need to have it spread around pretty widely. This is still not enough; the skill has got to be applied.

The cost of time is the enemy of first-class work. I was a publisher's production manager for enough years to find out where the pressures hurt most. There really is a very great deal to do, and a very high proportion of it is urgent. You have to meet schedules, you have to get your estimates right, you have to give instructions so comprehensive that you cover nearly all the possibilities of something going wrong. Nobody has ever covered all the possibilities, but you can try. Besieged by visitors, surrounded by telephones all ringing at the same time, buried under great mounds of typescript, proofs, artwork and complaints from the vice-president's favorite author, the production man has to clear a little corner in space and time to dream up the style of the book's typography, and sketch it out in such a way that a man he's never met will understand what he's after. In the face of all this, you need real determination, if you're going to deliver the editions at the right time and at the right cost, and still see to it that every copy in every edition is as well-made as lies in you to make it.

I'd go further than this. From my own experience, I'd also say that the circumstances have to be right. Not ideal, perhaps, or even easy, but adequately right. You may know how to do good work, and you may be determined to do nothing that isn't good work. You still need allies within your organization, and a market that your company can manage.

I don't think even this is enough. I think you even need allies outside your own organization. The forces opposing good quality work, in the printing and publishing trades and in every other kind of trade, add up to a lot of pressure. We need to confront them with some kind of corporate pressure in favor of good work. If each of us gets his own problems licked, he's done a good job; if he contributes something to other people, of a like mind, to getting their problems licked, he's done much more than a good job.

Now I'll try to summarize the points at which, in my belief, some corporate pressure of the kind I've mentioned might help quality in book production to survive. And this may be the best point for me to say what I mean by quality. The highest quality in book production, in my view, is accuracy, consistency and faithfulness of reproduction, of both text and illustration. Good proportions; orderly arrangement; sound materials honestly used; clarity; and grace—these are high qualities in book production. But let's never lose sight of the purpose of our work, which is to communicate, not to impress.

Let's go back to the imaginary situation I was talking about some time back. You were called in to help a publisher produce his books better.

You've set fire to his paper and wrecked his profits, and you'll need to do some pretty good work if you—and he—are going to survive the holocaust. You'll need to have a system of book production administration that runs like a sewing-machine, if you're going to produce books at the right time, at the right cost, and above all of the right quality. When you try to set up this system, you are likely to find out, if you haven't done so already—and I have found this out for myself—that an oasis of efficiency can't live in the midst of a desert of incompetence. In publishing, for example, if the company's general management, and above all its editorial department if it's separate from the management, if these parts of the firm aren't functioning as well as you want your book production to function, you can't do a good job. A good job isn't the same as a good effort. Efficiency means actually working well, not trying to work well. However we judge other people, we have to judge ourselves by results.

So my first point is this. Getting together to talk about all this is something done; writing articles and books for the converted is something else done. But what's needed most is to formulate a case for good bookmaking which will come home to general management.

People tend to talk about management as though it were all a deep-laid plot to make them absolutely miserable. That isn't management, it's bad management; Lord knows it exists, but let's not give it the wrong name. It's a part of good management to set up the circumstances of our work in such a way that each of us looks forward to getting back to the office after the night at home.

We need to convince the general management of our organizations that our companies should be places where there is leeway enough for good work to be done. We need to be able to spend enough money on the right suppliers and the right materials. We need enough staff—heaven *knows*—we need enough staff! We need the quality of the books we produce to be a matter of pride to the firm as a whole. One year, long ago, I produced every week a set of specimen settings of forthcoming books, and placed them before the board of directors at the weekly meeting. In that year, not one of them made any comment. I used to meditate the possibility of setting the chapter title one way up and the text the other, but I don't think they'd have noticed.

Second point: In book production, both as a publisher and as a printer, I seem to spend a lot of time sorting out queries about the text. In fact, I've spent quite a bit of time actually writing odd parts of books—nobody ever noticed, I'm glad to say. Now this, surely, is the editor's job; it's for him to establish a correct text, and make sure that it gets correctly printed. My experience has been that some editors have to spend so much time flinging out the nets to catch unwary authors that they never get round to caring much about little items such as spelling and punctuation—let alone the headings in scientific and technical books, which so far as I can see are usually written by dervishes.

We're coming to a time when the long training in spelling and punctuation and such-like which the printing industry imposes on its entrants may no longer be applied to book composition. Keyboarding is by no means the same as typewriting, but it could become very like it if we don't watch out. A good printer's composing room applies to manuscripts a consistency and a correctness in detail which are a very real aid to clear communication. Here again, I'm glad to say, nobody notices very much. When the printer doesn't do this any more, they'll notice all right, but perhaps they won't care.

If *we* care about this particular quality in books—and I for one believe it to be among the most important qualities of books—we have to make sure the publishers' editors care too. Marking up copy, to severe and even scholarly standards of consistency and correctness, is less exciting than chasing lady authors round the corridors of the Algonquin, but in the long run it matters far more. I'm working on this point myself, and hope next year to write at least part of a manual to show how these matters can be regulated.

I don't want to be nasty about editors. But I do think this business of the consistency and clarity of the text should be their first concern, and I don't think that in all publishing outfits it is.

Third point: The training of book designers. This is quite a big subject, but there are three matters only that I'd like to put forward, under this heading.

In my view, the appreciation of printing types and their successful selection are best based on instruction in the practice of lettering and hand-writing of the formal kind. When you've *made* letters with care, you know how they ought to be. Edward Johnston's book should be on the desk of every typographer, and all subsequent manuals should be compared with his before being relied on.

The apprentice book designer should not be allowed to suppose that his artistic sensibility is going to see him through. Book design is an ancient form of industrial design, and it has accumulated a pretty impressive body of literature. Much of this literature is American, and I suppose most of it is out of print. Books I recommended in print—in my own book—include De Vinne's *Practice of Typography*, published in 1904; Goudy's *Typologia*, 1940; Bruce Rogers' *Paragraphs on Printing*.

This study of the literature is particularly important in the States, because you don't have here the availability of historic printing that Europe can offer. There is a fine show of manuscripts and incunabula at the Morgan Library just now, and in general wealthy people have brought over here some of the finest books ever made. But we in Europe can pick up slightly tattered examples of not particularly rare old books, without being wealthy. I once bought from a barrow, for twenty-five shillings, a book printed in 1513 by Aldus Manutius, in the first of all italic typefaces. From the same barrow at another time, for five shillings, I got the large octavo prayer book which Baskerville printed in 1762. And from another barrow, my wife bought for one shilling and six-pence, or about twenty cents, a tiny and exquisite book of verse printed in roman and italic types by Bodoni in 1792.

Whether from books, or from examples of printing, or best of all from both, we can learn all we need to know. Many of us, including myself, have had no training in design. We need to bear in mind that eloquent passage in Updike's *Some Aspects of Printing* (Rudge, 1941):

"It seems to me that a right taste is cultivated in printing, as in other forms of endeavor, by knowing what has been done in the past, and what has been so esteemed that it has *lived*. If a man examines master-pieces of printing closely, he will begin to see why they were thought masterpieces, and in what the mastery lay. He will perceive that all great printing possesses certain qualities in common; that these qualities may be transferable in some slight degree to his own problems. And then he will find himself braced and stimulated, into clearer, simpler views of what he can make out of his task. When he sees the books that have delighted all generations, and begins to comprehend why they were great pieces of typography, he is beginning to train his taste. It is a process, which once begun, is fed from a thousand sources, and need never end."

In speaking of book designers, I don't think we should think only of publishers. Book printing is becoming more and more diverse, and technically more and more abstruse. There may come a time when the publisher's designer will have to keep his eye on the editorial, the visual, aspects of design, and leave much of the technical planning to the printer. It may be all but impossible for the designer to know all he needs to know about the techniques and machines that are going to be used. If this does come about, the printer should know more than he tends to know now about the requirements of good design. He should be ready to meet the publisher's designer halfway or better. I don't, however, believe that the control of book design should ever be allowed to fall into the printer's hands.

We shall still get nowhere without my fourth point: If quality work is not in demand, it withers away. If any publisher knows a printer whose quality is entirely satisfactory, let that publisher foster that printer. Let there be patience and clear instructions about schedules and information. If the printer isn't talented on this point, let the publisher persevere to make him so, not turn to other firms who may be cheaper and slicker but don't print so well. Good work does cost more than bad; but costs (and I don't mean prices) can be attacked by a steady flow of well-planned work. Prices will follow costs downwards, or at least remain a bit steadier than would otherwise be possible. Leonard Shatzkin has been writing articles bearing on this point, in *Publishers' Weekly*.

Let me close with another quotation from Updike. I have already used it to close a speech and even a book, but I for one am still not tired of what he wrote: "The practice of typography, if it be followed faithfully, is hard work—full of detail, full of drudgery; and not greatly rewarded, as men now count rewards. There are times, when we need to bring to it, all the history and art and feeling that we can, to make it bearable. But in the light of history and of art, and of knowledge and of man's achievement, it is as interesting a work as exists—a broad and humanizing employment, which can indeed be followed merely as a trade; but which, if perfected into an art, or even broadened into a profession, will perpetually open new horizons to our eyes, and new opportunities to our hands." [Daniel Berkeley Updike, *Printing Types: Their History, Form, and Use*, Vol. II, © 1922, 1937, Harvard University Press.]

Fernand Baudin.

TYPOGRAPHY—
EVOLUTION AND
REVOLUTION

by Fernand Baudin

FEWER AND FEWER people use the term "typography" to signify specific techniques for the cutting of punches, the striking of matrices, the casting, the composing and printing of type. It is now commonly used in graphic art magazines to cover the whole field of visual communications: traffic signals, pictographs, symbols and posters as well as newspaper layout, advertising, or, eventually, book typography. If "typography" is no longer to imply punches and so forth, what then could and should it stand for? I suggest that the real, the proper meaning implied should be "the multiplication of copies." Indeed, I take it as self-evident from everything we know about Gutenberg, Fust and Schoeffer, that these greatest of communication experts were primarily concerned with the multiplication of texts and not with creating any number or kind of new letter signs or symbols. If anything, they tended to reduce their numbers, and for very practical economic reasons. They were content with reproducing, multiplying whatever letter designs there were. Nor were they primarily concerned with aesthetics. They started their technological revolution by designing a Bible that just

Fernand Baudin of Belgium is a typographic designer and writer on typographic subjects, consultant to Culture et Civilisation, Brussels publishers, lecturer at leading art schools in Belgium and France, and European review editor of the *Journal of Typographic Research*. Lecture given November 1, 1967.

looked and read like a Bible. And we all know that they had enough artistic sensibility and tact to choose the best among any number of appropriate handwritings for their common purpose, or rather for the common purpose and pursuit of their hoped-for customers.

Today, typography is a technology that we are outgrowing. New technologies are emerging to serve the same purpose: multiplying copies of what is essentially *writing*. (I shall have more to say about this later on.) At this stage, allow me to insert an interpolation: I can see no point in minimizing or exalting our present technological progress. That it is progress, at least in its own technological context, I do not wish to question. However, I do wish to point to a fast-growing discrepancy and disproportion between the fantastic technological apparatus for multiplying any kind of communication, and the intrinsic—scientific or otherwise—value of the so-called message.

(On the other hand, it would be a mistake to suppose that technology is the sole revolutionary element. Let us be reminded that sometime in the first two centuries A.D., the scroll was superseded by the codex. There is too little factual information to warrant any comment upon the why and how of this revoluton. But, in its way, a revolution it was: it made for more transportable books, easier to consult for study and reference, for the introduction of critical apparatus and for propaganda. The Christians were not the last to avail themselves of the advantages of this new book form.)

The indiscriminate use of this word typography has had some nasty consequences. I shall cite three examples:

(1) For more than thirty years eminent graphic artists, practitioners as well as theoreticians, have been advocating a universal letter type, and, eventually, their own tentative version of it. Somehow they failed to win universal acceptance. This has nothing to do with any question about their talent, nor with the graphic qualities of their projects. Others, no less eminent in theory and in practice, urge the necessity for proper, competent, i.e., aesthetic new signs and symbols of their own making, to meet the growing demand in scientific and not-so-scientific communications. And all this, of course, in the name of Progress, Evolution, Revolution and the overthrowing of the language barrier.

I wish them well, for we are all interested in their success, even if it is not for the same reasons. Yet we must perforce admit that, with or without the help of specialists, new symbols have been invented, ever

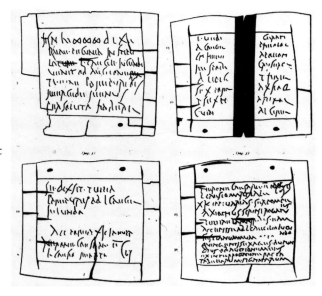

A quittance, 57 A.D., for 3,480 sesterces; three tablets bound by seals. The arrangement is part of the information.

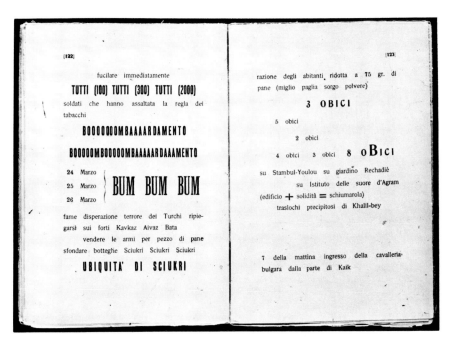

Pages from *Zang Tumb Tumb* by Marinetti, 1912; "poets and futurists should be free to indulge their wildest extravaganzas. . . ."

since writing was invented. And that not only scientists, but also dancers (as choreographers), musicians (traditional or otherwise), customs officers (who, in France at least, are responsible for road signs), sailors (with semaphore and Morse alphabets) and so on, have been and will tend to be dispensing with the assistance of designers.

(2) These two widely diverging tendencies, the one towards a universal alphabet, the other towards the multiplying of graphic symbols, appear to me as a perfect example of a circuitous argument; so circuitous that wherever you enter the typographic merry-go-round, one thing only is certain, that each side feels it is on the road to Progress, by evolution or revolution.

Where and why does the argument start circling? No doubt because the word typography has been used improperly. The result in this case is a mistaken view, a confusion, between the province of linguistics and the province of graphic art. With all respect and reverence where they are due, even the greatest artists are bound to make mistakes when they fail to put the horse before the cart, and especially when they wish to rush in where linguists fear to tread.

In other words, as Charles Peignot pointed out last year, a language is first created or just exists as a linguistic system. Only afterwards can it be written, drawn, painted, designed, multiplicated, etc., with more or less talent by various scriveners, graphic artists or calligraphers. In language, then, it is the abstract relatedness of abstract functions, not the visual aspect, that matters primarily.

(3) Before pointing out a third consequence of the indiscriminate use of the word typography, I may as well, at this point, state clearly what I am driving at. What I called the circuitous argument, the typographic merry-go-round, results in fact from a mistaken view about the true nature and function of writing and technology. Writing is not primarily a graphic art but a social function, while typography is not primarily an art either, but a technological means to accelerate and multiply writing in its social function.

Here, the subject of research is involved. How did psychologists get themselves into a blind alley where legibility is concerned? Thinking that the main issue was the design, the shape of the individual letters or alphabets, they have been researching for three quarters of a century. Their conclusion is that there is no significant difference in the relative legibility of any set of printing types designed to fulfill an identical function and compared under the same conditions of light, distance, etc. This will not surprise anyone more or less familiar with palaeography, or, for that matter, with the history of type. Any consistent system of standardized alphabetic or other signs can be made legible, readable and beautiful as well. And the how-to-do-it of legibility is something that any scribe or composer can master.

I don't mean to suggest that psychological research is worthless. One significant and practical result of psychological research is to be seen in the use of perforated tape for computer setting, obtained through due analysis of the operator's mental process while reading his copy and composing on the machine. Nor do I suggest that legibility at the composer's level is all there is to readability, and that, as a consequence, we could dispense with anyone else for the adequate treatment of copy.

It is also evident to me, as it is to all of us, that the aesthetic aspect of typography is quite properly the concern of typographers. But, it is only fair to add that there are other aspects as well. Indeed, many competent people have addressed themselves to the economic and technical aspects of typography. But scarcely anyone has ever inquired into the social function and significance of *writing* proper as distinct from any technology or calligraphy. (I know only of one exception: Istvan Hajnal: *L'enseignement de l'écriture aux universités médiévales*, Budapest, 1959, Maison d'édition de l'Académie des Sciences de Hongrie—to whom I am deeply indebted.)

We have no statements whatever from Gutenberg. One may only wonder if it would have occurred to him to inquire into legibility. But it may be taken for granted that he cared a lot about the social function of writing—so much so that he toiled for years and years, spending fortunes, eventually, to invent typography. It is quite obvious that there were, to say the least, as many different styles in handwriting in his time as there are different styles of printing types now. He had to make a choice. And we know that he made no mistake about that. He chose the most adequate letters for his Bible, Psalters, Indulgences. Adequate, here, means not just legible or beautiful but socially acceptable. And it is clear that this was perfectly congruent with any aesthetic considerations. Why should it be different in our time and with our technology?

All this is familiar ground indeed. It would also be trite to recount even briefly all that has been said about the impact of printing on the diffusion of knowledge and for that matter on the mind of man. Where

POIGNANT, ANTE (*pouà-gnan*, encore *po-gnan* au XIXᵉ s., in LITTRÉ). *adj.* (« Pointu » vers 1138 ; fig. au XIIIᵉ s. ; anc. p. prés. de *poindre*, « piquer »).

‖ **1°** *Vx.* Qui point, pique (Cf. BUFFON, in LITTRÉ).

« A cet instant du solstice, la lumière du plein midi est, pour ainsi dire, poignante. »   HUGO, Misér., V, I, XVI.   1

‖ **2°** *Fig.* Qui cause une impression très vive, très aiguë (souvent pénible*). V. **Navrant.** *Douleur* poignante* (Cf. Cessation, cit. 2 ; injuste, cit. 4), *Poignante émotion* (Cf. Offrir, cit. 20). *Amour passionné* (cit. 11) *et poignant. Éprouver un brusque et poignant besoin* (cit. 30). *La tentation la plus poignante* (Cf. Frôler, cit. 9). *Visage empreint d'une haine poignante* (Cf. Hideux, cit. 6).

« Elle était douce comme les bêtes gracieuses et agiles aux yeux   2
profonds, et troublait comme, au matin, le souvenir poignant et
vague de nos rêves. »   PROUST, Plaisirs et jours, p. 62.

« ... comme le captif qui, comptant les derniers jours et sachant   3
que bientôt ses chaines vont tomber, regarde soudain avec une
émotion poignante les murs de sa cellule... »
                                          DUHAM., Salavin, V, II.

— *Une scène poignante*, très émouvante, à la fois prenante et dramatique*. *Lecture poignante et exaltante* (cit. 1). *Poignants contrastes* (cit. 8). *Les réalités poignantes de la vie* (Cf. Fil, cit. 36). *Des adieux poignants, déchirants.* — *C'est poignant, cela perce, serre* le cœur.*

« Il y a quelque chose de plus poignant à voir brûler qu'un palais,   4
c'est une chaumière. Une chaumière en feu est lamentable. La dévas-
tation s'abattant sur la misère, le vautour s'acharnant sur le ver de
terre, il y a là on ne sait quel contresens qui serre le cœur. »
                              HUGO, Quatre-vingt-treize, I, IV, VII.

ABOVE   Entries for a single word in a dictionary may come out as a jumble unless the designer or printer has a sense of format.

Hajnal opened new fields for research was in insisting on the social importance of plain writing, not as calligraphy nor as typography, but as a mental process and as a social function.

The very intention to put a thought on paper affects the thinking process—determines a mental attitude of its own. It fosters rational thought. Even irrational thoughts take on and communicate some rationality through the process of being translated and transferred into written form—because writing itself, as such, is essentially a system of standardized signs, which stand for one or many more languages. One would, further, take an incomplete view of writing, readability and communication, if one relied only on the letters or signs, while neglecting their arrangement, the total form and design of the text matter as a whole book, diploma, or whatever. This total view, this overall arrangement, affects the impact, the meaning, and probably gives a better, fuller, expression of the whole social context than the forms and style of the individual signs.

Surely, written thought and language are utterly distinct from spoken language in the several ways they affect—and are affected by—the whole of their social context. Wherever writing is applied it tends to rationalize at least that sector of society where it is applied—not least in that it preserves (however temporarily) the present; creates a link with the past (however near); and contributes to the shaping of the future (however short its proximity). And this on the smallest individual, local, tribal scale as well as on the largest, the universal, scale.

Therefore, a proper subject for research, for study—not necessarily or exclusively historic—would be how and why various societies or groups handle their writing—what they choose to put on record and how they arrange their records (commercial, legal, religious); what status they give their scribes—slaves or mandarins or priests; how they came to prefer any special format and with what kind of practical or other results; what is the final outcome, visually, to be sure, but also socially and practically; and how the effects were felt inside the society or group under study and on its more or less distant neighbors.

It should be apparent that any single individual, however great his personal talent and endowments, is dependent on society, on writing, and not conversely—at least not on a comparable scale. It should be even more obvious that writing, seen in this light, as a method of rational, standardized thought, has proved itself more efficient as an agent of social progress than any oral tradition so far.

There is, further, no obvious reason why writing and printing should have developed as they did in our countries rather than as they did in other countries.

There is at least a chance that the presentation, the scaling up or down of the various parts of a whole piece of writing, printed or not, may be more important and socially significant than the design of any individual hand or letter style.

By the way, as a check, let me point to the fact that, with unfailing instinct, the first thing the overall subversive Dada movement assailed was language and typography, not by turns, but at one and the same time, clearly suggesting that written language is a fundamental aspect of social life.

It may be best to be explicit about what kind of writing I am being so insistent.

Let us call it *common writing*, as distinct from all-too-current or personal lack of consistency, of any degree of style or formality; as distinct also from any all too individualistic calligraphics.

It should also be clear that reason and rationality are not synonymous with rationalism. The kind of rationality I mean is the one that ensures that not only commercial, industrial, juridical, administrative and scientific texts, but even the most irrational ravings of the wildest enthusiasts and egotists are made systematically legible and protected by copyright.

And this leads me to remark, by the way, that any culture, however irrational its subject or import, tends towards a rational expression. The measure of its success as a culture is exactly the measure of the degree of rationality it achieves in its expression. Therefore there cannot be a fundamental clash between two or more cultures, but only an emotional clash between two or more exponents of diverse aspects of culture.

What are the eventual consequences of my insistence on the social meaning of writing? How is writing to be affected by our new technologies? Are we confronted with an evolution or a revolution? And where? How is technology going to affect writing as such? At present and in the near future?

In the first place there is no obvious reason why technology should spell disaster for writing. Writing was not debased by typography. Typography somehow took over a scriptorial tradition. It left us a heritage that is already put to profit by the new technology, so that the technological revolution does not in fact deflect in any sense the scriptorial evolution. As to the problems of communications, as far as language is concerned, the overthrowing of the language barriers is not properly a job for graphic artists. Whether the linguists are going to make it is another question. Let us hope that they know what they can possibly do about it. In any case, the roman alphabet is gaining ground. The question is whether it is wise for any one, graphist or linguist, to interfere with this.

It is natural that the alphabetic symbols fall short of meeting the needs of scientific communication. They were not made or intended to do that in the first place. It is no less obvious that scientists, dancers and customs officers do not care as much as they should for the aesthetic designs of their signs.

This is no reason for graphic artists to be obsessed with these scientific or other symbols. Common language, common writing, cannot afford to be neglected. However important it is in our society, scientific language is *not* going to supersede ordinary speech nor written language. Our society as it is, like any society, depends far more on common language and communications than on any specialized use of symbols—for the simple reason that without common language there is no society, and without society, there is no art, no science, no technology, no commerce, no industry, no law, no administration.

Writing is so familiar, so matter of fact, that we fail to realize that it is the very complex product, the end achievement of generations of mostly learned and specialized people. The last among the learned were the humanists. They were steeped in reverence for language and its written form and expression. As our culture grew more and more scientific and less and less philologic, learned men, i.e. scientists and even philologists, ceased to be interested in writing and typography.

For years, the bulk of written communications has been no longer printed but typewritten. There is every sign, by now, that the multiplying of copies is going to be moved from typographic shoulders to the shoulders of typists. Whatever else this may entail, it calls for at least as much attention as the designing of new symbols. Indeed the question arises: can we expect more attention and interest by executives and typists, when scientists fail to give any sign of it? Especially when indifference to plain language (spoken language, let alone writing) is already giving cause for alarm in the universities?

Since some things, especially those we call *cultural*, do not, by definition, take care of themselves, I suggest that some consideration be given to the training of many more people, operators and typists, in composition skills. This will probably happen as a matter of course. I also suggest that the designing of common written language, of writing as an intellectual discipline, as part and parcel of a mental process that needs education and culture, be taught at the university level. There are cogent reasons for that.

In the first place, the scriptorial tradition that typography transmitted was the product of the medieval and renaissance universities. Writing was taught at Bologna until the XVI century at least.

Now, our technology is already experimenting with machines that will some day be able to decipher handwritten messages—not scrawls, but disciplined, standardized symbols. This may be a technological revolution. But it calls for a new scriptorial evolution. What we need, then, is not a flashback to medieval times, but a new scriptorial tradition. To instruct more people in the composer's ability, as I said, will not do. Legibility, readability are not enough. These are not just calligraphic achievements. Because writing is not just orderliness in the transcription of signs, in the proper execution of a manual task. Writing is a way of thinking, a mental attitude. Only when thought is formed, constructed in an orderly way, can a corresponding orderliness be found and given to its transcription, to its layout, to its design. The layout itself then is not primarily an aesthetic consideration, but a psychologic and intellectual discipline. This is more than can be expected from typists or from operators.

It should be clear that such a complex subject as writing as an instrument for rational thought and social organization should not be confined to any kind of specialized publication, whether graphic or scientific. It calls for the cooperation of specialists in many branches of linguistics, communication, psychology, history, technology. That would be in itself quite a revolution!

Beatrice Warde.

TYPOGRAPHY—ART OR EXERCISE

by Beatrice Warde

I wANT to thank Doctor Bob for suggesting the title of this talk, the sort of end-of-term talk which, at this festive season, ought to have a little more informality and at the same time a little wider range than a scholarly lantern-slide lecture. So I seized upon this opportunity with pleasure as a sort of double thread upon which I could string certain pearls of memory from my fifty years of association with typography. To be apt for this famous Heritage series, those memories would have to be of moments when I was conscious that something was being handed over to me by some master whom I revered; something being "passed on" as a kind of legacy from the immediate past that would be worthy of my passing on in turn.

There is something thrilling in that very notion of receiving by inheritance ideas and discoveries and the fruits of experience—or even the physical objects which exemplify the beliefs and convictions which pass to us as precious legacies. For when we do that we are using a power which is unique to Man: the very faculty by which he climbed up out of the animal kingdom of Nature into his own human nature. Of all the hundreds of thousands of species of living animals there is only

Beatrice Warde (1900–1969), writer, lecturer, eloquent promoter of print, in 1927 became editor of the *Monotype Recorder* in England. Her writings are sampled in *The Crystal Goblet* (World, 1965) and the *Monotype Recorder*, Vol. 44, No. 1, Autumn 1970. Lecture given December 18, 1968. Edited by C.B.G. from her partially written text and a recording of the lecture.

one, *homo sapiens*, who breaks the iron rule of Nature, that you cannot "inherit acquired characteristics." If you take a pair of mice and paint them blue and cut off their tails and breed them, and do the same for a thousand generations, the thousandth litter will still be mouse-colored with long tails. But if you take a male and female member of the species *homo sapiens* and teach them some blue language, and cut off their respect for history, and then let them breed, you will find that the very first generation of their offspring is using blue language and showing the crippling effects of being robbed of the power to learn from the mistakes and achievements of their forebears.

So in preparing this talk I looked specially for those memories in which I was being handed something precious—an idea, or a physical object symbolizing the convictions and beliefs behind it—something that I could take as a valuable legacy or heritage, and something which might throw some light on the question we are asking ourselves here: Shall we look upon typography as an exercise in design—presumably an exercise in the smooth transference of ideas from mind to mind through the visible word—or is there any other sense in which it can be called an art?

That question has been exercising me ever since the day, many years ago, when my friend and former colleague Peggy Lang said casually in conversation, "But printing isn't an art, it's a craft." I was so taken aback by that that I could only riposte, "Printing is not a craft, it's an industry." That, of course, is only an example of the jiu-jitsu of debate, where you use the opponent's thrust to topple him over. But I was so shaken that I pulled out the "A" volume of the great *Oxford English Dictionary* and read right through those three folio pages of triple-column small print in which are set forth the seventeen distinct senses in which you can use the word "art." When I had done that I decided that printing must be one of the "of" arts, like the art of conversation or the art of cooking or what they teach debutantes, the art of entering a room: something that *must* be done with skill and know-how, and *can* be done with graciousness and pride.

But—up at the very beginning of that long entry was the etymological note on the origin of the word "art," and there I found something that made my eyes pop, for it seemed to have an unexpected bearing on the nature of typography. I want to put it to you in the form of a riddle: *Can you see the connection between the word "art" and the word "arthritis"?*

If not, look again, for it's staring you in the face. Arthritis, as some of us know to our cost, is the name for an inflammation of the joints, and it uses the ancient root *ar—*, "to fit," going on to *art*, "skill." Now we'll come back to that very ancient word for "joint," the Greek *arthros*, and you see how it diffuses into the idea of "joining"—fitting together. Now who was the first man whose skill at fitting together and joining was literally a matter of life and death? It was of course the armorer; because if your armor didn't fit, the enemy's spear would get through and you were for it! *Arma virumque cano*—but if the *armor* hadn't held, the *man* would not have survived.

Well, that action of skill has been inextricably mixed with the idea of art ever since, and it is possibly the oldest collection of ideas. Meanwhile, men sorted themselves out into layers and were called "civilized," and invented writing. In the greatest *civitas*, that of ancient Rome, they used the word *ars* in an ever widening sense, but with an extraordinarily interesting split down the middle, fragments of which still survive: they distinguished between the servile and the liberal arts.

The "servile arts" were those suitable to be practiced by slaves, and they dealt mainly with material things. The slaves could fit together paving stones, they could join mosaics. Then came the term "liberal arts;" it still survives, but in those days it had teeth in it, because it meant the arts reserved for freemen and freedmen. And those were the verbal arts. The freeman was permitted to join together words into sentences—grammar; to join sentences into syllogisms—logic; and to fit arguments to the audience and to the occasion—rhetoric. These were the *trivia* of the Middle Ages, the three arts of which I who stand before you am a bachelor, as many of you, too, are. This distinction was in existence when printing came in the form of picture printing in the late Middle Ages and when typography came in the form of word printing and ended the Middle Ages. And then, later, at the time of reveille, we have a distinction between the artists, which meant the students at the Sorbonne, and those painters and sculptors and other people who were known as "artisans" in those days.

Well, you know, with that bit of information I was able to comfort a distinguished poet whose stuff appears in *transition* and elsewhere, who was making his living writing copy in an advertising agency, and whose heart had nearly been broken by a fiend in human form whom he referred to as the "art director." It seems that the poet would spend the whole afternoon or day condensing what was really a sixty-word idea into the narrow compass of thirty words. This is an agonizing sort of task which can only be done by a poet or by using the poet's technique, because the poet distills what he has to say, whereas the prose writer spreads it out in his easier and longer manner. Well, having performed this great feat, the poet in question discovered that he was being asked to take out twelve indispensable words from his masterpiece, so that they would fit into something called "the panel," and there be put into extremely repulsive type, as small as possible, by a man who did not read—probably *couldn't* read in any sense that we would use—but who had a very clear idea of the pattern within a rectangle. Well, I was able to comfort the poet by that bit of research of mine, and by pointing out that it was only a couple of centuries ago that the word "artist" got its reference to painting (especially oil painting), drawing, sculpture, and so on, which is now its common, accepted meaning.

If we were to equate art simply with oil painting, as some do, we would have to admit that the artist is the potential enemy of the typographer. Calling in a painter to illustrate a book is very much like calling in a tiger to entertain at dinner. The tiger has its own ideas of what constitutes a good dinner. And the artist has his own primeval and subconscious suspicions and jealousies of the rival method of communication by the code of the phonetic alphabet. You have to keep an illustrator on a very taut leash when he is cavorting on a page that faces text, if he is not to swallow at one bite the attention which you were reserving for the author.

Now I have to speak of some of the rather annoying feats of experimental typography. I only do so in passing because they have been developing tentatively during my fifty years—perhaps more boldly today, but I think that we cannot worry about them. Let me take just a few examples—we can't spend this whole discussion on oddities. One is the fashion or fad, which is certainly not over, for pushing the text so far away from the gutters as to show that all the space which you could have for a margin you had used at the least needed place—namely, the gutter. Then we have to think of the growing fashion for what I call sardine spacing—a natural reaction against the mutton quad after the 4 point quad, but not a healthy reaction at all. It is very much promulgated by those people who say to you, when you object to it as being too thick, not allowing air between the sentences, "Ah, but see how much better the page looks upside down!" I've had that said to me, several times.

And then, of course, there is the nasty custom of setting paragraphs full out, and not indenting the first words, which of course can completely destroy that construct known as a paragraph. A writer can work all evening constructing a good paragraph, which has a beginning, a middle and an end, and which needs before it that breath of slight knowledge that something else is happening, which breaks the thread and starts the next thing. Anyone who sets a paragraph flush is insulting the art of letters and is seeing the thing, as it were, upside down. I have some very nice examples of how that was tried and then withdrawn, hastily and under a heavy fire of protest, both from the authors of articles in certain magazines and from the readers of them, who object to having to discover from the context where the paragraph begins and ends. I'm sorry to say that one of the most interesting examples is the *Penrose Annual* of about two or three years ago, where you have not only the unindented paragraph, you also have unjustified lines and beyond that the determination not to break any words, so that the difficulty of finding out how the author has shaped his article becomes very distracting, and the unjustified pages set forth with such moral fervor show some lines which stick out pugnaciously and other lines which come in, only because that is where the words happen to fall. It represents the defeat of the computerized composing machine because only man can decide where that line comes down on the right hand—which is drawn, and has been since the beginning of printing, in order to give you a chance to write on the margin, which you cannot do with a ragged right-hand margin looking at you.

If this were a lantern-slide lecture, I would have a lot of fun demonstrating some of these eccentricities, and showing how effective they can sometimes be in the sort of printed matter that comes to us free and can be freely thrown away—but how tiresome they can be in the serene framework of the typography of the book, a thing which the reader wants enough to pay money for and to keep. The reading public does vote on the look of its books. Its ballot papers are called "folding green," and it keeps electing what it considers recognizable.

What is the reason behind these irrational practices? I think it is that they were introduced by painters, image-makers, "artists" in the modern sense: people trained in art colleges, people who once dreamed of having one-man shows in galleries, but who later condescended to step down into the graphic arts. At any rate, they have the temperament of the pictorial artist. Now if there is one duty that God has laid upon the

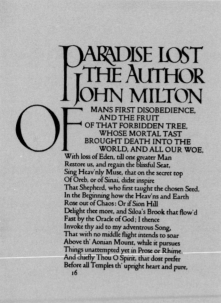

LEFT Doves type, with calligraphy in red, from *Paradise Lost*, Doves Press, 1902. Reproduced from *The Cambridge University Press Collection of Private Press Types* by Thomas Ralston; Cambridge, The University Printer, 1951; by permission of the Printer of the University of Cambridge.

RIGHT The "Subiaco" type of the Ashendene Press, from *Les Amours Pastorales de Daphnis et Chloe*, Ashendene Press, 1933. Reproduced from *The Cambridge University Press Collection of Private Press Types* by Thomas Ralston; Cambridge, The University Printer, 1951.

Mrs. Warde's most quoted piece of writing is "This Is a Printing Office." It is seen here in a reproduction of the original broadsheet, 1932, written and set to show Monotype's Perpetua Titling. The ornament, "words," and "friend you stand on sacred ground" were printed in red.

THIS IS

A PRINTING OFFICE

CROSSROADS OF CIVILIZATION

REFUGE OF ALL THE ARTS
AGAINST THE RAVAGES OF TIME

ARMOURY OF FEARLESS TRUTH
AGAINST WHISPERING RUMOUR

INCESSANT TRUMPET OF TRADE

FROM THIS PLACE WORDS MAY FLY ABROAD
NOT TO PERISH ON WAVES OF SOUND
NOT TO VARY WITH THE WRITER'S HAND
BUT FIXED IN TIME HAVING BEEN VERIFIED IN PROOF

FRIEND YOU STAND ON SACRED GROUND

THIS IS A PRINTING OFFICE

painter, or one supreme thing we ask of him, it is power to give us the shock of freshness, the tingle of something seen or realized for the first time. If he can't give us that little shock, that sense of disturbance, he might as well go into bookkeeping. As Morison once said, "The artist is the only man in modern society who is paid to do what he likes." What he likes is to disturb us, pleasantly or not, by a visual message; and we like that quality in his paintings. So of course he is the last man to enjoy that disciplined exercise in the code-transmission of words—that is, typography—with all its conventional signalling of purpose and kind by format, by style and by orthography.

Instead of lantern slides I have brought a few things which I call palpables, or tangibles. A palpable is something that, as the word implies, you can feel and move with your fingers, weigh and enjoy with your hands. I very much believe that, enormously valuable as slides are to an educated audience when they deal with specific points, they amount to as damaging an element in the education of typographers as any that I can think of except perhaps the little halftones in *Graphis*. I mean that they are out of scale, and scale is more important in typographic work than it is in almost any other kind. Slides are also two-dimensional, wheras all printed matter is three-dimensional, as you know, and its solidity and movability are part of its value. And finally, of course, they are luminous; but the light comes from them, it does not bounce off the page.

As to my "palpables," I will show two objects which, to me, symbolize the beginning and the climax of the typographic renascence that has taken place in my lifetime.

One is the last book of the great private presses of the Revival of Printing that began with the Kelmscott Press. It is the noble *Bibliography of the Ashendene Press* of that great artist-printer, St. John Hornby. Hornby handed me this book himself and pointed to the conspectus of the types of the Press, all cut by hand at his own commission for his private and exclusive use. Ah, but not all. There among them you see Monotype Poliphilus and Blado. Hornby pointed to them, then closed the book and handed it to me, saying, "We were the pioneers; but now the torch passes to you people at Monotype. You must keep it alight."

And we did take up that torch of revival, knowing that we could carry it down the mountain into some dark valleys of "ordinary" printing. Good faces and prouder design began to transform first the trade book of the 1920s, a mediocre, miserable thing; then the schoolbook which was supposed to look horrid because it was good for you; and last, even that most vulgar and squalid-looking type of book, the cheap Bible, which of course is a marvel of condensation, and generally about as moldy-looking a job as you can see; but all the great Bible houses of England in turn commissioned decent typefaces and pulled themselves together to bring out Holy Writ in something like an appropriate style.

I have called Hornby an artist. Why? Because he had the artist's urge to do the whole job himself with his own hands; the determination that if he had to have a crew of helpers, as any printer must, any praise for the result should be shared with the crew, but that any blame should rest solely on him—even to the point of destroying an entire edition of 300 precious copies on its way to the binder because of a slight set-off that appeared in one signature. Bruce Rogers was also quite ready to destroy, or to have destroyed, at any rate to remove his thistle (his personal device) from any work which in any aspect at all fell short of that vision which he had for it as a designer. I do not call any work a work of *art* unless it can be signed *in toto* by one man—saying not simply "Give me credit for the thing," but "If you don't like it, you know whom to blame." "No credit without blame" is one of the best mottoes that never has yet been adopted.

You may know that line that the London pavement artists so proudly chalk under their pathetic sketches of a sunset over Westminster Bridge. When they've done that rather gaudy affair they put under it, "All my own work." That is almost the only statement that could be written under the signature of a great artist at his moment of highest inspiration. Now we see why painting is called art today. Because since the Industrial Revolution, putting oil on canvas is almost the only remaining act of one man's skill in which there is any concentration of excitement and interest, whereas before the Industrial Revolution everything was done by art—that is, by the hand, one-by-one singly; now, of course, things come out in multiples. The man in the street certainly has a good instinct in talking about *art* and *artists*, and meaning *painting*. Because that is just about what it is.

I've spoken about palpables. I now want to show the nearest thing to an impalpable that art paper can make; it is not a message but a synopsis, the synopsis or corpus of the famous Times New Roman type, which not only is very well printed, but is a piece of right reason in design. I saw this thing emerging, I saw the first letters of it being drawn in on the back of a menu by Stanley Morison. It is an example in the rational evolution by trial and error, by constant experiment, and above all by work on the printing press, of a design which has gone rather well and I think done more than any other one face to improve the standards of modern typography.

There is an interesting connection with what we call, rightly, the Revival of Printing in the early days of those great masters like Hornby. The emphasis is on the word "printing." The implication is that printing means not only that supreme moment when the inked form meets the paper, but everything which led up to it and is part of the whole. In this way it was worked back from the press—an enormous press which went 100 miles an hour or something—and what happened under that press was what dictated this remarkable, legible and handsome typeface. And that I did get from Morison while I was enabled to watch the thing evolving when it was a very hush-hush matter of which none of us could speak aloud for over a year, while the six thousand experimental punches for Times New Roman were being cut at the Monotype works—all of us sworn to secrecy.

Among my other tangibles I have the letter that I received the day after Sir Sidney Cockerell's death, *from* Sir Sidney Cockerell, printed at the Stanbrook Abbey Press some months before his death. It is an extract from his will. He sent it only to his intimate friends, but he had so many friends, and this is all about friendship. By the way, at the age of ninety-four he said that he wrote in 6 point because it took less muscular exertion!

I have brought several lovely things also from private presses. One I was given recently when I was lecturing at an exhibition held in Loughborough Technical College. You might be surprised to know how many distinguished, original and interesting private presses there are in that one small district of England, around Loughborough. The private press keeps alive the tradition that what you do with the human hand leaves a certain impression upon the imagination and the mind and the heart; the hand, the palpability of printing and the feeling that comes out of the hand that never comes purely from the eye. I am perpetual honorary vice-president of the Small Printers Association, and this is very dear to me because it consists mainly of small by-street printers in England who want to have private presses—that is, they want to *be* private presses, and every month they exchange bits and pieces which they have proudly designed and printed among themselves; it's very much like the old Printers' International Specimen Exchange which was in Henry Bullen's library at the American Typefounders when I was starting my career there as his assistant. I've also brought along a copy of S. H. Steinberg's very fine *Memoir* of Stanley Morison which he wrote for the British Academy; Steinberg, of course, was the author of that incomparable history of what printing did to civilization, *500 Years of Printing*, the essence of which you find also in *Printing and the Mind of Man*, the record of the exhibition under that name.

There are some other things, including *The Token of Freedom*, which I got done in about two-and-a-half weeks in the middle of the blitz, to be given to the British children who were being bustled off to America so they would be safe. (*Safe*, mind you! Safe! Hah! They were going into a neutral country and being bombarded by Goebels' propaganda! And they called that safe!) So I thought perhaps they'd better have a little passport to take with them. I took a part from that wonderful anthology *The Pattern of Freedom*, edited by Sir Bruce Richmond, and turned it into this book at very short notice. What it illustrates typographically is the fact that if you're doing an anthology of poetry and prose, you must have done some research into what hanging initials are supposed to be for. They are quite important in a job like that.

It would not be proper to end without some reference to the black velvet background against which all lecturers in this series have been holding up the pearls of memory or of admonition: the black background of negation. I am talking about the present-day cult of disinheritance which to some extent has been gaining ground and affecting all the fine arts and a great deal of our other thinking in this century—about the determination to cut away anything which could be called a legacy from the past, if possible. In some cases it is perfectly possible. In the case of painting you can cut off 30,000 years in one stroke by ignoring what has come down to us from the Aurignacian cavemen who represented buffaloes and ponies—and very well, too—and saying, "I do not want my painting to look like anything else; I want it to look like what it is—paint!" And that of course is what does thrill you in the abstracts, the spatters, all the other things of that kind. But it's terrible when a printer says, "I want my typography to look like type." That's the *last* thing it should look like! It should look like a man telling you something, it should look like a scene out of *Hamlet*, it should look like anything, but you must not see it as type—not if you're a reader, at any rate.

This cult of disinheritance has affected typography in a special way.

Let us not confuse it with the cult of eccentricity, that is, of the mere juggling of our conventions, putting the type margins into funny positions and so on. The rule of this cult is different; it is in a way a method of determining that any printed thing—any object for that matter, but specifically any printed thing—shall first of all and above all and supremely signal not what kind of thing it is, not what class of people it is for, not the degree of respect and pride or of shame with which it is presented to its public. First of all and above all, it must signal the time in which it was produced, or at least make perfectly sure that nobody could imagine for a moment that it could have been produced in any time but our own, or by any people except our own generation, since presumably our forbears would not have thought of anything like that. It depends on the use of a very iron-jawed type and a general style that indicates that this is an iron-jawed industrial age with no time for frivolity. It is a moral sort of style and was once called *die neue Typographie*—although the author of the book of that name, the celebrated Jan Tschichold, has spent the rest of the years since the early 1930s in disavowing it and speaking of it as "the sins of my youth." Tschichold is now a very pillar of what he called the Anglo-American tradition, but perhaps we can overlook that little fact because what used to be called *Bauhaus Stil* is not only, in typography, gaining ground, but has in effect conquered, in its modifications, the whole realm of industrial and business and commercial printing and a good slice of publicity and advertising printing as well. And the contemporaries have brought that tide of rejection of the past right up to the printing of continuous reading matter—the books and other things that people pay money for.

The notion of what you might call nihilism is the second reform movement of this century. The eclectics, from William Morris right on through Stanley Morison to our present day, felt that the freedom to choose was an important thing. But freedom can descend into libertinism, and it can also sometimes, in typography, descend into frank thievery, as when you purloin a woodcut from a title page for no other reason than that you think it will enchant your readers; it does, but you cannot call it a moral thing to do.

The "disinheriting" reform movement is intensely moral, almost frighteningly so. We're not told what would be nice and pleasant to do, we're being told what we *ought* to do. Again and again you will find in the reformist or disinheriting school of typography admonitions about what is right and what is wrong to do.

Let me end with something that this reminds me of: a passage from Sellars' and Yeatmans' famous book, *1066 and All That*, which is an account of what you remember about history, not what happened—the motto of it is, "History is what you remember." And some of the things that everybody does remember are excruciatingly funny. In this particular connection I think of the passage in which the authors explain the difference between the Cavaliers and the Roundheads. It is first pointed out that the Cavaliers were noted for their "gay attire," whereas the Roundheads or Puritans were noted for their "somber garments." True enough, and there's a little thumbnail illustration which shows you the effect. Then the authors sum it up even better by saying, "The Cavaliers were wrong but romantic, whereas the Puritans were right but repulsive."

Well, I think on the whole many of you agree with me in that, looking back over time, I have always preferred, if necessary, to be wrong rather than repulsive. And—who knows?—perhaps we weren't wrong after all!